The Circassians of Turkey

The Circassians of Turkey

*War, Violence and Nationalism
from the Ottomans to Atatürk*

Caner Yelbaşı

I.B. TAURIS
LONDON • NEW YORK • OXFORD • NEW DELHI • SYDNEY

I.B. TAURIS
Bloomsbury Publishing Plc
50 Bedford Square, London, WC1B 3DP, UK
1385 Broadway, New York, NY 10018, USA
29 Earlsfort Terrace, Dublin 2, Ireland

BLOOMSBURY, I.B. TAURIS and the I.B. Tauris logo are
trademarks of Bloomsbury Publishing Plc

First published in Great Britain 2019
Paperback edition first published 2021

Copyright © Caner Yelbaı 2019
Caner Yelbaı has asserted his right under the Copyright,
Designs and Patents Act, 1988, to be identified as Author of this work.

For legal purposes the Acknowledgements on p. vii constitute
an extension of this copyright page.

Cover design: Adriana Brioso
Cover image: Adapazarı-Düzce region, South Marmara or Greece where a group of
Circassians were deported from Turkey due to their anti-Kemalist activities during the
Turkish-Greek War of 1919–22. From the author's private collection.

All rights reserved. No part of this publication may be reproduced or
transmitted in any form or by any means, electronic or mechanical,
including photocopying, recording, or any information storage or retrieval
system, without prior permission in writing from the publishers.

Bloomsbury Publishing Plc does not have any control over, or responsibility for,
any third-party websites referred to or in this book. All internet addresses given
in this book were correct at the time of going to press. The author and publisher
regret any inconvenience caused if addresses have changed or sites have
ceased to exist, but can accept no responsibility for any such changes.

A catalogue record for this book is available from the British Library.

A catalog record for this book is available from the Library of Congress.

ISBN: HB: 978-1-7883-1447-3
PB: 978-0-7556-4367-7
ePDF: 978-1-8386-0017-4
eBook: 978-1-8386-0018-1

Typeset by Deanta Global Publishing Services, Chennai, India

To find out more about our authors and books visit
www.bloomsbury.com and sign up for our newsletters.

Contents

List of Illustrations	vi
Acknowledgements	vii
Note on place names, names, abbreviations	ix
Maps	xi
1 Introduction	1
2 'Rebellion' or 'civil war': Circassian paramilitary activism during the Turkish–Greek War of 1919–20	21
3 Civil war in the empire: Adapazarı–Düzce and Yozgat incidents (1920)	41
4 Replacement of the bandits and irregular forces with the regular army, and exclusion of Çerkes Ethem from the nationalist movement	67
5 The Circassian Congress, bandits and the Gönen–Manyas deportations	99
6 The 150'ers, Circassians and the Turkish state 1924–38	127
7 Conclusion	175
Notes	185
Bibliography	234
Index	246

Illustrations

Maps

1 Circassian settlements in Turkey, after 1864. (Source: Zeynel Abidin Besleney, 'A Political History of Circassian Diaspora in Turkey 1864-2011'.) PhD diss. (SOAS, University of London, 2012) xi
2 Map showing the main places where the incidents took place. (Source: Author) xii

Figures

1 *Cumhuriyet* newspaper 19 October 1935. 'Cursed Assassins Under Justice! Villainous Çerkes Ethem!' 154
2 *Cumhuriyet* newspaper 24 October 1935. 'Istanbul's Hatred for the Traitors!' 155
3 *Cumhuriyet* newspaper 23 October 1935. 'Villains are being Cursed!' 156
4 Minorities (Armenians and Jews) made demonstrations for Atatürk! *Son Posta,* 28 October 1935 157
5 Assassination suspects, *Son Posta,* 18 February 1936 158
6 *Cumhuriyet* newspaper 1 August 1932. 'Miss Turkey Keriman was Chosen as Miss World' 166
7 *Cumhuriyet* newspaper 4 August 1932. 'Turkish Girl who Conquered the World!' 167
8 *Cumhuriyet* newspaper 3 August 1932. 'The Turkish Girl Who Became Miss World!' 168
9 *Cumhuriyet* newspaper 31 August 1932. 'Thousands of People welcomed Miss World!' 169
10 It was declared via the *Cumhuriyet* newspaper that the local municipality of Gönen banned speaking in languages other than Turkish. 'In Gönen Everyone will Speak Turkish' 21 May 1936, *Cumhuriyet* 170

Acknowledgements

I am profoundly grateful to my supervisor, Professor Benjamin C. Fortna, for his encouragement and guidance in addition to his sustained support and confidence in me. I feel incredibly lucky to have him as my doctoral supervisor. I would also like to thank Professor Konrad Hirschler, Professor Erik Jan Zürcher, Professor Eugene Rogan, Dr Angus Lockyer and Dr Ryan Gingeras for their valuable comments on this book. I am grateful to two referees for their comments and detailed suggestions.

I have benefitted from the help of Zeynel Abidin Besleney, Sefer Berzeg, Muhittin Ünal, Baki Çule, Sedat Reşad, Ahmet Vedat Güneş, Mustafa İmam, Murat Papşu, Bekir Yılmaz, Dr Yorgos Dedes, Gamon McLellan, Prof George Hewitt, Rengin Yurdakul, Elbruz Aksoy, Halil İbrahim Erbay, Hasan Genç, Khalid El-Awaisi, Müzeyyen Şirin, Ümit Şirin, İsmail Şirin, Meltem Şirin, Semih Şirin, Arzu Çınaz, Cihan Çelik and İlteriş Çelik. I would also like to thank some of the many friends for their support during these long four years in the UK and Turkey: Ayşe Zeynep Nayır, Ayşe Kara, Aydın Erken, Kuban Kural, Yakoob Ahmed, Ozan Ahmet Çetin, Sebahattin Abdurrahman, Talha Çiçek, Elis Gjevori and Ömer Faruk Büyükkurt.

I am also grateful to the staff of the Prime Ministry's Ottoman Archives; the Prime Ministry's Republican Archives; the Turkish Military History and Strategic Studies archives (ATASE); the staff at the archives of the Institute for the History of the Turkish Revolution (TİTE); the SOAS Library where Dominique Akhoun-Schwarb and Kobir Ahmed were extremely generous with their time and help; the Western Thrace Minority Culture and Educational Company (BAKEŞ); the Centre for Islamic Studies (İSAM); the Atatürk Library; the Şamil Educational and Cultural Foundation; the Turkish Grand National Assembly; the Caucasus Research Culture and Solidarity Foundation (KAFDAV); the British Library; the National Archives and the Parliamentary Archives; Adımlar Café of Eskişehir; and the Ministry of Turkish National Education which provided financial support. This book is derived, in part, from articles published in [MIDDLE EASTERN STUDIES] on [12 September 2018], available online: http://wwww.tandfonline.com/[https://doi.org/10.1080/00263206.2018.1473249] and [JOURNAL of BALKAN and NEAR EASTERN STUDIES] on [02 September 2018], available online: http://wwww.tandfonline.com/[https://doi.org/10.1080/19448953.2018.1506297]. Special thanks go to Sophie Rudland, Rory Gormley and Sorcha Thomson at I.B. Tauris, and Leeladevi Ulaganathan for their patient help on this project.

I would like to thank my grandmother, Şaziye Yelbaşı, and my aunt, Meryem Erdem, who ensured my comfort and hosted me while I was conducting field work in Ankara. Finally, I would like to thank my parents, my father Recep Yelbaşı and mother Gülümser Yelbaşı, and my brother Jankat Yelbaşı for their enduring and unwavering support.

Note on place names, names, abbreviations

Note on place names and names

Place names and names are rendered according to the modern Turkish usage, that is, not by strict transliteration. Therefore, names are given as Abdülhamid not Abdulhamid, and Paşa not Pasha.

Abbreviations

ATASE	General Staff Military History and Strategic Studies Archive in Ankara, Genel Kurmay Başkanlığı Askeri Tarih ve Stratejik Etüd Başkanlığı Arşivi
ATASE/ATAZB	Atatürk Collection, Atatürk Kolleksiyonu
ATASE/İSH	Turkish War of Independence Collection, İstiklal Harbi Kolleksiyonu
BCA	Prime Ministry's Republican Archives, Başbakanlık Cumhuriyet Arşivleri
BOA	Prime Ministry's Ottoman Archives, Başbakanlık Osmanlı Arşivleri
CUP	Committee of Union and Progress, İttihat ve Terakki Cemiyeti
KAFFED	Federation of Caucasian Association, Kafkas Dernekleri Federasyonu
TGNA-TBMM	Turkish Grand National Assembly, Türkiye Büyük Millet Meclisi

TİTE   Ankara University, History of Turkish Revolution Institute Archive, Ankara Üniversitesi Türk İnkılap Tarihi Enstitüsü Arşivi

PRPRO/FO   Public Record Office/Foreign Office, National Archive, London, Kew Gardens

Maps

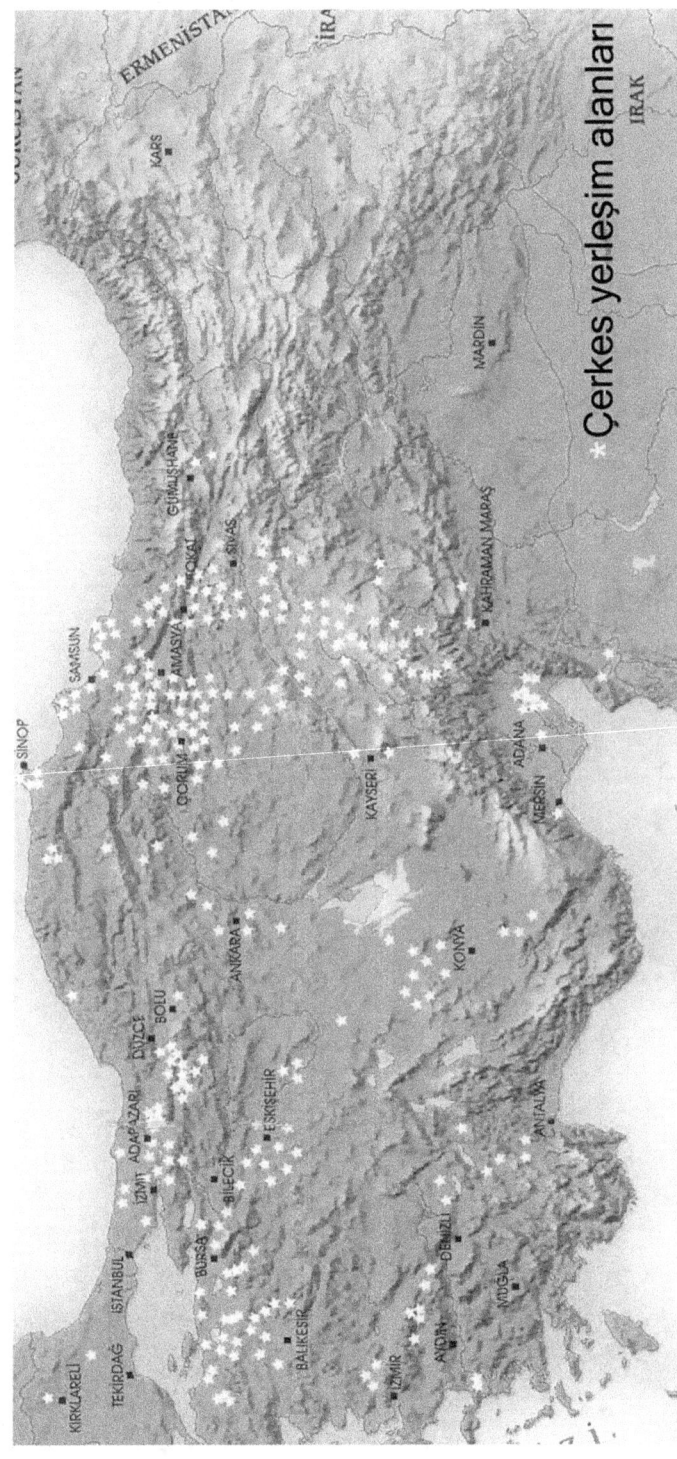

Map 1 Circassian settlements in Turkey, after 1864. (Source: Zeynel Abidin Besleney, 'A Political History of Circassian Diaspora in Turkey 1864-2011'. PhD diss. (SOAS, University of London, 2012)

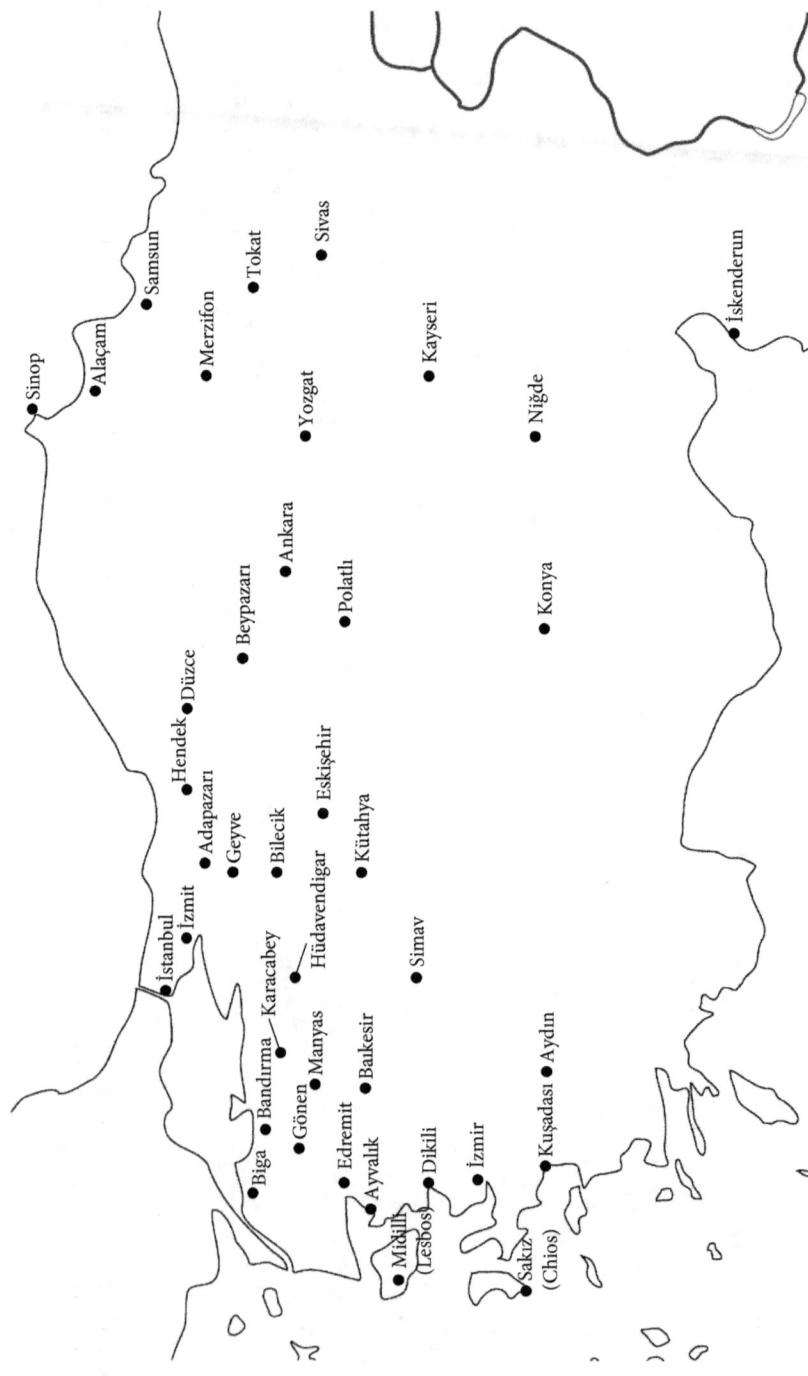

Map 2 Map showing the main places where the incidents took place. (Source: Author)

1

Introduction

The Circassians are the second largest non-Turkish ethnic group residing in the modern republic of Turkey, after the Kurds. Their population numbers about three million.[1] The Circassians hold a unique place in Ottoman–Turkish history, with 90 per cent of them, approximately a million people, having been exiled to the Ottoman Empire during the Russian expansion into the North Caucasus in the nineteenth century.[2] Following their exile, which is symbolically traced back to 21 May 1864, the date on which the Russian tsar declared the Caucasian War to be over, the Circassian elites became integrated into the Ottoman military and bureaucracy, achieving significant positions. Ordinary Circassians became either infantryman in the Ottoman military or farmers in the regions under the control of the Ottoman state.[3]

The Circassians did not have a well-organized state structure in the North Caucasus before their exile. The lack of a unified state allowed neighbours to attack the region without having to face serious resistance.[4] Geographical limitations did not allow them to practice agriculture, but they were able to practice animal husbandry and trade in various goods, including slaves. The markets were widespread. Russian forces started to take control of the region, ultimately gaining total control from the 1760s onwards.[5] The Russians believed that it was not a simple task to deal with them. They did not simply aim to conquer the region but also wanted to assimilate the inhabitants of the region.[6] However, in time, the Circassians began to be seen as 'savage' and 'eternal' enemies who had to be decimated,[7] and it took the Russian forces about one hundred years to gain control of the region – which they did by 'commit[ing] even more egregious acts of terror'[8] – and, finally, expel almost the whole Circassian population. The Circassians were being radicalized during this period by the poor conditions they faced on their transfer from their homeland to the Ottoman regions, where they were faced with incompetent state facilities and a bureaucracy that worsened their situation.⁹ Although the Ottoman state needed these newcomers in the military and to work in the agricultural sector, it was not able to both deal with them en masse and prevent the spread of epidemic diseases. Consequently, huge numbers of Circassians lost their lives.

There is still some discussion among the North Caucasian groups of Turkey about the term 'Circassian'. Historically, the British used 'Circassian' to refer solely to the Adige people, who comprised of more than ten tribes, among them Abzakh, Besleney, Bzhedug, Hatuqwai, Kabardian, Mamkhegg, Natukhai, Shapsug, Temirgoy, Ubikh and Znahey. On the other hand, documents show that the Ottomans generally used Circassian, or 'Çerkes' in Turkish, to describe all of the North-West Caucasian groups, namely the Adige, Ubikh, Abkhaz and Abaza and, in some documents, the Chechens and Dagestanis. Although, in some parts of Turkey, Abkhazians also call themselves Circassians, one cannot infer that all Abkhazians accept the Circassian identity as a supra-identity.[10]

With the reinstitution in 1908 of the Ottoman constitution of 1876, the Circassian elites benefitted from a new liberal atmosphere prevailing in the empire. They established a Circassian school and published a periodical focused on their history, culture and language and on the problems faced by them at that time within the empire. Subsequently, on 1 May 1910, they were granted permission by the Ottoman government to teach their language to pupils attending their schools.[11] However, this liberal climate did not endure. For nearly eleven years without cessation, the empire was at war on different fronts; from 1911 it fought against the occupation of Tripolitania by Italy, then in 1912–13 it was involved in the Balkan Wars, then it took part in the First World War of 1914–18, and then between 1919 and 1922 it was involved in the Turkish War of Independence.[12] There was also a coup d'état in 1913 by the Committee of Union and Progress (CUP),[13] following which it gained control of the empire incrementally until the end of the First World War.[14]

The aims and the central questions

Although there was general chaos throughout Anatolia after 1918, it should be underlined that this book limits its scope to Central and Western Anatolia. On the eastern front, nationalist forces struggled against the Armenian army. In Southern Anatolia, the French army, with the help of local Armenian bands, also aimed at carrying out an occupation. Moreover, throughout Anatolia, local conflicts between bands, local forces, police and the gendarme were widespread. To study all these regions and conflicts is beyond the scope of this book, which focuses principally on key important Western and Central Anatolian conflicts involving Circassians. Specifically, Yozgat, Ankara, Düzce, Adapazarı, İzmit, Gönen and Manyas are included, as these places were where incidents broke out. The Anzavur, the Adapazarı-Düzce, the Yozgat and the Çerkes Ethem incidents, the attempt to prepare for Circassian autonomy under Greek occupation, the Gönen–Manyas deportations and the Circassian opposition to the Kemalist regime are the topics highlighted and studied in this book.

During the republican period, the state and its institutions failed to allow academics and researchers to study the bloody Turkish War of Independence or the early republican period in any detail with objectivity. Until the early 2000s, the controversial topics of this transformative period, from empire to nation state, were off limits to independent researchers inside Turkey. The authoritarian approach of the state to this topic created a barrier to researchers. Those who tried to circumvent it were punished by the state. For example, economist Fikret Başkaya, who wrote a well-known and critical book on Kemalism and the early republican period,[15] was sentenced in 1993 to twenty months in prison, under the prevailing counter-terrorism legislation. This was because the book criticized Kemalism from a leftist perspective, arguing that the Kemalist movement was no more than a Bonapartist and pragmatic movement. Similarly, a journalist, Hakan Albayrak, was also sentenced for claiming in his column that the Islamic funeral prayer was not conducted when Atatürk died, even though eight days later he corrected his earlier comment and said that the Islamic funeral prayer had indeed been held; Albayrak was sentenced in 2004 to fifteen months under the law 'Crimes against Atatürk'.[16] In the last decade, however, a great number of books have been published relating to this period, describing the experiences of the different religious and ethnic groups of Turkey. While there are a number of books that have been published on the most significant non-Turkish group inside the country, namely the Kurds, there is a dearth of academic studies on the Circassians of Turkey.

This book aims to introduce a new perspective on the existing historiography. Although over recent decades there have been some worthy, novel discussions relating to Kemalist historiography in both Turkish TV programmes and popular history magazines, there has been limited historiography originating from the academic domain. This study aims to break new ground in this area, focusing in detail on the political and historical context for the emergence of the activities of Çerkes Ethem and Anzavur Ahmed, the Gönen and Manyas exiles, and the Circassian opposition to the Kemalist regime and its repressive policies against the Circassians during the single-party periods. With few exceptions, none of these topics could hitherto be, or have been, studied, with objectivity by either the Turkish academy or internationally.[17] With some exceptions, existing works were heavily influenced by the Turkish 'one nation' ideology, based on Kemalism. Thus, they either ignore the presence of the aforementioned issues or accept them only to then bring them to view at a shallow level, with discussions centring on who was 'progressive' or 'backward' in the conflict.

The book will underline the presence of the Circassians in this specific period of Ottoman history, 1918–38, showing how the period after the First World War, the era that witnessed the transformation from empire to nation state, was a painful experience for the non-Turkish community. The study of the Circassians in this period helps to understand better the troubled years of the Ottoman collapse and the emergence of the Turkish nation state, in which the Circassians were actively involved – they were either fighting to save the empire or, later on, resisting the creation of the Turkish nation state.

In the broader context, the book will utilize concepts relating to theories of civil war and political loyalty and ask the following questions: First, where do the Ottoman/Turkish or loyalist/nationalist[18] struggles and civil war fit into a worldwide context? Secondly, what were the dynamics at play, in terms of the shifting loyalties among Circassian elites and ordinary people, for both the state and the ethnic identity of the Circassians during this period?

Civil war has been defined as armed conflict that leads to at least a thousand deaths.[19] It is typically a struggle between different groups or authority-wielders within the boundaries of a state.[20] It is possible to state that civil war can be divided into two categories: 'old' and 'new' civil wars. In old civil wars, there were mutual political aspirations for participants whose aims were delineated clearly from the outset.²¹ Violence was not venerated; it was merely accepted as a necessary stepping stone for attaining the political aims of the group.²² In contemporary civil wars, on the other hand, a clearly delineated aim emerges among interested groups. The struggle for leadership and the lack of hierarchy within groups has also been a problem in contemporary civil wars.²³ These factors all contribute to uncertainty in the struggle between different groups and authorities.

It is further useful to understand the Turkish civil war in a broader historical context, by comparing it with another civil war, in this case one that was taking place in Russia. Similar to the Kemalists in Turkey, the Bolsheviks believed that their revolution in October 1917 signified a radical break with the past, necessitating the establishment of a new order in the country. There were some striking similarities between the Russian and Ottoman civil wars and, interestingly, both victors in the civil wars, namely the Bolsheviks and Kemalists, used similar terminologies to depict them. Those supporting the Bolsheviks and Kemalists were termed progressive and those against them were labelled backward, reactionary or loyal to previous regimes. This terminology framed the boundaries of the political language in domestic politics for many decades to come in Turkey.²⁴

The second central question of the book concerns how Circassian political loyalty changed during this transformative period. Although the Circassians relied on the Ottoman sultan/caliph, considering that after the First World War political authority was represented by two governments – the Ottoman Porte in Istanbul as a de jure government and the Ankara government as a de facto one – the loyalty of the Circassian people was, contrary to traditional accounts, split between the two governments. The ordinary Circassian people, generally speaking, supported the loyalists, while the majority of the military elites and the CUP members backed the nationalists. It is also possible to assert that for some of the Circassian elites, the loyalty of their ethnic Circassian identity later became more vital and pronounced. As will be shown in this study, they tried to set up an autonomous Circassian structure under Greek occupation as a buffer zone between the Greeks and Turks in 1921. Until that time, Circassian identity and its loyalties to the Ottoman state were not in conflict. The concept of Ottoman identity, which was in fact a multinational identity, allowed the Circassians to identify themselves clearly. However, after the Greek occupation, some of the Circassian notables thought that the Ottoman state's days were limited, and that the time had arrived for them to establish an autonomous structure under Greek occupation. This was partly because they feared that if they returned to Central Anatolia, the nationalists of Ankara would not give them sufficient space within the new state and would execute them for their opposition to Ankara.[25] They decided to take a step based on the Wilsonian principles[26] popular at the time and set up an autonomous Circassian state structure. However, this decision was not supported by the vast majority of the Circassians.

This book argues that the majority of the Circassians, like most of the people in Anatolia at the end of the empire, were dependent on the decisions taken by the Ottoman government, which was seen as the legitimate government by the people in Anatolia. Being aware of this and wanting the people's support, the Kuva-yi Milliye[27] and the nationalists of Ankara did not attack the Ottoman government in public at the beginning of their movements. Moreover, they used the rhetoric that Kuva-yi Milliye was fighting to save İstanbul and the sultan from the Alliance's occupation. Given this atmosphere, the Circassians expressed their support for the Ottoman government but distanced themselves from the Kuva-yi Milliye and the nationalists, who were seen as the successors of the CUP, which was blamed for the disastrous results the empire faced in the previous couple of years.

While ordinary Circassians may have distanced themselves from the nationalists, Circassians in the bureaucracy, army, Special Organization and paramilitary organizations were divided into three groups. The first group played an important role from the beginning to the end in the resistance against the Alliance and Greek occupation in Anatolia. Among the members of this group were people such as Rauf Orbay,[28] Bekir Sami (Kunduh),[29] Bekir Sami (Günsav),[30] Yusuf İzzet Paşa (Met, Janutuko),[31] İbrahim Süreyya (Yiğit)[32] and Cemil Cahit (Toydemir).[33] The second group, which involved people such as Çerkes Ethem, Çerkes Reşid and Kuşçubaşı Eşref, joined the national struggle at the beginning and prevented the chaos in Anatolia (like Çerkes Ethem), but later on it left or was excluded from the national struggle. It might be said that the second group was also close to Enver Paşa and it was at the centre of the Enver–Mustafa Kemal leadership struggle. The third group comprised of former Special Organization agents and soldiers who participated in the

First World War as members of the Ottoman army and Special Organization; however, they went against the nationalists of Ankara from the beginning of 1919 since they saw the nationalists, such as Ahmed Anzavur, Sefer Berzeg and Maan Şirin, as rebelling against the Ottoman government. They showed their opposition by organizing an anti-nationalist movement in the South Marmara and Adapazarı-Düzce regions.

One could see that ethnicity and Islam played roles in the Circassian mobilization, both when they were with the nationalists or against the nationalists, as Gingeras emphasizes in his book. In the case of Circassians, ethnicity facilitated the intra-community network. It made it easy for them to gather. However, it is difficult to say that their motivation was based on their ethnic identity. Whether intentionally or not, the Circassians became a part of the power struggle between İstanbul and Ankara, a power struggled that saw the transformation of the empire to a nation state. They were instrumentalized by the power centres, such as the governments in İstanbul and Ankara, and by their own local leaders at the time. The politics in the majority Circassian regions were related to the interior or exterior community struggles, local disagreements, intra-community networks and relationship with the state and religion. In this specific time period (1918–38), the transition of the state from one particular shape to another was instrumentalized and used in the power struggle between Ankara and İstanbul.

One of the arguments of this book is that the paramilitary activism of the Circassians from the end of the First World War to the Turkish War of Independence and the early Turkish Republican period completely changed their relationship with the 'state'. Here, the state refers to both the centres of power – the Ottoman Empire and the Turkish Republic. The Turkish Republic, particularly in its early days, aimed to shape society and the state with a top–down modernization and secularization project. As the loyal refugees (*muhacirs*) of the Ottoman state, Circassians were the human sources for the Ottoman army, Special Organization and agricultural production. Their elites were also relatives of royal household. Although their settlement process from the 1860s onwards created widespread problems, from epidemic to starvation, for the Ottoman state, their 'loyalty' to the state had not been questioned by it. However, after the chaotic and devastating period of the First World War and the Turkish War of Independence, they were not welcomed by the new Turkish Republic. They became the subject of ambivalent policies of the republican rulers.

In the early republican period, the Kemalist elites, on the one hand, did not desire the exile or deportation of the Circassians from Turkey. Although they had only recently come (about sixty years ago, from 1860s onwards) to Anatolia, they were seen by the regime as Anatolian. The state system was not designed to create race-based ethnic citizenship. Rather, it proposed to dissolve the different identities and assimilate them into the Turkish one. The only way for a Circassian in the early republican period to participate in daily life without the interference of state officials in public places was to accept the Turkish identity and assimilate with the Turkish people. As Charles Tilly emphasizes in his article on state making, 'state making' is a process in which 'agents of the state' eliminate or neutralize 'their rivals inside those territories'.[34] In this case the Circassians were seen as rivals due to their relationship with the Ottoman state (or Ottoman past). The Kemalists wanted them either eliminated or neutralized – that is, turned into loyal citizens – by the new Turkish Republic.

It can be said that the nation-building process has one purpose: to destroy all the existing nations and create a single national identity in the given territory. In the Turkish nation-building process, the different identities of the post-Ottoman Empire *bakiyes* (or the non-Turkish people) had to be assimilated into the Turkish identity. However, as underlined by Anthony Smith, the national identity in many cases became the source 'of instability and conflict in many parts of the world'; it was the main cause of long-lasting conflicts,[35] as was seen in the creation of Turkish identity in the early republican period. Turkish identity was not welcomed by the non-Turkish groups in Anatolia and caused conflict and tension between the state and society.

The existing historiography of this period in Turkey's history is very problematic for a number of reasons. The Turkish War of Independence is still treated as a movement supported by most people, except those who were 'backward' or 'collaborators' with the 'Greek and British occupiers'. However, recent studies show that local dynamics varied massively from district to district and among different ethnic groups. In South Marmara, the relationship between the state and the residents of the region was already strained following the First World War, particularly due to the disastrous results of the war on the Anatolian people, which included epidemics and food shortages.[36] The existing situation weakened the state's authority in this region and led to an increase in intra-regional struggles between the Turks, Circassians, Albanians and some Greeks, a significant number of whom were exiled or deported during the war. In particular, the Circassian–Albanian conflicts during the 1900s were among the most serious for the region. Moreover, until the Battle of Sakarya in 1921, the resistance movement was not expected to succeed against the Greek army, as it was supported by the Allies. The region was ruled by Greek authorities for more than two years, which shows that further scholarly research is still necessary to understand fully local anti-resistance movement activities and the local population's relationship with the Greek authorities.

One of the most significant books of the period relating to the activities of the Circassians and the post-Balkan War in Anatolia is Ryan Gingeras's *Sorrowful Shores: Violence, Ethnicity and the End of the Ottoman Empire, 1912–1923*.[37] The book was one of the first to adopt an alternative approach to study in detail the internal struggles in Anatolia during the Turkish–Greek War of 1919–22. Gingeras consulted a number of memoirs written by witnesses during this period and studied some of the key protagonists who played a prominent role in the period, as well as relied on archival sources. One of the missing parts of the story in the historiography of this period relates to the internal conflicts that transpired locally in parts of Western Anatolia, a place that Gingeras also focuses on in his book. What differentiates this book from Gingeras's book is that this book claims that a power struggle had an important place during these years. For instance, Çerkes Ethem and Mustafa Kemal's struggle seemed to be a conflict for power. Kuşçubaşı Eşref's opposition to the Kemalist rule was also a part of a power struggle. However, this does not mean that ethnicity did not play a role during this period. As will be seen in Chapter 4, the Ankara government's deportation of the Circassians from Gönen–Manyas region was based on ethnicity.

Paramilitarism and Circassians

Bandits or paramilitary groups do not obey authority; they remain outside the control of the absolute power and, hence, have the potential to rebel against authority.[38] Not having control over all the land and over all citizens renders those in power vulnerable. As will be seen in the following chapters, the ones in power, that is, the Kemalists, needed local patrons on their side to gain dominance in the name of law and authority over the central government in Ankara, since they were not all-powerful. Çerkes Ethem[39] was needed to exert power initially.

Just before the First World War, the South Marmara region was already a battleground for different brigand groups. There were the Albanians, who began to move to the region in the years after the Ottomans lost the Balkans in the Ottoman–Russian War of 1877–78; there were also the Circassians and Turks and the other local people who did not have a good working relationship ever since the mass migration, with inefficient state policies and the lack of security in the region causing problems between them. Each of these communities had armed groups to defend themselves against the other groups, since the state did not have enough power to protect people and provide security in the region. This situation helped the Circassians and the other groups to mobilize their armed people when they needed them, such as during the War of Independence.

One of the armed groups was under the control of Çakırcalı Ahmet Efe. Efe had great support from the local people since he was the symbol of resistance against the lawlessness and unequal treatment meted out by the state.[40] The local rivalry between the local Turks, Circassians and Albanians turned into a conflict and grew rapidly. To protect the local people from the cruelty of the Circassians and Albanians, Efe aimed to take vengeance on them. He killed approximately forty innocent Albanians and Circassians, thus exacerbating the problem and giving rise to a blood feud among the people.[41] Subsequently, Anzavur Ahmed,[42] Kuşçubaşı Eşref[43] and Sami,[44] who would come to be well known, mobilized local Circassians in the region to kill Efe and his relatives in revenge. Efe was finally killed in a skirmish in November 1911.[45] This event demonstrates that the Ottoman state did not have the power to protect the life of its own subjects. It can also be seen that during these years the bandits were always one step ahead of the regular armed forces. They had the support of the people and were better armed and equipped than the regular army and gendarme. Although local Circassians did not have the capability to handle Efe themselves, they could rely on their armed people to save their lives when the state could not.

One of the aims of this study is to examine the process of Circassian mobilization during the Turkish–Greek War of 1919–22. During that period, both the de jure government of the Ottoman Empire in Istanbul and the de facto government in Ankara used paramilitary groups against one another in their attempts to gain control over the country. This struggle between the two governments and the use of paramilitary groups made the conflict akin to a civil war, particularly in the affected Adapazarı-Düzce and South Marmara regions,[46] which experienced widespread chaos. This state of civil war and the associated chaos have generally been disregarded by scholars, particularly those responsible for producing the official (Kemalist) historiography of Turkey. According to Kemalist historiography, which was created and developed by the regime in the late 1920s and 1930s based on Atatürk's famous *Nutuk* speech[47], there was no attempt to differentiate approaches to engagement in rebellions initiated against the 'national struggle' and 'collaborators' working with foreign forces. This chaos and the internal struggles that occurred during the Turkish War of Independence undermines the very notion of a republic created by the Kemalist regime, which emphasized the 'nationalist' and 'total war' features of the war against the Greek troops during the republican period.

High-ranking CUP members, Ottoman bureaucrats and military men who used paramilitary groups to form lines of resistance against the Greek troops beginning to occupy Western Anatolia in May 1919 were already planning their moves before the end of the First World War.[48] They had been concealing arms for later use against the Alliance in case of the possible occupation of Anatolia after the Mudros Armistice (October 1918), the armistice that was signed between the Allies and the Ottomans. South Marmara was a key area for processing arms, and its depots were responsible for organizing the resistance movement and armed struggle against the possible occupation of the Anatolian portion of the empire by the Alliance. It was also a region in which people were already well armed, due to various intra-regional conflicts originating from the 1910s.

In the days following the end of the First World War in October 1918, high-ranking members of the CUP escaped the country to avoid facing charges for war crimes. After the war, the Allies allowed Greek troops to occupy İzmir in the west of Turkey in May 1919. The Ottoman army was weak at that time, as its soldiers had become increasingly ravaged after suffering war throughout the entirety of the preceding last decade. The Ottoman military had suffered large-scale losses, casualties and deserters during the First World War. It was also enduring serious economic hardships and food shortages. At a time when morale and motivation were exceedingly low, the various paramilitary groups that emerged were initially perceived as saviours and protectors against the Greek occupation. They were considered useful as a means to deter further Greek offensives until the army would be ready to engage the Greek troops again. Thus, war-weariness was one of the greatest threats to the nationalists.[49] The Anatolian people suffered scarcity and economic difficulties because of the war; furthermore, as some army officers wrote in their memoirs, people in Anatolia hated soldiers and the practice of military conscription in the post-First-World-War era.[50]

The paramilitary unit, as a form of resistance against occupation, was a key feature of the early resistance movement in Anatolia. As has been mentioned previously, the Anatolian people were already sickened by war having suffered lasting periods of conflict over the previous ten years. Although a group of high-ranking military men, prominent CUP members and local paramilitary leaders aimed to protect Anatolia, the people of the region were not voluntarily willing to support the resistance movement against Greek occupation. The only concern of the majority of the people was survival, rather than coming together around the resistance movement to fight against occupying forces. People were tired, and suffering from war, lack of food, disease and infirmity. They were unwilling to fight anymore. The populations of Anatolia viewed the high-ranking military men and officers as responsible for the catastrophic situation they encountered.[51] Under such conditions, the role played by the paramilitary groups and brigades was crucial. The paramilitaries were more acceptable to people than the regular army. Moreover, soldiers preferred to fight as members of the irregular forces since they did not have to wear military uniform, the hierarchy was not so important as in the regular army and the salary was much higher.[52]

On the other side, the Greeks were also war-weary. Military service had been made compulsory in 1911, and they had engaged in several wars over the last ten years, including the Balkan Wars, the First World War and the Turkish–Greek War of 1919–22. Some soldiers recruited into the army in 1911 had still not been discharged, and an attitude of anti-militarism was pervasive among the soldiers in the Greek army.[53] Moreover, the Turkish–Greek War had triggered a domestic struggle between the Greek forces and the country's politicians. The loyalists who wished to remain neutral disagreed on the subject of the occupation of Anatolia; the supporters of Venizelos, the Venizelists, backed the occupation.[54] Due to the difficulties associated with wartime conditions, the extended duration of a state of war and conditions at the front, the Anatolian campaign turned out to be a misadventure for the Greek army, as reluctance and anger spread among Greek army soldiers.[55]

There were many paramilitary groups in South Marmara that were made up of Circassians. One important question that has hitherto not been adequately dealt with is this: Why did a large number of Circassians join paramilitary groups? Without understanding the Circassian presence in the Ottoman Empire, it is impossible to understand the paramilitary activism of Circassians after the First World War. It should be emphasized here that the Circassians had become accustomed to war before being exiled to the Ottoman Empire, having been engaged in a long struggle against the Russians from the mid-eighteenth up until the late nineteenth century. Without a formal state structure, particularly those who used to live in North-West Caucasus, the Circassians tribes (*boy*), fought a long guerrilla war against the Russians in the North Caucasus.[56] In the post-exile period, their skills led them to be recruited into the army, to fill a gap in the Ottoman military's needs. They were also used by the Ottomans to counter the rebellions in the Balkans and Anatolia, and during the reign of Abdülhamid II, formed part of gendarme forces. As Fortna emphasizes, the Russian attacks and their expulsion from the North Caucasus radicalized them, making it easier for the Ottoman government to recruit them for voluntary or irregular paramilitary groups.

The class structure was a characteristic feature of the Circassian community, and it affected Circassian participation in the Ottoman army. The Circassians can generally be divided into two different classes, *warq* (aristocracy) and *tfokotl* (peasantry).[57] The existence of slavery and the class structure continued even after the Circassians converted to Islam and were exiled to the Ottoman Empire. The system of slavery among the Circassian community was employed by the Ottomans when incorporating them as soldiers into the Ottoman military. Due to the increase in the slave trade in the nineteenth century from the North Caucasus to the empire, the Circassians were considered key human resources, able to fill the empire's needs. This meant they were able to move to the higher echelons of the Ottoman military and bureaucracy, until recruitment practices altered to incorporate professional training during the late nineteenth century.[58] During the reign of Sultan Abdülhamid II, a new law was issued by the Porte aiming to abolish slavery and recruit manumitted slaves into the military. According to this new legislation, the state would pay the price of the slave to the owner, and then the slave would be recruited into the army, assuming the owner accepted.[59] This policy increased the number of Circassian foot soldiers in the Ottoman military. There were also Circassians from upper-class families who joined the Ottoman army and royal military school, becoming a new elite class in the Ottoman Empire, and who used 'lower class' Circassians to solidify their own position at the centre of the empire. This situation provided an opening for them in their new country. The elites became part of the power centre and lower-class Circassians became either villagers or foot soldiers. Nonetheless, scholars have argued that slavery affected some enslaved families even during the War of Independence period (1919–1922), pointing out that during this period enslaved families, on the urging of their owners, fought the nationalists.[60] Undoubtedly, the elites benefitted from this situation until the end of the patron–client system at the beginning of the 1920s.

Notably, however, the Circassians already had a long history of interaction with the Ottoman Empire. Long before they moved to the empire en masse, their women served as slaves in the Ottoman harem. Girls were kidnapped and sold by slave traders or were simply given away by the girls' own families to the Ottoman aristocracy in the hope that it would help them become part of the Ottoman elite. This was especially true in the case of the Abkhazian and Ubikh tribes. This allowed some Circassians to become part of the Ottoman Empire via the harem.

The Porte used slavery both to meet its need for white women slaves for the harem and to move Circassian men into the military. The Abkhazians and Ubikhs, in particular, used the harem and the military to obtain positions inside the empire, as they had a more distinct hierarchical social structure than the other tribes. The existence of Circassian women in the harem provided an important means for the Circassians to enter the Ottoman bureaucracy and the military. Circassian slave girls became concubines and wives of high-ranking bureaucrats and military men, even the sultan. The latter role was an important one for a slave girl and her family. She could become the mother of a prince, or a *şehzade*, which would then have a positive impact on her relatives' careers in the Ottoman military and bureaucracy.[61] This was the case for Anzavur Ahmed, whose sister was one of the wives of Abdülhamid II; he was raised to the rank of *Paşa*.

Arguably, the Circassians were systematically organized to participate in the armed activities of the state – they were part of the military and Ottoman Special Organization (*Teşkilat-ı Mahsusa*), for instance. The Ottoman Special Organization was established by Enver Paşa in November 1913 to battle insurgents in the Balkans.[62] The organization consisted of paramilitary groups and was used for 'intelligence-gathering, warfare, propaganda and special organisations, political assassinations, clandestine operations and suppression of non-Muslim groups'.[63] It was initially hoped that the organization would remain under Enver's control, although on the surface there was little to suggest that the insurgents were working for the Ottoman Empire. The Caucasus Revolutionary Committee, which was associated with the Special Organization to perform counter activities in Iran and Russia, particularly in the Caucasus, so as to free the region from Russian control, had recruited dozens of Circassians from Anatolia to implement its policies.[64] Thus, it is reasonable to suggest that their changing cultural features enabled them to adjust to the regular and irregular armed activities of the Ottoman Empire and the Turkish Republic. This situation echoed what they had encountered in previous decades, prior to being exiled to the Ottoman Empire in the eighteenth and nineteenth centuries. Their long struggle against Russian occupation, colonization and atrocities in the North Caucasus, the difficult conditions of their exile from the North Caucasus to the Ottoman Empire and their struggles to integrate into their new settlements and with their new neighbours made daily life tough. These ruthless conditions led to the emergence of a 'war-like' Circassian culture. The ethnic and personal network played an important role during the First World War. Enver Paşa, in particular, chose people on the basis of their loyalty to him and not simply on the basis of their military capability and experience. This opened a new pathway for the Circassians going forward, as will be seen in the case of Eşref and Çerkes Ethem.[65]

In the post-First-World-War period, dozens of those who fought in the Ottoman army under the Special Organization returned home. Many of these fighters, such as Anzavur Ahmed, Maan Ali, Çerkes Davut and Çerkes Bekir, were *alaylı* – that is, they had not studied in military schools and so did not have well-organized connections with the executive of the CUP, as their relationship with it had been broken in the post-First-World-War period.[66] Whatever they observed during the First World War made them anti-CUP and therefore against the national movement in Ankara. These individuals became the leading figures of the anti-nationalist movement in 1919 and 1920.[67] However, huge numbers of Circassians also fought in the national movement for the Ankara government's army, and worked in the bureaucracy, becoming MPs in the assembly.[68]

Chapters of the book

The first chapter of the book is the introduction (this chapter).

Chapter 2 examines Circassian participation in the civil war period from 1919–20 – that is, during the so-called period of 'National Struggle'. Although this was largely a war between Greek and Turkish troops, there were several battles fought between the followers of the Nationalists and the Loyalists. Both sides used paramilitaries as a tool to achieve control over the country. Çerkes Ethem and Anzavur Ahmed were two important leaders at this time. Çerkes Ethem, the majority of whose soldiers were Circassians, was influential in suppressing the movements against the nationalists of Ankara, from South Marmara to Central Anatolia. Meanwhile, another Circassian, Anzavur Ahmed, also had a significant impact on the Circassians, as a leading figure responsible for mobilizing the Muslims of the South Marmara against the *Kuva-yi Milliye*, while emphasizing Islamic solidarity among the people of the empire. This chapter further argues that because the people of the region felt a large degree of war-weariness, Ahmed Anzavur gained their support following a successful propaganda drive. He mobilized the Circassians of the region using his connections with the community, by employing religious rhetoric and by drawing on the emotional attachment that the Circassians had to the Ottoman sultan and the caliphate.

Chapter 3 focuses on the Adapazarı-Düzce incidents, the Yozgat incident, and in response to these two incidents the pro-nationalist activities of Çerkes Ethem and his growing impact on the political problems facing the Ankara government. The Düzce-Hendek region proved to be a major battlefield for the Circassians who supported the Istanbul government and for those who supported the Ankara government.[69] The loyalist Circassians of the Adapazarı-Düzce region rose against Ankara, attempting to seize control of the region. Due to Ankara's lack of an effective military force, Çerkes Ethem was called upon to suppress the uprising. In doing so, he caused an internal Circassian conflict in Düzce that resulted in about fifty people involved in the uprising being sentenced to be hanged. At the same time, Ankara was threatened by another uprising in Yozgat, led by a local landowner from the Çapanoğlu family. Ethem was invited once more by Ankara to restore order in Yozgat. This chapter argues that Ethem increased his military and political power in Anatolia and Ankara, particularly in the assembly, through his suppression of these three incidents (Anzavur, Adapazarı-Düzce and Yozgat), which in effect saved the national movement from the destruction caused by Istanbul-backed incidents in Anatolia.

Chapter 4 focuses on the exclusion of Ethem from the nationalist cause in relation to the Enver Paşa–Mustafa Kemal conflicts, and the impact of the so-called Green Army Society on this. As Chapter 3 notes, the increasing political and military power of Ethem concerned Mustafa Kemal and İsmet (İnönü), mainly because they wanted Ethem to act as a military man only. However, political opposition against Mustafa Kemal in Ankara, and outside it, from those such as Enver Paşa was worrying; indeed, Enver did eventually attempt to use Ethem against Mustafa Kemal. The supporters of the Green Army had in fact asked Ethem to join the movement, as he already had military power, and it was hoped that this would give the movement increased political influence. From this perspective, Ethem seemed to be more of a threat to Mustafa Kemal than a manageable military man under his control. Ethem and his brothers' harsh policies towards anti-nationalist groups were also used by Ankara as proof that they were harming the nationalist cause. Thus, when Mustafa Kemal decided to change the military order and commanders at the western front in October 1920, a feud broke out between Çerkes Ethem, Tevfik and Reşit, on the one hand, and İsmet, Refet and Mustafa Kemal, on the other.

Chapter 5 details the activities of one-time governor of İzmit, Çule İbrahim Hakkı, the Circassian Congress and the Gönen–Manyas deportations. After his relationship with the Istanbul government deteriorated irreparably, İbrahim Hakkı addressed the issue of Greek occupation forces in Western Anatolia. He changed his political stance from that of loyal Ottoman statesman to a believer in Circassian autonomy under the Greek occupation forces in Western Anatolia. However, his ambitions were not realized because notable Circassians and the general mass of the Circassian people did not favour autonomy. This chapter also sheds light on Circassian armed opposition to the Kemalists in Western Anatolia during the period 1922–23, when forces tried to wage a counter-revolution against the Ankara government. It will also focus on the Ankara government's response to this opposition, namely the forceful exiling of fourteen Circassian villages from the region as a form of collective punishment.

Chapter 6 explores the anti-nationalist activities of Circassians from 1924 onwards, and the drawing up by the Ankara assembly of a list of *personae non gratae* (*Yüzellilikler*) in April 1924. Those who were against the nationalists from the beginning and those who were excluded by the Ankara government engaged in anti-nationalist activities. Although in the past certain groups may have had disagreements, they now had a common enemy: the Kemalists. Çerkes Ethem, Tevfik, Reşit, Kuşçubaşı Eşref, Çerkes Sami, Çule İbrahim Hakkı and Maan Mustafa, a group of Circassian and Abkhazians from the Western Anatolia region and some other Muslims from Anatolia were the driving opposition force. This opposition first began in the Greek-occupied zone of Western Anatolia, but then spread beyond Turkey, as members of this group were declared *personae non gratae*. This chapter will also focus on how the list of *personae non gratae* was determined by the Grand Assembly of Turkey, and the motivation behind the decisions made by the assembly, since about 86 of the 150 persons on the list were Circassians. This chapter will also discuss the impact of Kemalist nationalization and modernization projects on the Circassians as a distinct non-Turkish Muslim group in the country. The years following the War of Independence saw the Kemalist elite attempt to revive the nation-building project proposed by the CUP, while also increasing the authoritarian policies that remained from the previous era. The experience of the first few years was sufficient to persuade the Kemalist elite that the country was unprepared for a pluralistic political system, although it may well be possible to argue that the Kemalist elite had never aimed to implement a pluralistic system in the first place. The prohibition of non-Turkish languages as part of the infamous 'Citizen, Speak Turkish!' campaigns, and the exclusion of those with Circassian identity from the public places will also be the focus of this chapter.[70]

The Circassians suffered from state oppression in the early republican period, but their suffering was in fact much less when compared to the other minority groups. However, they did face persecution due to their closeness to the Ottoman state, especially through the harem and the military and the intelligence services and because of the Çerkes Ethem incident. For high-ranking Kemalists, politicians and statesman in the early republican period, Circassian identity was associated with either 'backwardness', the Ottoman state or the 'traitor' Çerkes Ethem. They were seen by the republican elites as a reminder of the bad old days of the Ottoman Empire and the civil war between the Ankara and Istanbul governments. Chapter 7 aims to answer, first, why the Circassians, from the time of the Turkish War of Independence period to the creation of the Turkish nation state, were opposed to the Kemalists and, then, the why they did not face similar pressures and violence as the Kurds faced in the early republican period.

2

'Rebellion' or 'civil war': Circassian paramilitary activism during the Turkish–Greek War of 1919–20

Civil wars and violence in the period 1918–23 were widespread in Europe. Thus, the civil war in Turkey – it should be noted that the statement that there was a civil war is itself disputed, with mainstream Turkish historians rejecting it – was not unique to Ottoman--Turkish history in the post-First-World-War era. Civil war and domestic violence were prevalent across the European continent, from Russia to Britain, Spain and the Ottoman Empire during 1918–23. At the beginning of the First World War, the conflict, as was the case traditionally, was between states and their armies. However, after the war, violence was directed principally against civilians and intrastate actors by their own governments.[1] The widespread use of violence turned this war into a 'European civil war',[2] as the worsening conditions brought about by warfare, conflicts between revolutionaries and counter-revolutionaries spread across the continent.[3] In Russia, for example, there was the conflict between the Red, White and Green armies at the end of the First World War. In Italy, the territorial and economic profits gained during the First World War were insufficient to satisfy the nationalist fervour of some Italians. Their disappointment resulted in violence, eventually bringing Mussolini to power.[4] In Britain, soldiers joined in riots, which erupted in January and August 1919 in major cities.[5] There was also a struggle between the Irish nationalists and the British army in Northern Ireland at this time.[6]

One can observe similarities between the two great multinational empires; the Russian and the Ottoman Empires. Generally speaking, the Ottomans and Russians comprised the two main rival groups competing for power inside the empire during this period. Both empires experienced civil wars, the existing regimes: the White army in Russia against the Bolsheviks, and the loyalists in Turkey against the nationalists.[7] The creation of a narrative (historiography) was also important for both the empires of the successor states. It can be said that all the leaders – Lenin, Mustafa Kemal Atatürk and Stalin – worked on the production of a 'national history' for their countries, viewing themselves as 'revolutionary leaders'. The writing of the nation's history was considered a necessity by the leaders and politicians of the authoritarian states.[8]

The civil wars (or 'rebellions' as they are termed in official Turkish historiography) were framed by the leaders in the official school history textbooks and their own memoirs as demonstrating the 'backwardness' of the old regimes and their supporters.[9] In the post-war period, when the Bolsheviks and Kemalists seized the power necessary to realize their agenda, the state was seen as the chief instrument of social and economic transformation, and both were based on single-party regimes and statist economic policies.[10] This chapter examines the influence of the Circassian presence on both sides in the civil war between Istanbul and Ankara.

The domestic problems and the conflict in the Ottoman state during the period of the Turkish–Greek War (1919–22) have generally been bypassed by mainstream Turkish historians. Although local opposition(s) to the nationalist resistance[11] was nuanced inside Anatolia, varying from province to province and district to district, all the uprisings have generally been viewed indiscriminately by historians as 'rebellions'.[12] Mainstream Turkish historians and leading officials of the period have been reluctant to address the issues of domestic conflict and violence in their books and memoirs. Where they do mention conflicts, they underline the 'ignorance' and 'backwardness' of 'the rebels' and their 'collaboration' with Greek and British occupiers or the Istanbul government without fully analysing the reasons for these mass movements. To define the period, particularly 1920, as a time of 'civil war' is more suitable than referring to it in terms of 'rebellion', because the anti-nationalist movement received mass support and the national movement had no absolute and legitimate authority during the period, only taking power as the de facto government in Ankara/Anatolia.

The First World War led to the almost total destruction of the Ottoman Empire.[13] Post-war conditions weakened the empire, in terms of not only manpower, population and productivity but also economics. Inflation rates were high, scarcity of food was rife and chaos was widespread in Anatolia. Large numbers of people in the capital, the provinces and the districts opposed the CUP, holding it responsible for the disastrous events in Anatolia. The existence of the CUP in Anatolia was increasingly a challenge for many people.[14]

During the First World War, unrest, robbery, burglary and kidnappings were widespread in the South Marmara region.[15] The lack of state authority led to an increase in the number of bandits committing crimes in the region. There were large numbers of Circassians among the bandits. Due to their dense population in the South Marmara, they were characterized by a 'war-like culture', inherited from decades of war and exile before they settled. This, along with clashes with other groups in the region, made them a highly influential force in South Marmara.[16] Before the First World War, conflict was already brewing between the Circassians and Albanians. Throughout the First World War, the tension was exacerbated among Circassians, the Albanians and the Turks of South Marmara. The reasons for these tensions were mainly competition for advantage over other groups or for positions as local administrators, which provided a great opportunity to gain access to state facilities to overcome the harsh conditions of war.

In the days following the First World War, the *Kuva-yi Milliye* and its loyalist opponents emerged as newly armed groups, adding to the number of armed groups already operating in South Marmara. The bandits and armed groups in the region were incorporated into these two new groups from their initially small and fragmented units. Although ethnic differences were important to the formation of these two different groups, their main distinctive features could be categorized as either nationalist or loyalist. This chapter provides a background to the Turkish War of Independence and then explores the nationalists' efforts to create a line of resistance against Greek occupation in South Marmara using paramilitary groups. Finally, it will examine the origins of the anti-nationalist movement and the mobilization of Circassians and other Muslim peoples in the region.

Turkish War of Independence: Historiography and problems with sources

The Turkish War of Independence remains a controversial period in Turkish historiography. Undoubtedly, the history of the period is mainly a product of *Nutuk* – the 'Great Speech' of Mustafa Kemal Atatürk. Erik J. Zürcher claims that fifty thousand copies of *Nutuk* were published in the days following the CHP Congress in 1927 at which Atatürk gave the speech.[17] These fifty thousand copies were published for the 1.4 million literate people of Turkey; given today's number of literates in Turkey, publishing fifty thousand copies back in 1927 was the equivalent of publishing and promoting 2.5 million copies of a book today. From the mid-1930s until the 1950s, the Turkish War of Independence period was taught in public schools and universities as *İnkılap Tarihi* or 'History of the Revolution'. The course was taught by politicians,[18] some of whom were hard-line Kemalists, such as Recep Peker and Mahmut Esad Bozkurt, and it was used as a tool to disseminate official state ideology. The main sources of the lecture were Atatürk's *Nutuk*, which was also a useful source for creating a 'national history' of the 'nation'. In fact, the textbooks were prepared by people close to government circles.[19] Textbooks were influenced by romanticism, French positivism and German historicism, which gave the Kemalist political leaders what they needed to create a national history for the newborn nation, full of heroism and pragmatism as a basis for a strong state.[20]

It can also be said that publications emanating from the Turkish General Staff also had a huge impact on the creation of a historiography for the Turkish War of Independence, because, until the 1980s, publications by General Staff on the period were the main sources available, due to restrictions placed on accessing archives in the country. They published a significant number of books and journals, which included important documents about the war.[21] However, it is not possible to know which documents were chosen for publication by General Staff. The archives were disregarded and not effectively organized in Turkey until the 1990s. Still, in the absence of archival documents, other publications, such as memoirs, began to expand in the early 1950s to become a significant source for the Turkish–Greek War historiography. Nevertheless, from the 1950s onwards, the main source for the period was Atatürk's *Nutuk*, due to restrictions on publications and in the press. There are several problems with relying on the *Nutuk*, mainly because it gives a one-sided explanation of the incidents without much objectivity. Numerous historians use *Nutuk* as a principal source, without ever questioning its veracity as a 'historical memoir' or document.

The lack of social history and informative works related to the First World War and the Turkish War of Independence period are other explanations for the existence of 'official' Turkish historiography.[22] The historiography of the era was shaped by the authorities (politicians of the Republican Party), who sought to give political legitimacy to their policies.[23] One of the main resources of the period, besides archival documents, includes memoirs written by high-ranking military figures who fought during the War of Independence and by state officials from the early republican period. Certainly, however, memoirs are not always reliable sources. In Turkish historiography it can be said that they are generally more problematic than usual because of the emphasis given to 'the single man' Mustafa Kemal by early republican elites and successor generations. For instance, Hıfzı Veldet[24] mentions in his memoirs that when the British forces occupied the assembly in Istanbul in March 1920, they (Hıfzı Veldet and his schoolmates) were both worried and surprised.

> One day in March 1920, a friend of ours, Memduh (Payzın), came to us crying and said '[The] English [have] occupied Istanbul [and] martyred our soldiers when they were sleeping.' Everyone was thinking about Istanbul and their family and relatives, and consoling each other. We swore to take revenge from the English and fight the Greeks while we were crying. After that surprise when we were conscious, we thought 'Mustafa Kemal Paşa surely could take requisite measures, we believed him to be like a prophet.'[25]

Hıfzı Veldet's attitude towards Mustafa Kemal reflects the typically unrealistic and fictional approach of the early republican elites to the period, in general, and Mustafa Kemal, in particular. In March 1920, Mustafa Kemal was a former Ottoman army general and the only head of the national representative committee, the *Heyet-i Temsiliye*.[26] However, the approach taken by Hıfzı Veldet places Mustafa Kemal centre stage, as the sole figure already responsible for predetermining his policy responses to future incidents.

Here, I argue that the nationalist resistance to Greek forces was not organized by the people themselves in Anatolia. The resistance was not a result of the process of a series of congresses carried out by local people to protest against, and then mobilize in opposition to, the Greek occupation in Eastern Anatolia. In fact, the potential for armed resistance was already apparent to the CUP, as it calculated the potential risks from an Allied occupation of Anatolia during the First World War. The Karakol Society, established by the CUP on 13 November 1918, was one example of this. The aim of the society was to keep the empire united under the CUP's control.

Everyone involved in establishing the society was a member of the CUP.[27] The resistance movements in Anatolia were a top–down project carried out through the medium of resistance associations called Defence of Right Societies (*Müdafa-i Hukuk Cemiyetleri*). The associations in Western and Eastern Anatolia were set up by members of special organizations, Karakol, members of CUP and local notables.[28]

Although the Kemalists were once members of the CUP, Kemalist historians have consciously denied the role of the CUP in the nationalist resistance.[29] The CUP was the most powerful political party at the time, despite the majority holding it responsible for the existing political situation. It could still mobilize a broad range of people from different backgrounds within society – from members of armed militias or groups to bureaucrats and high-ranking military personnel. The role of the CUP has been ignored in mainstream historiography because its last days were filled with wars, conflicts and exiles and its members were engaged in a power struggle with their old allies: the Kemalists.[30] Such a background was not a convenient backdrop for the 'new' republic of Turkey. Moreover, the Kemalists were already in conflict with the remaining CUP members from the 1920s, up until the alleged assassination attempt of Mustafa Kemal in 1926.[31] Therefore, mainstream historians did not pay sufficient attention to the role played by the CUP during the pre-republic period.

Organizing paramilitary resistance against the Greek occupation

Before Greek forces occupied İzmir, paramilitary groups and arms had already been prepared by a group of Ottoman officials to provide resistance against the potential occupation of the region by Alliance members.[32] During the First World War, the CUP hid a number of arms in West Anatolia. In contrast to the official historiography, a national struggle of resistance began before Mustafa Kemal went to Samsun on 19 May 1919. Some commanding officers and state officials, who were former members of CUP, or who had been close to the CUP, were already seeking to go to Anatolia due to the prevailing threat of the possible establishment of an Armenian state in Eastern Anatolia or the occupation of Anatolia by Alliance members. Kazım Karabekir, Mersinli Cemal Paşa, Nurettin Paşa, Cafer Tayyar (Eğilmez), Kazım Özalp and Rauf Orbay were some of the most prominent figures. Rauf Orbay also helped to coordinate resistance between different groups in Anatolia against the Greek occupation.[33] Another important individual in this group was Kazım Karabekir, who had arrived in Anatolia before Mustafa Kemal. On 13 March 1919, Kazım Karabekir was appointed a commanding officer of the Fifteenth Army, which was later renamed the Ninth Army, in Erzurum.[34]

It can be said that the War Office and the General Staff of the Ottoman Empire supported the resistance movement from the outset. During this period, key efforts were led by Cevat Paşa (Çobanlı) (19 December 1918–2 April 1919), Mersinli Cemal Paşa (10 October 1919–25 January 1920) and Kavaklı Ahmet Fevzi Paşa (Çakmak) (3 February 1920–16 March 1920). Indeed, the Anatolian movement gained large-scale support from the War Office and General Staff.[35] Bekir Sami (Günsav) Bey was appointed to bring together Ottoman soldiers who had dispersed when the Greeks occupied İzmir and to take specific measures to organize combat units.[36] Kazım (Özalp) Bey[37] was also nominated by the General Staff as the commander of the 61st division. He was also encouraged by the War Office to provide resistance against Greek troops while avoiding massacres directed against the non-Muslims in the region.[38] In South Marmara, Rauf Bey (Orbay) also met Çerkes Ethem,[39] with the aim of creating a line of resistance composed of paramilitary groups made up of Circassians, who were already armed as they had been fighting with the Albanians in the region.

It can be said that there was no coordination between the different local resistance groups to counter the occupation of Anatolia. It is also important to emphasize that the main aim of local resistance movements was to battle against Greek and Armenians soldiers and bandits.[40] Although French and Italian soldiers occupied a number of areas, no major battles occurred between these forces and Ottoman soldiers.[41] It must also be mentioned that the national movement did not always view France and Italy as enemies. Kazım Özalp states in his memoirs that 'the French and Italian military officials M Deuran and Mr Parciel behaved in a friendly way and helped us' (*Kuva-yi Milliye*). Other foreign military officials came to Balıkesir seeking information about the activities, numbers of soldiers and the establishment of a nationalist resistance: 'I did not have any doubts about bringing them to the fronts and showing them our national forces' actions'.[42] Even British forces preferred not to come into conflict with the *Kuva-yi Milliye*. They tried to achieve their political objectives in Anatolia without fighting.[43]

Both the Ottoman government and the de facto government of Ankara (the *Kuva-yi Milliye*) also avoided conflict with the British.[44] In addition, a group of Ottoman politicians and governors believed that the continuing existence of the Ottoman state was dependent on British support. These politicians and governors believed that if they created problems for the British forces in Anatolia, they would risk losing the entire state, because they were too weak to resist Britain.[45] For example, Ali Kemal, the minister of interior, supported an agreement with the British, choosing not to fight against the Allies and the Greeks – even if they occupied the land brutally. Otherwise, he claimed that it would not be possible 'to save the fatherland'. He was antagonistic towards the *Kuva-yi Milliye* and its policies. One of his telegrams to the local pro-*Kuva-yi Milliye* governors reveals that his aim was to inhibit the progress of the nationalists: 'Your way is a dead end, you will lead to massacres of the Muslim elements of the state. We cannot do anything while having war (against them).'[46] In contrast, he also explained the committee of Balıkesir's resistance movement; he stated that they (the officials of the Ottoman government) had to order them not to resist, since they (the officials) were under pressure from their occupiers. However, he also advised the national resistance committee that they should rise against the Ottoman government because resistance was their right.[47] The Ottoman state was already suffering from a lack of manpower and as a consequence of financial and military losses incurred during the First World War, it could not survive a British attack. The British officials similarly demanded that the Ottomans halt their military actions directed against the Greek troops in South Marmara, warning that otherwise, the Greek troops, backed by the British, might improve their situation, with the result that they would be able to occupy as far as Central Anatolia.[48]

The British presence created a dilemma for the Istanbul government. Although the Ottoman rulers were striving to keep the empire united under its control without losses, to succeed in its aim, compromises had to be made to the British in terms of sovereignty. A British presence for thirty to thirty-five years was considered a preferable option to the dismemberment of the state.⁴⁹ With this policy, the palace would enhance its power, which was very low under the CUP's rule. The members of the Liberal Entente held a similar position relative to the palace (The *Hürriyet ve İtilaf* or the Liberal Entente was the ruling party in the Ottoman Empire in the post-First-World-War era.). They sought ways to improve their relations with the British, working towards signing a peace agreement to avoid further trouble for the empire and its subjects.⁵⁰

In the days following the Greek occupation, local organizations were established under the title 'The Resistance against the Occupation and Annexation of Greek Forces', in Western Anatolia. The local resistance was organized by military men, local governors and notables in South Marmara.⁵¹ The first congress of local resistance groups was held between 27 June and 12 July 1919. The aim of these local congresses was to organize local lines of resistance against the occupiers and to protect people's possessions. There were no direct connections between local congresses in different regions due to a lack of collective intent and leadership.

In the districts and towns, the notables were the most important assistants of military commanders. In the days following the First World War, local notables were hesitant about, and resistant to, becoming involved, as they were sickened by war like many others in the empire. Moreover, some of the local notables did not necessarily agree with the intention to conduct paramilitary attacks against Greek forces. This changed, however, when Greek forces occupied Western Anatolia and no fewer than one hundred thousand Greeks settled in the region. Now, local notables began to fear for the loss of their possessions.⁵² They began to support the local resistance movement and paramilitary groups in order to safeguard their possessions and privileged positions, which were threatened by the Greek occupation.⁵³ In addition to their economic power and the great amount of land they owned, the notables had large numbers of workers who were employed on their lands.⁵⁴

The newspapers in Istanbul began to criticize the high-ranking military commanders for the decisions they had taken during the First World War. The pressure felt from the press, coupled with the existence of Allied soldiers in the capital, discouraged the military and those related to the CUP and its war policies in Istanbul. Moreover, the Greek occupation of Western Anatolia and the presence of Allied forces in Istanbul forced high-ranking military men to leave the city for Anatolia. Although Mustafa Kemal tried to take his place in the Istanbul government as minister of war, he was unsuccessful, and he ultimately left Istanbul, settling for the role of an inspector in Samsun. Notwithstanding the nationalist fervour that persuaded high-ranking bureaucrats and military men to resist the occupation by going to Anatolia, it was not until the official occupation of Istanbul by British forces that large numbers of these officials chose to leave Istanbul.[55] After the occupation, they felt they had no place left for them in Istanbul; they had few options open to them; either they would be arrested by British forces and sent to Malta as political detainees or they could leave Istanbul for Ankara.[56] It seems that the occupation of Istanbul hugely influenced their decision to go to Ankara.

The rise of the anti-nationalist movement in South Marmara

The population of the South Marmara region consisted mostly of refugees who had travelled to the region in the mid-1860s. One of the largest groups in the region was the Circassians, many of whom had been settled in the region by the Ottoman Porte in the second half of the nineteenth century after the Circassian exile. During the days following the *93 Harbi*, or the Ottoman–Russian War of 1877–78, an increasing number of refugees flooded into the region. These included Turks, Albanians, Circassians and Bosnians. From the 1860s to the 1920s, the influx of refugees completely altered the social and economic characteristics of the South Marmara. Meanwhile, the non-Muslim residents of South Marmara were either exiled or left the region voluntarily, between 1910 and the early 1920s. Their migration, or exile, also led to further major changes in the region. The Turks, Circassians, Albanians and Bosnians had already previously fought one another, and from early 1910, the relationship between the different groups had been worsened due to weak state structures and the arrival of many more migrants in the region fleeing from the effects of the Balkan Wars.

In the months following the end of the First World War, Anzavur Ahmed, a member of the Ottoman Special Organization, was appointed the governor of several districts in the South Marmara region.[57] Although at the close of the First World War, Anzavur was working with the nationalists to control the Circassian bandits who were creating chaos and endangering the region, later he moved to the anti-nationalist cause, because his demands were not being satisfied by the nationalists.[58] During the Greek occupation, Anzavur Ahmed mobilized many people with the support of some high-ranking Ottoman politicians working against the *Kuva-yi Milliye*. He used discourse laden with Islamic references, emphasizing the importance of the caliphate and the Ottoman sultanate, while simultaneously attacking the declarations of the *Kuva-yi Milliye* in Anatolia by accusing it of being a continuation of the CUP. Anzavur Ahmed clearly used key nationalist figures' links with the CUP in his speeches in order to mobilize the masses against them. He referred to the wartime and pre-wartime policies of the CUP, drawing analogies with *Kuva-yi Milliye* in a bid to disgrace the latter in front of the people. He declared that his aim was to save the country from the CUP and its policies and to end the Greek occupation with a loyal army.[59] Conversely, Hacim Muhittin (1881–1965), a leading figure for *Kuva-yi Milliye* in Balıkesir, stated that the aim of Ahmed Anzavur was actually to arrest him and other *Kuva-yi Milliye* members (during horse races in Balıkesir/Savaştepe) to send them to Istanbul. He also believed that Anzavur's movement would ultimately lead to a Turkish–Circassian conflict in the region, and that British forces would then take advantage of the situation to gain control of the region.[60]

Certainly, in 1919, a short while before Anzavur arrived, chaos persisted in the region, particularly in Karacabey, as struggles between the Circassians and Albanians worsened.[61] Armed clashes were taking place between groups, and many of these continued for days on end, with people engaged in the widespread plundering of one another's villages and farms.[62] A significant number of people were killed on both sides. The conflict between the Albanians and Circassians spread to other districts in the region, such as Kirmasti.[63] Overall insecurity provided a significant opportunity for Anzavur's opposition[64] to mobilize the masses to counter the nationalists. In addition to the security problems affecting the region, members of the *Kuva-yi Milliye* forced people to pay taxes beyond what they could reasonably afford; they also confiscated their horses and seized property belonging to villagers and residents in the region.[65]

Clashes between the Circassians and Albanians were an acute problem in Kirmasti and Karacabey. However, Bekir Sami believes that the underlying dispute between the Circassians and Albanians in Kirmasti and Karacabey was not 'ethnic' in nature.⁶⁶ However, even if the reasons for the conflict between the Circassians and Albanians were due to ethnic differences, this cannot provide a basis for generalizing about the events in the entire South Marmara region. The basis of the conflict for the groups was about gaining local authority over the groups in the region while trying to restrict other groups' living space. The participants in the Anzavur incident consisted of several groups; this provides evidence of the veracity of Bekir Sami's argument. Many of those who took part in the Anzavur incident were Circassians, Pomaks, Albanians and Turks. They participated because Anzavur Ahmed's rhetoric focused on Islam and the sultan/caliph, although he used these as symbols rather than attaching any deeper meaning to them, as will become clearer later.⁶⁷ It is apparent, however, that although problems existed between the different ethnic groups, an emphasis on Islam, loyalty to the sultan and an anti-CUP stance convinced them to work together against the *Kuva-yi Milliye*.

Anzavur was also backed by several groups in the capital. He used the presence of the British in the region to push his anti-nationalist agenda. Britain also aimed to use Ahmed Anzavur to save the Dardanelles and the Straits for themselves. The threat from the nationalists around the Dardanelles forced the British to support Anzavur's movement in the form of military equipment.⁶⁸ The Ottoman government, the Damad Ferit cabinet itself, also promised military assistance to Anzavur Ahmed to oppose the *Kuva-yi Milliye*.⁶⁹ Anzavur Ahmed was further supported by other groups, some of whose members were agents or volunteers of the Special Organization of the Ottoman state and who had been pardoned by the state for past crimes committed while in criminal gangs.⁷⁰ He also began to recruit armed persons to counter the *Kuva-yi Milliye*.⁷¹ Anzavur Ahmed used Islamic rhetoric while also claiming that the *Kuva-yi Milliye* was a continuation of the CUP – a group, which he claimed was comprised of freemasons.⁷² He also presented himself to the sultan as the one able to liberate the Aydın province from Greek occupation and protect the country from further losses in provinces that might potentially become part of an independent Armenia.⁷³

As apparent in a report sent to the War Office, the reasons for the widespread unrest in the Bursa/Hüdavendigar province of South Marmara and its surroundings during the post-First-World-War period could be expressed as follows:

- The gendarmes are not forceful and reliable;
- The residents of the region are from very diverse ethnic and religious backgrounds, like 'the tower of Babel';
- Due to the continuation of many new waves of migration, many people are homeless and suffering from famine;
- Worse still is the 'bandit activism' of some groups, which opens a door to foreign intervention in the region; and
- Those who have been appointed as members of the military tribunal have not come to the region to begin their duties.[74]

On 12 November 1919, Anzavur Ahmed captured the Susurluk district of Balıkesir.[75] One of his aims in doing so was to end the *Kuva-yi Milliye* and to arrest its members.[76] He gave a speech, which emphasized his plans to abolish military service so that he could protect the caliphate; and he requested that soldiers either leave the district or join him.[77] The *Kuva-yi Milliye*'s response to Anzavur Ahmed's movement was clear. In the beginning, the *Kuva-yi Milliye* avoided conflict with Anzavur Ahmed because the latter had already received the backing of many people in a short period. Some military commanders were sent by the *Kuva-yi Milliye* to induce Anzavur Ahmed to join their national movement. However, they were unsuccessful.[78] It is important to explore what the *Kuva-yi Milliye* meant to Ahmed Anzavur as an ordinary Ottoman '*alaylı*' (soldier) and a former member of the *Teşkilat-ı Mahsusa*. In a telegram to the Ministry of Interior, Anzavur Ahmed stated that, because of the CUP's policies over the last ten years, people were witnessing an ongoing and terrible situation in the empire, while the *Kuva-yi Milliye*, which was organized by the very same people, was now provoking ordinary people to seek revenge against the Greeks and the Entente. They were nothing more than bandits who had come together and organized the *Kuva-yi Milliye*. The group also ruled the state without consideration for the legitimate Ottoman government. They collected money from the poor while living lavishly themselves.[79]

On 14 November 1919, he sent a letter to Colonel Kazım Özalp to demand Özalp's neutrality in his fight against the CUP and the Greek troops.[80] A day later, Anzavur Ahmed and his troops encountered the *Kuva-yi Milliye*.

He was then defeated, and he left the region.[81] On 22 November, Anzavur Ahmed captured Gönen and arrested a number of officials, including the first lieutenant and governor of the district Ziya (Şahan) Efendi and *Kuva-yi Milliye* member Esat Bey.[82] The mostly Circassian-populated villages around Gönen and Manyas areas either willingly or forcibly participated in Anzavur's movement; these villages included Muratlar, Keçeler, Bayramiç, Üçpınar, Karalar, Çerkes Keçidere, Karaağaçalan, Aynalıdere, Hacı Menteş, Sızı Hasan Bey, Çerkes Çalı Oba and Asmalıdere (Turks were resident in the village).[83] Çerkes Ethem participated in the battle against Anzavur Ahmed.[84] On 26 November he came to Gönen, and Anzavur Ahmed was again defeated.[85] Gönen and its villages were held by *Kuva-yi Milliye* on 2 December; up until this time, Anzavur Ahmed had lost 120 of his men in conflict.[86]

On 6 December 1919, nearly eighty armed people under the leadership of the gangs Suphi and Kara Hasan of *Kuva-yi Milliye* were sent to arrest Anzavur Ahmed; they ended up looting the farm of the wife of a prominent Circassian gang leader named Şah İsmail and some other Circassian villages.[87] Another group of armed people also joined the Suphi and Kara Hasan action against the Circassians. The situation in the region transformed into an ethnic conflict between the Circassians and Turks. The local governors tried to minimize these conflicts and sent an advisory council to the Circassians, in which two Circassians took part – (Big) Ahmet Fevzi Paşa and Hurşit Paşa.[88] The advisory council spoke to local people in order to calm the situation, and this prompted the discharge of the rebels arrested in the region by the local governors.[89] On balance, it can be stated that during the Anzavur incident, the approach of the Istanbul government was self-contradictory. Initially, there was no determined policy towards the *Kuva-yi Milliye*. There was no doubt that different political groups existed in Istanbul, all vying for power.[90] Even in the government, different policies were applied by different ministries. Two ministries in particular – *Dahiliye Nezareti* (Ministry of Interior) and *Harbiye Nezareti* (War Office and its local branches) – espoused very different policies. The military commander of local units, such as the War Office, demanded a harsh repression of 'the rebels' without any sympathy.[91] Meanwhile, the local governors of the region, that is, those from the Ministry of Interior, aspired to send an advisory council to Anzavur Ahmed in order to placate him.[92]

It can be said that from the very beginning a connection existed between the War Office in Istanbul and *Kuva-yi Milliye*. When Britain asked by the Ministry of War to remove Cemal Paşa and Cevat Paşa from their offices, Mustafa Kemal, even though he had been removed from his duties, supported resistance against the British demands. The War Office was part of the national movement. The nationalists and the War Office itself engaged in a partial collaboration, and despite the frequent cabinet reshuffles in Istanbul, this collaboration continued until the official occupation of Istanbul by British forces in March 1920. It is also noteworthy that the nationalists viewed themselves as the 'saviours' of the state. Indeed, it can be seen from archival documents that the nationalists were already considering themselves the legitimate governors of the state, long before they opened the assembly in Ankara on April 1920. In fact, their attitude led to confusion in the existing historiography, due to the often-contradictory language used – language that presented them as both reliant on the Istanbul government *and* against it. Although they were officials and the military men of the Ottoman state, they accused Istanbul of not taking the necessary measures to stop the chaos in South Marmara. The people who vied against the nationalists were characterized as 'opponents' (*muhalif/karşıt*) by the former; however, it can be argued that those opponents were not against the legitimate government of the country, that is the one in Istanbul. They were, in fact, against the *Kuva-yi Milliye* and later the Ankara government.

Particularly with regard to Biga, it can be said that the town's local officials did not support one side in the conflict between the *Kuva-yi Milliye* and Ahmed Anzavur. Although the *Kuva-yi Milliye* consisted of military men, bureaucrats and state officials, besides the guerrillas and irregulars, the local governors of Biga still did not support it.[93] It seems that in the town there were two distinct groups tussling for authority, while the local officials of the town were changing sides according to who was winning. On 20 February 1920, Anzavur Ahmed captured Biga and seized arms, which had been snatched earlier by the *Kuva-yi Milliye* from the Akbaş arsenal.[94] Many Circassians arrived in Biga with Anzavur from their villages.[95] Significant numbers of people from the districts of Gönen and Biga joined Anzavur's movement towards Yenice, where arms were being stored by the *Kuva-yi Milliye*.[96] Hamdi Bey,[97] who was a nationalist and a former governor of Edremit district, aimed to prepare a regiment from Biga and to tax the people of Biga for the expenses of the regiment.⁹⁸ However, the potential taxation troubled people who had already undergone economic hardships; thus, it caused an increase in support for Anzavur Ahmed.⁹⁹ Due to this support, the *Kuva-yi Milliye* failed to resist the anti-nationalists in the region. The arsenal was blown up by the *Kuva-yi Milliye* because they did not have enough soldiers to protect the arms and felt threatened by the possibility of Anzavur gaining access to them.¹⁰⁰ By April, Anzavur took control in Gönen,¹⁰¹ Bandırma¹⁰² Karacabey and Kirmasti. The impact of his movement reached Adapazarı, where the people, a majority of whom were Circassian, then began to conspire against *Kuva-yi Milliye*.¹⁰³ His movement thus became widespread throughout the region.

The actions taken by the *Kuva-yi Milliye* against Anzavur Ahmed were on occasion quite harsh. On 6 March 1920, a group of people from *Kuva-yi Milliye* burnt down three Circassian villages and the houses of Circassians who had been allied with Anzavur Ahmed.¹⁰⁴ Indeed, until April 1920, the *Kuva-yi Milliye* did not have much support in the region and the anti-nationalist movement was still strong. Therefore, to solidify their position in the region, the *Kuva-yi Milliye* commanders took additional steps, hardening their policy and rhetoric against the Circassians in order to 'warn' them of the consequences if they persisted. Bekir Sami emphasized that Circassians should be loyal to the state, meaning the *Kuva-yi Milliye*, otherwise they would be annihilated. He emphasized this by going to Kirmasti and Karacabey and claiming that a 'betrayal' would result in the Circassians being annihilated.¹⁰⁵ When a concern was raised among Circassians about the *Kuva-yi Milliye*, Bekir Sami tried to convince them that they were safe by saying that half of the leadership in the *Kuva-yi Milliye* were Circassians. The aim of *Kuva-yi Milliye* was nothing more than to achieve an independent Turkey.¹⁰⁶ However, Bekir Sami did not consider the ordinary people's thoughts regarding the *Kuva-yi Milliye*. Ordinary Circassians felt themselves close to the sultanate and caliphate, contrary to the Circassian elite who were once members of the CUP and who had then taken a role in the *Kuva-yi Milliye*. Bekir Sami nonetheless emphasized the role of the elite Circassians in the *Kuva-yi Milliye*.

Some military units were permitted to imprison, punish and even execute (without the necessary judicial process) those who opposed the *Kuva-yi Milliye* and supported Anzavur Ahmed.¹⁰⁷ The nationalists did in fact discuss the process of military tribunals. However, it emerged that military men did not aspire to conduct proper judicial processes; they saw this as wasting time.¹⁰⁸ The commander of the 172nd Regiment, Lieutenant Colonel Kasap Osman (or Osman 'the Butcher'), asked Bekir Sami for his opinion concerning whether he should execute prisoners by shooting or whether he should judge them.¹⁰⁹ Two days after asking for Bekir Sami's opinion, Colonel Osman executed four individuals who had killed a *Kuva-yi Milliye* soldier in an exchange of fire, as an example to others.¹¹⁰

The lack of proper equipment and organized army units in the region led to an understanding among the *Kuva-yi Milliye* commanders regarding the importance of the irregular and paramilitary groups in carrying out resistance against Greek troops and the Anzavur Ahmed incident. Assistance against Anzavur Ahmed from Çerkes Ethem, who had already established a hundred-kilometre-long line of resistance against the Greek forces,¹¹¹ as well as Demirci Efe, was demanded.¹¹² Çerkes Ethem came to the region with two thousand armed men, while Demirci Efe sent six hundred cavalrymen to join the *Kuva-yi Milliye*.¹¹³ A group of Anzavur's armed men, under the command of Çerkes Ahmet Bey, a retired Ottoman army colonel, were followed to Biga wharf, where they were caught in the crossfire of the *Kuva-yi Milliye* before boarding a ship to escape from Biga.¹¹⁴ Anzavur was wounded and left the region for Istanbul. Those who supported Anzavur were later dispersed by Ethem's forces. Ahmed Anzavur did not represent an important threat to Ankara at this time.

It is noteworthy that Kazım Özalp referred to Ahmed Anzavur's armed men as 'brigands', even though they were under the command of a former Ottoman colonel who himself had been under the command of Kazım Özalp during the First World War.¹¹⁵ However, Kazım Özalp did not offer to explain why a retired Ottoman army colonel, Çerkes Ahmet Bey, had also joined Ahmed Anzavur. The answer to this might lie in Çerkes Ahmet's own Circassian network, a dislike of CUP/ *Kuva-yi Milliye*, his feelings or ties to the Ottoman dynasty, or local disputes with other groups. Kazım Özalp did not give any reasons for the actions carried out by his former colonel. He only emphasized that they (himself and *Kuva-yi Milliye*) were working to 'save' the fatherland, while the anti-nationalist movement was comprised of bandits, religious fanatics and bigots.¹¹⁶

Ahmed Anzavur's movement favoured a two-pronged tactic as part of a wider strategy of mobilizing the different people of the region. The first was centred on ethnicity and the second on Islam. That is to say, although Anzavur Ahmed underlined 'Islamic unity' and his rhetoric focused on the Muslims of the state, his main success came in mobilizing large numbers of Circassians.[117] Indeed, he focused on places populated by Circassians, such as Biga, Gönen, Kirmasti, Manyas, Düzce, Adapazarı and Hendek. It is also important to mention that not only ordinary Circassians but also Circassian notables supported Ahmed Anzavur.[118] These features of Anzavur's movement threatened the *Kuva-yi Milliye* because of the possibility they opened for a 'Turkish-Circassian issue' to develop in the region.[119] The *Kuva-yi Milliye* also needed the support of the armed groups in the region for their war against the Greeks, and could not afford the 'ethnic conflict' brewing among the subjects of the state.[120]

As noted above, the second important component of Ahmed Anzavur's mobilization strategy was his appeal for Islamic unity and better relations with the Ottoman Porte.[121] Such rhetoric influenced Muslim sentiment against the *Kuva-yi Milliye*. Anzavur also avoided the issues of taxation and compulsory military service, two unpopular policies employed by the *Kuva-yi Milliye*; this increased his support among ordinary people. In this regard, Anzavur Ahmed's movement was more of a threat to the *Kuva-yi Milliye* than the Greek occupation. The internal struggle in the South Marmara between Anzavur Ahmed and the nationalists could lead to a reduction in support for the *Kuva-yi Milliye*.[122] His criticism of Mustafa Kemal and his circle was especially harsh. He described Mustafa Kemal as a rebel. Anzavur Ahmed also promised that he would save the Anatolian people from Mustafa Kemal's cruelty for the sake of the fatherland and the sultan.[123]

The nationalists were fully cognizant of the Circassian support for Anzavur Ahmed. They attempted to divide the Circassians into two groups to strengthen the *Kuva-yi Milliye* in the region.[124] Otherwise, they thought they would be unable to pursue their activities in the region. It can also be said that there were differences between the *Kuva-yi Milliye* and Anzavur Ahmed in terms of their attitude towards the residents of the region. For instance, the *Kuva-yi Milliye* threatened and cajoled the local population through force to acquire their support against the Greek occupation and Ahmed Anzavur. By contrast,

Ahmed Anzavur sought the support of local people via non-coercive means. His written declarations against the nationalists were often enough to gain the backing of the masses in the field.

In the days and months following the First World War, violence and conflict became widespread throughout the South Marmara region, and bandits and gangs became features of daily life. The main characteristic features of these groups were their ethnicity, which separated them from 'others'. However, the conflicts were generally local and limited to their districts. With the Greek occupation of Western Anatolia, two new main groups emerged in the region: the loyalists and the nationalists. Existing armed groups later joined one of the new groups, while continuing their bandit activities. It is noteworthy that the loyalist movement was united on an Islamic basis. The loyalists mobilized people by emphasizing their ties with the caliphate and the sultanate. Circassian ethnicity also played an important role in the strengthening of the loyalist movement. Anzavur Ahmed used Circassian ethnicity to solidify his movement, which was based in towns populated by Circassians. Meanwhile, the national movement also tried to use Circassian ethnicity to gain an advantage. In the beginning, this was used to develop a line of resistance against the Greek occupation, and it relied on Circassian networks in South Marmara. However, with the emergence of the anti-nationalist movement, the nationalists encouraged Çerkes Ethem to battle against the anti-nationalists. The conflict between the loyalists and nationalists then became an intra-community struggle between Çerkes Ethem and Anzavur Ahmed. The conflict also forced the nationalists to think more deeply about the existence of Circassians in the region. As will be explored later, the Gönen–Manyas deportations can be seen as a deliberate nationalist attempt to reduce the density of the Circassian population in the region.

3

Civil war in the empire: Adapazarı–Düzce and Yozgat incidents (1920)

In the history of the modern republic of Turkey, the Adapazarı–Hendek–Düzce region came to the attention of the media twice, in 1996. The first such instance was when a ferry, Avrasya, which ran between the port at Trabzon, Turkey, and the port at Sochi, Russia, was hijacked. The aim of those who hijacked the ferry was to protest against the atrocities committed by Russia in Chechnya during the Russian–Chechnian War of 1996.[1] The incident received massive attention from both the Turkish and international media. Because the incident played out without an armed clash with the security forces and because none of the passengers were wounded, many North Caucasian groups in Turkey monitored the incident closely and welcomed the activists in İstanbul. The activists brought the ferry to İstanbul and left without engaging in a clash with the Turkish security forces. The leading members of the group were Circassian and Abkhazian from the Adapazarı and Düzce region.

The second incident that grabbed the attention of the media was the Susurluk incident (one of the biggest scandals highlighting the extent of the police–mafia–state nexus in Turkey), which followed a seemingly routine car crash in the Southern Marmara town of Susurluk. The bodies in the car included those of Abdullah Çatlı, who was wanted by Interpol, police chief Hüseyin Kocadağ and Sedat Bucak, an MP and a leader of a pro-state tribe from Southeast Turkey; all except Sedat Bucak were pronounced dead at the scene. A parliamentary committee was established in order to investigate the presence of this unlikely trio in the car crash. The committee conducted hearings with politicians, bureaucrats and suspects in the case. Additionally, individuals thought to be related to these people and their networks were also called upon to testify before the committee. Mehmet Hadi Özcan,[2] who was imprisoned as a leader of a local criminal group that was active in the İzmit–Adapazarı region, also appeared before the committee.

Below are some excerpts from his testimony:

> **Chair:** Several extra-judicial executions have been carried out in this triangle, Kocaeli, Sakarya (Adapazarı), Sapanca, and Istanbul, and it so happens that the mafia groups are all based in this region. Why is this?
> **Mehmet Hadi Özcan:** Because of the weather, I suppose! I don't know. [He was obviously making a reference to a well-known Turkish expression that is generally used to make fun of questions that one is asked, or to water down the seriousness of the matter being discussed.]
> **Chair:** We also like the weather, but …
> **Mehmet Hadi Özcan:** Indeed, it is all happening here, and they are all from around here.
> **Chair:** But I do not think that it is simply because of the weather.[3]

Evidently, the weather was not the cause. In fact, this was not the first time that the region had been the focus of attention. Almost seventy-five years earlier, in 1920, an incident took place in the region that threatened the very survival of *Kuva-yi Milliye* in Ankara. This incident was led by a Circassian-dominated group, which had close relationships with the Ottoman government. The Ottoman government later used this situation to weaken the Ankara-based nationalists. The nationalists first sent an advisory delegation to calm down those who had taken up arms, but the Ankara government chose to use military force to suppress them, killing several members of the delegation who were en route to a meeting with anti-nationalists. Although a certain level of calm was initially achieved in the region, anti-*Kuva-yi Milliye* sentiments prevailed in the region, and opposition to the Ankara government continued. This opposition movement continued until the 1940s, and became a transborder movement when its leading members were stripped of their citizenship and banished from the newly established Turkish Republic. This incident will be investigated in further detail in Chapter 6.

Although the Adapazarı–Düzce incidents appeared to be a limited opposition movement compared to other incidents of the era, both in terms of its geographical penetration and in terms of the after-effects of the incidents in the following decades, it retains a unique place in the historiography of modern Turkey. Indeed, the incidents broke out in a region that was situated very close to the headquarters of the national movement, thus forcing the

Ankara government to prepare for relocating parliament to the town of Sivas.[4] The leaders of the incidents were either killed by the nationalists, or they moved abroad and continued their opposition to the nationalist cause (later known as the Kemalist cause) over the following years. This chapter argues that the suppression of the anti-nationalist movements of Adapazarı–Düzce and Yozgat strengthened Çerkes Ethem's position in the nationalist cause. Moreover, it claims that, in order to unite the people against the Greek occupation and the anti-nationalists, Ethem took extremely harsh measures against the anti-nationalists, without differentiating between Turks, Circassians, Muslims or non-Muslims. It could be said that without Ethem's military forces and actions, it would not have been possible for the Ankara government to gain acceptance as the de facto government from the people of Anatolia. This chapter will demonstrate why the Adapazarı–Düzce incidents occupy a significant place in the history of Turkey, particularly during the transformation from empire to nation state. First, this chapter will examine the Circassian opposition to the Ankara-based nationalists in the Adapazarı–Düzce region. Secondly, it will focus on how one key paramilitary leader of the period, Çerkes Ethem, became one of the most powerful people in the country after suppressing another incident in Yozgat.

The Adapazarı–Düzce incidents

The Adapazarı–Düzce region was extremely important for both the Istanbul and Ankara governments, as gaining the support of the local people could change the balance of power for either side in the conflict. During the period after the First World War, there were many armed people and armed groups in this area. Geographically, the region was sandwiched between the territories controlled by the opposing governments in Istanbul and Ankara. Therefore, this was, strategically speaking, a very significant location. For the Ankara government, the region was a transit zone for sending Ottoman military arms from the arsenals in Istanbul to Anatolia. The main railway line from Istanbul to West and Central Anatolia passed through this region and, during the civil war, maintaining control over the railway line and the region was vital. Moreover, the Ankara government was greatly concerned about armed mobilization in the region, which, although both geographically and politically closer to the

Ottoman Porte, was only a day's journey from Ankara. The conflict, which initially surfaced in the Adapazarı–Düzce region, moved closer to Ankara with each passing day, where the government did not have a sufficiently well-prepared army.

The Adapazarı–Düzce region was also vital for Ankara-based nationalists in Istanbul, who passed through the region on their way to Ankara. The *Karakol*[5], which organized the nationalists' escape from Istanbul, was a powerful organization in the region, but was being threatened by Rum, Armenian bandits and Ottoman Palace-supported anti-nationalist Circassians. The local Laz, an ethnic group that originates from the Black Sea coast, were mobilized by *Karakol* against anti-nationalist groups in the region. Local small-boat captains, Ramiz and Rauf of Hopa, as well as Dr Refik of Trabzon, Meto Hüseyin and Mehmet Bey, were recruited to the nationalist cause by Karakol, and Yenibahçeli Şükrü was appointed as the general commander of the region.[6] Although Ali Fuat Paşa (Cebesoy)[7] believed that the significance of the incident was exaggerated by the Ankara government due to the reports that it received from local unit commanders, the incident was, nevertheless, the single biggest threat facing Ankara at that time. The Ankara government began to panic and, in an attempt to quell the incident, the government diverted army units from the western and southern fronts to the region, even though those troops did not have sufficient preparation and training for confronting the local anti-nationalists.

A group of Circassian notables attempted to gain control of the region. Their aim was to maintain their control of the region by holding on to the prominence that they enjoyed in the post–First-World-War period, and they sought the support of the Istanbul government. Some members of the Ottoman Palace, such as *Baş Mabeyinci* Yaver Paşa, contacted Circassian notables in the hope of convincing them to rise up against the Ankara government[8] with the help of well-armed local Circassian villagers in İzmit, Sapanca, Hendek and Düzce. One of the reasons the Porte had gained support so fast was the great respect and affinity the locals felt towards the Ottoman sultan and the caliph, as well as the presence in the Ottoman government, bureaucracy, army and security structures of a significant number of Circassians from the region, who commanded respect among the local Circassians and had relatives among them. Furthermore, the presence of Circassian women in the Ottoman harem also played a part here.⁹ Not only did the leaders of the incident gain the support of the local people, they were also able to influence the army units that were stationed in the region.¹⁰

The people of the region had no sympathies for CUP rule and considered the nationalists of Ankara to be a continuation of the CUP, which was thought by many to be responsible for the disastrous outcomes in the First World War. The fact that the region had been engaged in several long-lasting wars, from the Balkan Wars of 1912–13 to October 1918, when their involvement in the First World War ended, was another reason for the incident. Specifically, war-weariness was a problem in the region, which had been in a constant state of war since the early 1910s. Although the country was under occupation, many ordinary people were against military mobilization.¹¹ The local notables, on the other hand, took a less strict stance towards either the Istanbul government or the nationalists in Anatolia. For the most part, they depended on their own personal networks and on the dynamics of local politics. For instance, Sait Bey worked for the *Kuva-yi Milliye* in the Adapazarı region, but his local rival, Çerkes Hikmet, also sought a position in the local *Kuva-yi Milliye* branch; he was prevented by his rivals from joining the branch, which was also controlled by members of the CUP that Çerkes Hikmet opposed. Consequently, Çerkes Hikmet began recruiting people who supported the Istanbul government, rather than *Kuva-yi Milliye*.¹²

The Adapazarı–Düzce region first attracted the attention of Mustafa Kemal on 20 October 1919. In a telegram sent by the commander of the First Division, Mustafa Asım, to Mustafa Kemal, the former explained that a group of Circassian and Abkhazians led by Bekir, Beslan and Talustan Beys, had tried to recruit people in the town of Akyazı by declaring that they would not accept Mustafa Kemal as a replacement for the sultan, and had tried to set up a local government.¹³ Two pro-Ankara Circassians were sent by Mustafa Asım to gather information about the incident.¹⁴ A few days later, with the support of local Circassians and military units stationed in the area, the group was routed out of the town.¹⁵

Public order had already broken down in Adapazarı and the surrounding areas after the First World War. Some Circassians and Abkhazians were actively engaging in banditry in the region.¹⁶ In the early days of the national movement, a struggle between the Ankara and Istanbul governments had already begun in Adapazarı–Düzce over authority and control of the region. Çerkes Bekir of Adapazarı went to the region to recruit people to the Special Organization, which was controlled by the national movement at that time.[17] However, Bekir's propaganda for the nationalist cause was unsuccessful. The elders of the Circassian community in Düzce did not accept Bekir's offer of working for the *Kuva-yi Milliye*.[18] Approximately ten days later, he came to Adapazarı to recruit people; as in Düzce, his attempt ended in failure.[19] On 24 February 1920, Kuşçubaşı Eşref Bey, who used the title 'Commander of the Mujahedeen of Turkey' (Türkiye Umum Mücahidin Kumandanı) and had been appointed to the position of commander of the *Kuva-yi Milliye* forces in İzmit, Adapazarı and Bolu, came to Kandıra, a town in Adapazarı, with the objective of preventing any anti-*Kuva-yi Milliye* uprisings in the region.[20] Due to his ethnic origin and network with the armed groups in the region it could be said that Eşref was preferred by Ankara.[21] He arrived in Adapazarı on 3 April 1920 accompanied by dozens of mounted infantry soldiers[22]; he aimed to recruit local people for his troop but he was not sure what reaction he would get from the locals.[23]

However, he also failed in his attempt to gain the support of the locals for the nationalist cause. One possible explanation for this failure is that the local Circassian notables did not think that his family's rank in the Circassian hierarchy was high enough, even though Eşref was a well-known agent in the Special Organization and his family had links to the Ottoman Palace because of his father's role there.[24] One could be from the palace, but not a Circassian noble. Another problem Eşref faced in the region was his lack of strong local connection. He was very well-known among the army officers, Special Organization agents and soldiers but he did not have very well-working local connections in the Adapazarı region. He was known in Western Thrace and Arab lands by the local people and bedouins but it was difficult to say the same for Adapazarı. His family also did not have strong local connections. They worked and lived in İstanbul. As a result, Eşref was unable to gain control in Adapazarı. Çerkes Kanbulat Sait of Adapazarı was wary of Eşref's activities and mobilized a group to oust Eşref. Although this movement was initially directed against Eşref's activities, it later turned into an anti-*Kuva-yi Milliye* uprising. Eşref had to escape from Adapazarı with only thirty armed men. Those who failed to escape were imprisoned and beaten by the anti-nationalists, the majority of whom were Circassians.²⁵ Kanbulat and his helpers first moved to Adapazarı, but later headed towards Hendek. In the town of Çatalköprü, they destroyed the bridges that connected Adapazarı with Hendek.²⁶

On 13 April, anti-*Kuva-yi Milliye* Circassians and Abkhazians held a meeting in the Ömer Efendi village of Düzce and started another incident.²⁷ The telegraph lines were broken, military buildings were attacked and a captain and an officer were killed.²⁸ Military ammunition were taken over by the anti-nationalists; prisoners were released from the military prison and the town jail, and the anti-nationalists recruited people into their own gendarme force. They seized official positions in Düzce and appointed Berzeg Sefer Bey as governor and Maan Ali²⁹ as commander of the gendarme force, made Vahap responsible for subsistence and reinforcement (iaşe ve ikmal), and named Koç Bey as mayor of the town.³⁰ On 18 April, the leaders of the incident met in *Paşa Karyesi* and made a declaration, in which they openly stated that they were not hostile towards the Istanbul government.³¹ A group of the anti-nationalists, which comprised people from the twenty-seven different villages of the Düzce–Bolu region,³² attacked military units in Bolu and Düzce and seized their arms.³³ Since the local governor of Bolu also backed the anti-nationalist movement, he was able to convince them to go back to their villages. The Ankara government sent a group of MPs to negotiate with the local leaders and put an end to the anti-*Kuva-yi Milliye* movement; this group included Hüsrev, Fuat, Şükrü and Hüseyin Beys, and was accompanied by a cavalry detachment.³⁴ On 20 April, another group of anti-nationalists came to Bolu from Gerede to occupy the local governor's building and to complain about Ankara and local bureaucrats who were loyal to Ankara. As a result of this occupation, the anti-nationalists declared that they would not recognize any government apart from that of the sultan, and that they would not join any government army except that demanded by Istanbul. Communication channels would only remain open with Istanbul, and not with Ankara. In addition, the clerks of the Telegraph Office of Bolu would be replaced, and only the government in Istanbul would be allowed to collect taxes from the region.³⁵

The Ankara government sent its military detachments from Adapazarı to Düzce to suppress the incident, which was close to reaching the outskirts of Ankara, but they were defeated by the anti-nationalists, of whom there were more than two thousand (the majority of whom were Circassian).³⁶ In Düzce,

Hendek and Adapazarı, all senior nationalist military officers were arrested; more than eight hundred foot soldiers were discharged, and their arms and ammunition were confiscated by the anti-nationalists,[37] who were led by Berzeg Sefer Bey.[38] Lieutenant Colonel Mahmut, who was also Circassian, was sent by Mustafa Kemal to replace Kuşçubaşı Eşref and to convince the Circassians to end their anti-nationalist activities. Mahmut informed Ankara that Eşref's existence in the region and his freeing the prisoners worsened the situation in Adapazarı.[39] He left the Yağbasan village of Hendek on 21 April,[40] and was on his way to Düzce when he was confronted by a group of armed men, most of whom were Abkhazians. They were accompanied by other Abkhazian troops under Mahmut Bey's command. Initially, the meeting was friendly and Mahmud Bey's troops and the anti-nationalist Abkhazians began marching together towards Düzce. However, at some point on the 23 April 1920, an Abkhazian from the anti-nationalist group shot Mahmut Bey[41] and killed a further three people who were sent by Ankara as an 'advice council', with the task of reaching an agreement between the Ankara government and the anti-nationalists in the village of Budaklar of Hendek.[42] Following these incidents, no *Kuva-yi Milliye* sympathizers remained in the region.[43] The region was now entirely under the control of the anti-nationalists, who put forward the demands of the Istanbul government via the commander of the gendarme force of Bolu, Osman Nuri, on 24 April 1920.[44] They stated that the sultan and his government (i.e. the Istanbul government) were the only legitimate authorities in the empire, only the Ministry of War should have the authority to recruit people into the army, telegram communication should be opened with the Istanbul government and cut with Ankara, and tax should only be collected by the Ministry of Finance.[45]

Ankara subsequently sent a group of MPs and military men to the region. This group included Hüsrev (Gerede) Bey, whose memoirs are an important source for understanding the incident.[46] When the group arrived in Gerede, they were surrounded by anti-nationalists and were taken as hostages.[47] It is worth noting that Islamic rhetoric and rituals were practised by the anti-nationalists during the incident in order to encourage local people to rise up against the Ankara government. Although there were Turks among the anti-nationalists, the majority of the participants were Circassian.[48] The leader of the anti-nationalists, Berzeg Sefer Bey, visited Hüsrev Bey in prison, where he explained to him that he was against Mustafa Kemal and his friends because he wanted to prevent them from establishing a military dictatorship in Turkey.[49]

On 2 May 1920, Bolu was taken by the *Kuva-yi Milliye* forces, which consisted of five hundred cavalry and foot soldiers under the command of the Lieutenant Colonel Arif Bey.[50] Two days after Arif Bey had taken control of the city; it was surrounded by forces belonging to the Istanbul government. As a result, one hundred soldiers were captured as prisoners of war by the anti-nationalists. Arif Bey was forced to leave the city, which fell into the hands of the Istanbul government on 13 May 1920.[51] However, the nationalists did not cease their activities; they had different cells and networks in several other cities in Anatolia and used all possible means of collecting intelligence in the Adapazarı–Düzce region. For this purpose, Kuşçubaşı Eşref's brother Ahmed, a reserve officer, and his friend, Lieutenant Ahmed Adli Bey, travelled from Istanbul to İzmit, pretending to be merchants. However, on completion of their journey through the region, they were arrested by the Istanbul government on May 1920.[52]

By May 1920, the region had already become a centre of the anti-nationalist movement. This movement not only involved Circassians of Düzce; anti-*Kuva-yi Milliye* uprisings also flared up in Adapazarı and İzmit. Most of these involved three main opposition groups that were operating in the region. The first group was from the Düzce–Bolu region and consisted of Circassians and Abkhazians under the leadership of Berzeg Sefer. The second group was made up of the forces led by Ahmed Anzavur,[53] who was also active outside South Marmara and had the potential to pose a serious threat to the Ankara government in Adapazarı. He demonstrated this by organizing a raid on Boğazköy on 10 May 1920, in which he led around five hundred armed men, some of whom were from the villages of Hamidiye, Kemaliye and Kumbaşı in Adapazarı. He occupied the region for six days, attacking the troops of Ali Fuat Paşa with two thousand soldiers from the army of the caliphate on 15 May, and taking full control of the entire region on 24 May.[54] However, his victory was short-lived, as he was defeated two days later by a joint Cebesoy–Ethem force on 26 May, the latter of which had recently reached the town of Hendek.[55] Finally, the third opposition group was from the town of İzmit, where Çule İbrahim Hakkı[56] was the governor. [57]

As a response to the threat posed by the anti-nationalist Circassians, the Ankara government also attempted to use Circassians from other regions against them. With the outbreak of the incident, the nationalists in Ankara considered arming Circassians from the towns of Haymana and Bala (near Ankara) and deploying them in Bolu, but later concluded that arming the Haymana and Bala Circassians would pose security risks in the future, as they might join their fellow Circassians in Düzce and Adapazarı. Thus, these plans never came to fruition.[58] The Damad Ferid Paşa government in Istanbul also went to great lengths to persuade local Circassians in other parts of Anatolia to create difficulties for the *Kuva-yi Milliye*, which aimed to end the national movement before a possible civil war began. At times, the British also favoured the anti-nationalists. It is important to remember that the British put pressure on the Ottoman government to sign the peace treaty with the Allies before the Ottoman delegation was sent to the conference in Sèvres, France. In a meeting between Damad Ferid Paşa, a British military representative, and General Milne on 20 April 1920, it was stated that support in the form of ammunition and guns would be provided to Ahmed Anzavur's forces, and also to those of İbrahim in Yalova.[59] İbrahim, who was probably the commander of the gendarme force in Yalova, had approximately 1,500 soldiers. The plan was to combine these forces in order to create a bigger anti-*Kuva-yi Milliye* force in South Marmara.[60] During that meeting, it was also decided that Ahmed Anzavur would take Bursa from the nationalists before moving to Yalova in the north in order to join İbrahim and his forces. The aim of this plan was to enable them to solidify their presence in İzmit and re-occupy Eskişehir.[61] For that purpose, and to strengthen Anzavur`s position, Damad Ferid gave him the title of Paşa in April 1920.[62] Damad Ferid needed the support of the Circassians of İzmit, Adapazarı, Sinop and Central Anatolia in order to succeed in his anti-nationalist policies. He sent fixers from Istanbul to these regions to organize the local Circassians into an anti-nationalist cause.[63] Some local Circassian notables from the Adapazarı–Düzce area were invited to Istanbul to make promises and guarantee that they would be loyal to the Ottoman government and the Palace.[64] In addition, the British considered Anzavur to be a favourable person, as he enjoyed a great deal of support from local people and was not involved in any lootings or other such crimes.[65] One of the primary concerns of the British was ensuring the security of the Bosphorus under their occupation. Therefore, İzmit, a city located at the gates of the Bosphorus, had a significant place in British policy.[66]

A further British policy involved retaining control of Istanbul and the Çanakkale (Gallipoli) straits. Strategically speaking, the straits occupied a crucial position. If the British had the straits, they could control shipping traffic between the Black Sea and the Mediterranean. Moreover, this would ensure that the Ottoman capital, Istanbul, would remain safe under British occupation. Ankara believed that the British implemented this policy by backing the local Circassian notable Ahmed Anzavur, in order to create a buffer zone between their occupied territory and the *Kuva-yi Milliye*-controlled area in the Marmara region.[67] İsmet (İnönü) Bey also claimed that from the Black Sea town of Şile to the Gulf of Edremit in the Aegean Sea, the region would be secured by Ahmed Anzavur on behalf of the British forces. The aim of this collaboration was to prevent any armed conflict between the British forces and the *Kuva-yi Milliye* forces: Ahmed Anzavur would act as a barrier between them. The British aimed to turn the Marmara region into a buffer zone by saving it from nationalist forces. Furthermore, the Ankara government believed that, when the incident began in the Adapazarı–Düzce region, this concern caused Anzavur to move to the region so that he could mobilize more people against Ankara.[68] However, British documents show that Ankara exaggerated both the involvement of the British in the civil war between the Istanbul and Ankara governments and its support for the anti-nationalists in the region and their leaders, such as Anzavur Ahmed. The British representative in Istanbul was not willing to become involved in the struggle between the two governments, even though it formally backed the Istanbul government. The British also complained about their allies in Anatolia, namely the Italian and French forces, since the Italians were not against the nationalists of Ankara, and the French made it difficult for the British to pursue their policy.[69] It seems that, in such circumstances, Britain backed the Damad Ferid government in order to advance its own interests. It avoided having direct connections with the armed anti-nationalists in Anatolia, such as Ahmed Anzavur, because of the rumours surrounding its policies and the increasing level of anti-British sentiments in Anatolia.[70]

For Ankara, and particularly for Mustafa Kemal, the main enemy was not the British or Greek forces, but rather the Damad Ferid Paşa, his circle, and the domestic problems that Ankara believed to be the main threats to the continuity of the *Kuva-yi Milliye* movement.[71] The priority of the Ankara government was quelling the uprisings, rather than fighting the occupation forces; if it failed to retain control over Anatolia in this chaotic situation, it would be easy for the occupation forces to execute their plans. Nevertheless, the leaders of the nationalist movement, such as Mustafa Kemal, avoided making negative remarks about the sultan in public, even though the Ankara government was engaged in a civil war with the Istanbul government and the anti-nationalists. In the minds of the people, the sultan was not responsible for the disastrous situation in the empire. Although the nationalist forces were fighting the anti-nationalists, the Ankara government followed a policy of arguing that the Ottoman sultan/caliph was not free from British pressure in occupied Istanbul. According to Mustafa Kemal, the sultan and the Istanbul government were two different entities, as he once claimed in the assembly. The Istanbul government, which was reformed on the orders of the sultan many times during the occupation (due to British pressure), and particularly the Ferid Paşa cabinet, was held captive by the British. Mustafa Kemal noted that there was no need to send a delegation from the Ankara assembly to Istanbul to gain the support of the sultan for the national movement since the British occupation of Istanbul prevented the sultan from openly declaring his support for the *Kuva-yi Milliye* movement. The assembly was already looking for a way to meet with the sultan, and in order to do so, a secret contact would have to be found.[72] He further argued that, even if he learnt that the sultan was against the national movement, he would not believe it, and would ascribe any such declaration to British pressure on the sultan.

Çerkes Ethem in the Adapazarı–Düzce region

As a paramilitary leader, Çerkes Ethem, would become one of the most dominant forces of the era. He was initially close to the national movement in Anatolia, and had enjoyed a good relationship with the bureaucratic elites of that movement ever since his military service during the First World War, when he fought against the Russian and British forces in Iran and Afghanistan with the Teşkilat-ı Mahsusa, under the command of his older brother Reşit Bey.[73] Following the Mudros Armistice, Çerkes Ethem was in the town of Bandırma in South Marmara, where he was convinced by Rauf Bey (Orbay) to join the nationalist cause. He quickly organized his own paramilitary forces and set up the first lines of resistance against the Greek occupation. In addition, he developed his own strategies for collecting money from people in order to fund his paramilitary groups. Although he did use some resources that had been allocated to associations resisting against the Greek occupation to provide for the needs of his soldiers,[74] he generally sustained his military units using money that had been forcibly gathered from notables in the region. His policies were not welcomed by the notables, who did not agree to pay voluntarily. In the territories that he controlled, Ethem enacted a number of relatively severe policies. He would stage sudden attacks on towns experiencing disorder, or those considered anti-*Kuva-yi Milliye*. After an armed clash, he usually took control and created military tribunals to carry out the trials of miscreants. The decisions of these tribunals tended to be very harsh: this was the single biggest complaint that locals and his own forces made about Ethem. The ongoing war and armed conflicts raging in the region meant that the tribunals had been given the authority to execute death sentences without following the proper legal process.

Ethem Bey's paramilitary group consisted of a large number of Circassians. He and his brothers refused to join the standing army, the establishment of which was being proposed by people in Ankara who had a background in the regular Ottoman army. Indeed, his men had not been 'proper soldiers' in the first place, and they simply wanted to continue with their haphazard paramilitary activities.[75] Taxes were an important financial resource that Ethem collected from notables in the region, although his methods of doing so were very unpopular: he would arrest those who refused to pay tax,[76] and his militia would seize money, just like the common criminal bandits and paramilitary groups in the region. Ethem's militia was a powerful one, and it was based on a wide-ranging kinship network with other Circassians in the region; his social status as the son of a wealthy landowner also helped him to gain the respect of fellow Circassians.

After suppressing the first Anzavur incident, Çerkes Ethem was asked by İsmet (İnönü) Bey to move to the Adapazarı–Düzce region so that he could also quell the 'uprising' that was taking place there.[77] On the way to the Adapazarı–Düzce region, Ethem decided to go to the town of Manyas, where Anzavur Ahmed's supporters had gathered to escape from Ethem's forces. After the first attack by Ethem's forces on the town, approximately six hundred of Anzavur's men joined Ethem,[78] while the remainder either fled to Istanbul or were killed in the skirmish. These additions to Ethem's forces gave him a total of about five thousand cavalry men, all of whom had fine military equipment. In addition, he now had approximately five hundred foot soldiers.[79] On 29 April 1920, Ethem and his forces arrived first in Geyve, and then in then Sapanca and Adapazarı, where some people were sentenced to death.[80] He suppressed the disorder that was prevailing there and took control of the area. An imam, a military captain and ten civilians were hanged following a decision taken by his military tribunal.[81] By taking control, he prevented the anti-nationalist forces from raiding, and subsequently terminating, the assembly in Ankara. Those who were heading towards Ankara in order to attack the assembly dispersed because they lacked adequate support from other anti-nationalists.[82]

Although Ethem was a man who was concerned mainly with war, he was in no doubt about the necessity of becoming involved in political matters from time to time. On 23 May 1920, before putting an end to the incident, he prepared three letters for Sultan Vahidettin, Sadrazam Damad Ferid Paşa and the supreme military command in Istanbul. These letters clearly show why Ethem became involved in the nationalist struggle. In his first letter, which was written for Vahidettin, he argues that Damad Ferid was not an appropriate choice for the role of Sadrazam. Ethem claims that the caliphate and sultanate did not derive any benefits from Damad Ferid's method of administration and that his policies led to people in Anatolia killing one another.[83] Ethem also emphasized that, while the *Kuva-yi Milliye* aimed to save the sultan from occupation, Damad Ferid's policies divided people into different groups. Finally, he asked Vahidettin to dismiss Damad Ferid from the sadrazamship and to appoint people who had merit and were capable of doing the job.[84] Moreover, Ethem also prepared a letter for Damad Ferid himself, in which he told him that the Ottoman administration had never been ruled by anyone with such a low level of capability. He blamed Damad Ferid for the problems in the state and accused him of being a traitor, as his policies had led to people killing one another.[85] In his final letter, which was addressed to the supreme military commander in Istanbul, he also emphasized his concerns about Damad Ferid and reiterated his belief that Damad Ferid did not deserve the position that he held. Furthermore, he argued that Damad Ferid would never be capable of representing the Ottoman nation.[86] However, the delivery of these three letters to Istanbul was prevented by Ali Fuat Paşa, who wanted Ethem to avoid becoming involved in politics so that he could focus instead on fighting the Greeks and quelling any uprisings against Ankara. Nevertheless, these letters tell us that Ethem was not an apolitical fighter who had no understanding of politics. The language used in the letters shows us that, if they were written by Ethem, he was an educated man. Even if the letters were not written by him, they still prove that he was surrounded by people who were very capable and astute, and who understood the political issues faced by the empire.

One night, while Hüsrev (Gerede) Bey was in prison, Berzeg Sefer Bey sent Ahmet Ağa to negotiate with him, in order to reach an agreement with Mustafa Kemal on his behalf. Hüsrev Bey was secretly released from prison and was brought to the house of Abdülgani Bey, one of the leading figures of the incident. He met with Berzeg Sefer Bey and Koç Bey, the commander of the gendarme force in Düzce. Sefer claimed that he was surprised by the news of the Sèvres Treaty[87] and was filled with remorse about his initial hostility towards Ankara. Sefer asked Hüsrev Bey to negotiate with the Ankara government on his behalf and to ask for reconciliation.[88] Although he was against the *Kuva-yi Milliye*, he was also against the partition of the Ottoman Empire that the Allies had stipulated in the terms of the Sèvres Peace Treaty, which would divide and colonize the Ottoman Empire under the rule of the Allies. While Hüsrev Bey travelled to Ankara via the other side of the front, Sefer Bey met with Refet (Bele) Bey on 24 May to negotiate the terms for ending his uprising.[89]

Although the leader of the incident in Düzce almost reached an agreement with Mustafa Kemal on ending it, Ethem moved towards Düzce via Geyve-Sapanca-Adapazarı. Anti-nationalists demanded that Refet Bey, and not Ethem Bey, come to Düzce to meet with them so that he could evaluate the situation for himself. The leaders of the incident were concerned about the possibility of Ethem taking hasty action towards Düzce, so they also sent him a telegram warning him not to act, as they were close to reaching an agreement with the Ankara government.[90] However, Ethem ignored this request to wait, and moved towards Düzce. On 26 May, he captured the city without clashing with the anti-nationalists, who were planning to welcome him as a guest.[91] He sent a telegram to Mustafa Kemal in Ankara, which contained a list of anti-nationalists who would be hanged, and asked for Mustafa Kemal's permission to carry out the executions.[92] After a long discussion, Sefer Bey's execution was not approved by Mustafa Kemal, since he had assisted with Hüsrev Bey's release from prison.[93] However, on 27 May 1920, about fifty people were hanged by Ethem's forces, including Sefer, Koç, Abdülgani, Abdülvehap, Rüştü the murderer, Kamil, Mehmet, Ali Galip Beys, Gürcü Hoca and the major staff officer Hayri.[94] In addition to these local people, seven high-ranking officers from the *Kuva-yi İnzibatiye*[95] forces, who had come to the region to mobilize the people against the *Kuva-yi Milliye*, were also hanged on the 28 May. These officers were Major Hayri, Lieutenant Ali Cerrah, İbrahim Ethem, Şerafettin, Second Lieutenant Suphi, İsmail Hakkı, Katip Hasan, Deputy Officer Mehmet, Ali Cenap and Hurşit Beys.[96] On the following day, the MPs Hacı Abdülvahap Bey, Müfti Çerkes Ahmet, İvranyalızade Hacı Emin, Hacı Hamdi and Komiteci Çubukluzade Sabri and the lawyer Nuri Efendi of Mengen were executed in front of the governor's mansion.[97] In Bolu, gendarme lieutenant Fuat, trainee Fethullah of Bagdad, reserve officer Hafız İbrahim, Hafız Hamdi, Hayri Efendis, Yunus, Mehmet, Hafız Hakkı and Bayram were hanged by the *Kuva-yi Milliye* forces in the second week of June 1920.[98] In the following weeks, Hoca Sadık Efendi of Çarşamba, Kör Ali, Abaza Ethem, a Rum priest, Çolak Hamdi, Hafız Abdullah and Arif were also executed.[99]

The hanging of the Circassians in the Adapazarı–Düzce region by Ethem caused much debate among the Circassians of Turkey. As a paramilitary leader, he was responsible for executing a number of people before and after the Adapazarı–Düzce incidents. His forces usually hanged several people after taking control of towns, as was the case in Salihli, Gönen, Manyas and Yozgat. However, the sanctions that he applied in those towns were never as harsh as those that he chose to apply in Adapazarı–Düzce. According to Baki Çule, a native Circassian of Düzce,[100] disagreements of a personal nature existed between Ethem and Sefer Bey long before the incident. He stated that Ethem and Sefer liked the same girl – this girl first became Ethem's kaşen[101] but later married Sefer.[102] Consequently, Ethem violently punished Sefer Bey and his supporters, despite the fact that Sefer Bey had reached an agreement with the Ankara government. Ethem came to the region without considering the decision made by the Ankara government and established the military tribunal himself as a prosecutor to hanging people. Internal tribal struggles among Circassians, that is between the Şapsığ and Ubıkh subgroups, could also explain the disagreement between the two men. Indeed, there had been a longstanding struggle between Circassian tribes in the region concerning who held sway over the other tribes and families. As a member of the Şapsığ, Ethem was welcomed by the mayor of the Humetiko (a town), Hüseyin Remzi Bey, who was also a member of Şapsığ; Hüseyin Remzi Bey allowed Ethem to stay in his house during his time in Düzce. It could also be argued that some local leaders used Ethem to eliminate their regional rivals, as this would enable them to achieve or maintain dominance. Sefer Bey, on the other hand, belonged to one of the leading families of the Ubıkh subgroup. With the exception of one person, everyone around Sefer Bey was also Ubıkh. This situation led to tribal divisions between Circassians and the Şapsığ; Çerkes Ethem did not interrupt executions of Ubıkhs.

Although the nationalists only regained control of the Adapazarı–Düzce region for a very limited time, they still took severe measures. Those who supported the incidents were condemned to death by the *Kuva-yi Milliye*, whereas other anti-nationalists escaped death by moving to Istanbul. The Istanbul government was planning to turn this situation around by mobilizing anti-nationalists to join the newly established *Kuva-yi İnzibatiyye* force.[103] Approximately forty anti-nationalists had left the region and were seeking support from the Istanbul government.[104] The Istanbul government passed a law stipulating that compensation must be paid to those who suffered because of the nationalist attack in the Adapazarı region and were forced to leave the region.[105] It was not only people from the Adapazarı–Düzce region who moved to Istanbul after the capture of the former by Ethem's forces, but also those from the towns of Alaşehir and Salihli.[106]

To settle the chaos and prevent another incident, the nationalists tried to take further precautions in the region. Significant numbers of Circassians from the region joined Ethem's forces.[107] The commander of the Bolu region recruited approximately one thousand Abkhazians to the gendarme forces. He also demanded a cavalry regiment from Ankara, arguing that it would not otherwise be possible to keep order in the region, as the loyalty of the population to the sultanate meant that there was a risk of a further uprising.[108] The Ankara government did not consider the Abkhazians of the region to be trustworthy, and the Ministry of War warned the Ministry of Interior in Ankara that those Abkhazians who fought in the nationalist cause were expected to turn against Ankara.[109] The case of Abkhazians was also discussed in the assembly, where Hüsrev (Gerede), who had been captured during the Düzce incident, explained the origins of the problem in Düzce. The Circassians and Abkhazians were the leading figures of the incident and, in his opinion, the Circassians would regret what had happened, whereas the Abkhazians, especially those from the Nüfren region[110] (Halil Bey Village), lived as bandits, and did not fully accept the state's authority. They were particularly opposed to the constitutional monarchy since their relationships with the Ottoman Palace – where their daughters lived in the Harem – had already broken down in the days following the declaration of the constitution in 1908. Furthermore, he suggested that the Ankara government should cleanse the region of armed bands, including armed Abkhazians.[111]

However, the measures taken in the region were not firmly established, and Düzce once again became a gathering place for anti-nationalists. The second incident began on 19 July 1920, when a group of people rose under the leadership of Maan Ali and occupied Düzce. Within a short period, their numbers had grown to one thousand,[112] but Colonel Nazım of the Ankara government was, nevertheless, able to suppress the incident.[113] On 9 August 1920, another attempt to seize control of the local governor's offices took place in Bolu, this time by a group of about twenty Abkhazians. They based their actions on their belief that the Circassian and Abkhazian men of the region would be killed by *Kuva-yı Milliye* and their daughters and wives would be made into concubines.[114] This incident was also not successful for them and was suppressed by the nationalists on 18 August.[115] To strengthen its rule in the region, the Ankara government declared an amnesty on 30 August 1920. However, some people were excluded from the amnesty. These included Hacı Akmil and Maan Ali Bey of Düzce; Gürcü Süleyman Efendi of Hendek; Talo Sinan Bey, Çır Çır Bey, Kamil, Akçallı Hüseyin Çavuş and his brother Beslen of Akyazı; and Şirin Hazbuk Ahmet and Mustafa of Kayalar village. Furthermore, the governor of Bolu, a man named Osman, İzmit governor İbrahim Hakkı, along with Ahmed Anzavur and Captain Mehmet Hulusi, were all wanted dead or alive and their properties were confiscated.[116] Nevertheless, the anti-nationalist movement continued and, in the summer of 1921, hundreds of deserters from the surrounding area came to Düzce. The deserters consisted not only of Circassians and Abkhazians, but also of other Muslims who had moved to Düzce.¹¹⁷ For this reason, Ankara paid close attention to the Düzce region. The names of those who had launched the incident and had not been punished by Ankara were published in a list, and the villages of Abaza Aktepe, Çerkes Elmacık, Çerkesköprübaşı, Çiftlik, Cedidiyye, Çıpyak, Arapçiftliği, Büyükaçma, Dereliköy and Süleyman Bey were named as having played a role in the incident.¹¹⁸ Even at the end of December 1921, complaints against Circassians in Düzce and Adapazarı were still being made. For example, three hundred Circassian cavalry soldiers created disorder and disturbed the military units of the Ankara government in the region.¹¹⁹

In the days following the Adapazarı–Düzce incidents of October 1920, another incident took place in the Central Black Sea region of Sinop. A group of Circassians, which included ex-military officer Çerkes Kazım and a few of his friends from the town of Alaçam and the village of Karlı, became involved in banditry and joined a local group called *Bayram Çetesi*. The local governor then attempted to engage in ethnic cleansing (he used the words '*tathir*' and '*temizlemek*', which mean cleanse, to describe this process) by trying to remove all Circassians from the region, regardless of whether they were bandits.¹²⁰ However, this was not permitted by Canik governorships' *Mutasarrıflık*, who warned the local gendarme and armed forces that they should try to catch the members of armed bands, instead of removing all local Circassians from the region.¹²¹ At the end of the pursuit, Bayram and Çerkes Kazım were killed by gendarme forces (8 November 1920), who regained control of the area.¹²²

The Yozgat incident

Immediately after the Adapazarı–Düzce incidents, Ankara needed Ethem to suppress another anti-nationalist movement to the east of Ankara, in Yozgat. A local notable family, the Çapanoğlu family, rejected the nationalists' demand that they send representatives to the assembly in Ankara on behalf of the people of Yozgat.¹²³ To the Çapanoğlu brothers, the idea of sending representatives to the assembly was akin to rebelling against both the sultanate and the Ottoman government. Thus, they informed the nationalists that no representatives from Yozgat would be sent to the assembly.¹²⁴ At first, the general military staff issued an appeal to bring the Çapanoğlu brothers to Ankara. However, the vice governor of Ankara, Yahya Galip helped them to avoid coming to Ankara to stand trial because a member of the family, Celal (who was also the local governor of Tokat), had assisted Yahya Galip when he was in exile in Tokat during the time of the Abdülhamid II.[125]

Tensions between the Committee of Union and Progress (CUP) and the Liberal Entente further affected the emergence of the uprising. Edip Bey (1859–1925), an influential member of the Çapanoğlu family, was once a supporter of the CUP and an MP for the party.[126] In the Ottoman Assembly of the post-1908 period, he had slowly become an opponent of the CUP because he did not agree with some of their policies, and his criticisms eventually led to his expulsion from the CUP. He was not even allowed to return to the governorship, and was forced to leave the capital and return to his hometown on 5 January 1911.[127] Later on, he joined the Liberal Entente. The loyalist–nationalist differentiation in that region was not especially motivated by ideology or religion, but rather depended on individuals' personal and past political experiences. Thus, Edip Bey was against the nationalists due to the lack of authority in the region, war-weariness, and the fact that he was an anti-CUP activist.

At first, there were two incidents in Yozgat. One of these was between the Yıldızeli and Akdağmadeni regions, and was led by 'Postacı Nazım' or Nazım the Postman, and the other was between the areas of Zile and Çekerek, and was led by Aynacıoğulları.[128] These incidents were not initially related to each other, but later became widespread due to the persistent lack of authority in the region. In the early days, the Çapanoğlu family did not participate in the incident, but the developing situation later encouraged two Çapanoğlus, Celal and Salih Beys, to compete against the nationalists.[129] One of these issues transpired when the mufti of Yozgat and the Çapanoğlu family disagreed about the collection of money for the nationalists. The mufti informed Ankara that the family was against collecting money for the nationalist cause, and Kılıç Ali Bey was sent by Ankara to Yozgat to seize control of the region and to organize fundraising for the *Kuva-yi Milliye*. He came to Yozgat on 1 June 1920, and kept the Çapanoğlu family under close surveillance. Members of the family, including Celal, Edip, Salih and their brother-in-law, Mahmut (along with his sons Mekki, Şekib and Muhlis), were very disturbed by Kılıç Ali's policies. In response, they left the city and began to collaborate with the anti-nationalists

(8 June 1920).¹³⁰ A week later, they returned to the city in order to begin the uprising (14 June). Their first move was to release prisoners from the town prison.¹³¹

On this issue, it has been noted that Süleyman Sırrı once mentioned, in a secret session of the assembly, that Çapanoğlu Memet Ağa had been assigned by the sultan to fight against the Ankara government; he had been given a force of 1,500 men for this purpose.¹³² Indeed, the incident spread very quickly. Once again, Ankara did not have enough military power to gain complete control of the situation. When the family achieved full control of Yozgat on 14 (or 13) June, Ethem – who had just suppressed the incident in Düzce – was called by İsmet (İnönü) to overthrow the Çapanoğlus.¹³³ Ethem was welcomed by all the high-ranking politicians and military men at Ankara train station. A celebration in his honour was organized by Mustafa Kemal in the streets of Ankara, where he was declared the saviour of the people, or 'Münci Millet', in the assembly. In spite of this warm welcome, Ethem was not pleased to be in Ankara. He would rather have been in Salihli, so that he could administer the front and prepare for a potential Greek attack.¹³⁴ In the special meeting between him, Mustafa Kemal, İsmet (İnönü) and Fevzi (Çakmak), Ethem criticized the Ankara government and its leaders for not being able to quell an incident that took place next to their city. Furthermore, he accused them of not working hard enough to form a military unit and of sending manifestos to Anatolia, Istanbul and the Allied powers instead.¹³⁵ During this meeting, the rhetoric that Ethem used against the leaders of the Ankara government was unexpected and harsh. Mustafa Kemal, on the other hand, complained about disagreements in the assembly, believing that these disagreements stemmed from the fact that many people from different backgrounds were present, most of whom were emotionally connected to the caliphate. Hence, it was difficult to pass laws and take the necessary measures in the assembly to control the region.¹³⁶

On 20 June, Ethem moved from Ankara to Yozgat. On 23 June, he arrived in Yozgat and took control of the city on behalf of the nationalist forces on that same day.¹³⁷ After his attack on the Çapanoğlus, some of the leaders of that family left the battleground and escaped to the Aziziye (Pınarbaşı) region of Kayseri, a region that was mostly settled by Circassians. Other members of the family, namely Halid and Mehmed Celaleddin Bey, were also sheltered by

Circassians.[138] The governor and inspector of Yozgat were imprisoned. Ethem established a military court, which hanged twelve people, and hanged the Kadı of the town (the judge in the Islamic court).[139] Çapanoğlu Mahmut Bey, Çapanoğlu Vasıf Bey, Ceritzade Hüsnü Efendi, Kadı Remzi Efendi, Tevfikzade Ahmed Efendi, Hafız Şahab, his son Refet Efendi and Veysel (from the Tatar İmam village), were all hanged due to their participation in the incident; the other four people who were hanged were from Ethem's own forces, and were executed for looting during the suppression of the incident.[140] However, the families of those who took part in the incident could not be arrested; instead, they were sent to Ankara by Ethem. The houses and properties of those captured by Ethem were demolished. Lastly, those who could not be arrested were made to join nationalist forces. If they did so, their lives would be protected.[141]

Ethem let his people burn the Çapanoğlu family houses and farms.[142] On 24 June, he went to the town of Alaca. A Circassian village on the periphery of the town, by the name of Altıntaş, was surrounded by his forces. Ethem chose to carry out a raid on this village because its residents had fought against the *Kuva-yi Milliye* when they came to the region. Since the nationalists lost a significant number of men in that fight, Ethem wanted to punish the villagers. Therefore, twenty-three people were executed by firing squad.[143] It can be said that although Ethem had a significant number of Circassians within his forces, he had zero tolerance for Circassians who fought against nationalists. His brutality did not distinguish between Circassian and non-Circassian enemies, as he had already shown during the Adapazarı–Düzce and Anzavur incidents.

In the post–First-World-War order, there was chaos in the Yozgat region, just as there was in the Adapazarı–Düzce region, and in South Marmara in general, with killings and hangings becoming part of daily life. The governor of Yozgat, also known as 'The Crazy Kurdish Governor' (Kürt Deli Vali), announced that anyone who brought the head of a notorious local bandit called 'Circassian İlyas the Murderer' (Katil Çerkes İlyas) from the village of Arpalık of Sarıkaya to the town of Yozgat would be pardoned by the state, regardless of what crimes he might previously have committed. Another bandit from the region, Ebellioğlu Musa, along with his men and Battal 'the Black' ('Kara Battal'), pursued İlyas, and then ambushed, killed and beheaded him. His head was sent to the governor, but when the Circassians heard the news of his death, they exacted revenge by killing Battal and his mother.[144]

In the region, the horrific consequences of violence were very noticeable. With control of the region now in the hands of the nationalists, violence was not prevented; executions were rampantly carried out in the name of the 'law'. Following the suppression of the incident, an independent court was established by Ankara and this court hanged twenty-five people. The court usually tried people on one day and executed them the next day.[145] A number of people were also executed by shooting, without any judicial process having taken place. Rifat (he was known locally as *Düzceli Rifat*), a leader of a local Circassian band, and twelve of his men were exiled to Ankara because they took part in the incident. They were to be tried in court or kept under surveillance in Ankara. However, on the way to Ankara, they were executed by nationalists.[146] Only Rifat and one of his men escaped the execution.

Still evading capture by the nationalists, Çapanoğlu Edip Bey decided to find a way of meeting with the sultan in Istanbul, from where he could bring arms, artillery and military forces to fight against the *Kuva-yi Milliye*. He thought that, if he reached the port of Samsun on the Black Sea, he could make it to Istanbul. Along with Abdülkadir Bey and some of his men, Edip Bey moved from the town of Akdağmadeni in Yozgat to Samsun. Çerkes Kara Yusuf was their guide (*mihmandar*).[147] This region contained a high number of Circassian villages and settlements, which they used to overcome difficulties that they faced during their journey, as the Circassian villagers and fighters provided them with food, horses and accommodation. They travelled to Merzifon via Çorum, Tokat and Amasya. However, when they reached Merzifon, they had to go back to Yozgat. Samsun proved to be an unsafe place for them because the nationalist forces had already taken control of the city.[148] The party left using the same route that they had followed to get to Yozgat. A few days after their arrival in Yozgat, Edip Bey was arrested by local military forces of the Ankara government, and was exiled to Ankara, where he was to be kept under surveillance. In Ankara, he was not imprisoned, and was only required to attend the police station twice daily in order to show himself to officials.[149]

In Yozgat, the local power struggle was won by the Ankara government. However, the Çapanoğlu incident increased the friction between Ethem and Mustafa Kemal. An investigation by the military court held the governor (*mutasarrıf*) of Yozgat, who also had good relations with Yahya Galip Bey (the governor of Ankara, who had close ties to Mustafa Kemal at the time) responsible for not quelling the incident. Ethem sent a telegram to Ankara, in which he requested that Yahya Galip be called before the military court. However, his demand was rejected by Ankara on the grounds that Yahya Galib was too sick to make the journey to Yozgat.[150] One reason why this demand was rejected might have been the fact that Yahya Galib had not sacked the governor of Yozgat before the incident. Mustafa Kemal might have thought that if Yahya Galib were to be tried by the military court because of his bad governance, he himself could be called to appear before the very same court.[151] Mustafa Kemal, as head of the assembly, bore some responsibility for Yahya Galib's mistakes. He may possibly have thought that if he gave Ethem the opportunity to try Yahya Galib, Ethem would attempt to try him as well. Moreover, Ethem explains in his memoir that Mustafa Kemal's failure to remove Yahya Galip was a mistake, despite the mistakes made by the latter during his time as governor of the region.[152] Mustafa Kemal did not allow the military court to try Yahya Galib, and the incident turned into a power struggle between him and Ethem. This incident was the second issue to develop between Mustafa Kemal and Ethem, and was the beginning of a crisis of authority in the national movement.

Although the civil war continued after these incidents, the most important incidents, namely the Anzavur, the Adapazarı–Düzce and Yozgat, had all been suppressed by Ethem.[153] In the eastern part of Anatolia, Kazım Karabekir waged war on Armenian forces. During this period, however, the western and central parts of the Anatolian movement were somewhat weak against Greek forces and the anti-nationalist uprisings. In the absence of regular troops, irregular troops were vital. Having a larger irregular force allowed Ethem to succeed in suppressing the three most important incidents early on, which proved vital for the establishment of the Ankara government in this part of the state.[154]

The Adapazarı–Düzce region was one of the important places for the anti-nationalist movement during the 1920s. Traditionally, the people of this region were loyal to the Ottoman sultan. The Circassians were the predominant group of the region and, to them, the Ankara government and the *Kuva-yı Milliye* appeared to be the continuation of the CUP, which they held solely accountable for the disastrous outcomes of the wars over the past decade. The existence of the anti-nationalist movement in the Adapazarı–Düzce region deepened the impact of the civil war between the Istanbul and Ankara governments. In addition to the Adapazarı–Düzce incidents, the Çapanoğlu incident was also another significant problem for the Ankara government, which lacked the military power needed to overcome the disorder and defeat the anti-nationalists at that time. Çerkes Ethem was called on by Ankara to protect the nationalist cause and prevent its demise at a time when it was just emerging.

4

Replacement of the bandits and irregular forces with the regular army, and exclusion of Çerkes Ethem from the nationalist movement

Why is the so-called 'Çerkes Ethem incident' still considered an important subject in Turkish historiography ninety years later? As can be seen from the image uploaded on the webpage of Turkish General Staff (TGS) on 26 February 2013,[1] Ethem was welcomed at the Ankara train station by Mustafa Kemal himself in 1920. In a previous version of the image, the faces of Ethem and some of his soldiers were blurred.[2] Within a few days of the uploading of the picture on the TGS web page, a group of Circassians in Turkey reacted to the blurring of the image on social media by protesting (via Twitter). TGS then changed the image to the original version, which was clearer, placating the Circassian community. It is difficult to say that the release of the blurred picture was the result of an institutional policy at the TGS. The uploading of the image was a decision made by an officer or a sub-department, since if the TGS did have an institutional-wide policy concerning the Çerkes Ethem incident it would not have been possible for the author of this book to conduct research in the TGS military archives (ATASE) over the last few years. During this time, no restrictions were imposed on access to the archives, and every document in the catalogues relating to Çerkes Ethem was made available. Moreover, the head of the ATASE, a brigadier general, who I happened to meet at the institution, kindly asked me if I needed anything else for my research. During the period of my research, every single document I requested was uploaded to my account. This compares favourably with the policy on military archives that researchers had to contend with ten years ago. The working conditions at the ATASE for researchers today are more flexible. However, some officials within the TGS have yet to adjust to this policy, as evidenced by the aforementioned issue concerning the blurred picture uploaded onto the TGS web page. It is possible the TGS has an ambivalent policy: on the one hand, it wants to open the archives to everyone; on the other, it still maintains certain ideological barriers regarding particular topics, affecting some sub-departments and individuals within the TGS.

As mentioned in the previous chapter, Ethem suppressed the three important anti-nationalist incidents threatening the government based in Ankara, as all large-scale domestic threats targeted it. Mustafa Kemal then aimed at taking control of the entire assembly and the western front. The regular army was being prepared by Ankara, and the war against Armenian forces in the eastern front was ending. In view of this situation, the relationship between Ethem and Mustafa Kemal began to change. Mustafa Kemal, as the head of the assembly and fast becoming an unrivalled leader of the Anatolian movement, had gradually increased his power with regard to military and political issues.

Aside from the danger from Ethem and Enver Paşa (the latter was seeking a way to return to Anatolia), there was no significant threat to Mustafa Kemal's ambitions. Mustafa Kemal initially aimed to control and use Ethem, although he quickly learned that this was no easy task. He concluded at the end of December 1920 that the best option was to exclude him from the Anatolian movement altogether. This chapter argues that there were several reasons why the relationship between Çerkes Ethem and Mustafa Kemal had deteriorated, resulting in Çerkes Ethem's exclusion from the national movement. One reason was the increasing significance of Ethem's military victories on the western front and the political impact this was having in the assembly, particularly after he successfully suppressed the incidents. Although, as a military man, Ethem did not have political ambitions, he was fast becoming one of the most influential people among the political circles of the time. Due to the absence and imprisonment of a large number of prominent CUP members by the British, Ethem's military success against the anti-nationalist groups heightened his importance to the political opponents of Mustafa Kemal in the assembly. Although Mustafa Kemal had influence over the members of the assembly, he frequently encountered significant opposition to some of his decisions among members.[3] Ethem was surrounded by the opponents of Mustafa Kemal, some of whom were careerists, while others were looking for an opportunity to strengthen their own positions against him. They attempted to use Ethem to solidify their movement and to balance Mustafa Kemal's influence. However, this attempt along with Mustafa Kemal's intolerant approach to anyone who opposed his own authority and Tevfik's (Ethem's brother) uncompromising stance towards the regular army led to open conflict between the two sides and the exclusion of Ethem and his brothers from the nationalist core. Indeed, the mismanagement of the differences that arose between the irregular troops under Ethem and Tevfik and the regular troops under İsmet and Refet Beys was an important reason for the exclusion of Ethem and his brothers. This chapter will first examine the reasons for the struggle between Mustafa Kemal and Enver Paşa and its impact on the general policy of the Ankara government towards the North Caucasus and towards Çerkes Ethem. Secondly, it will study the Green Army Society, an organization that gradually became an obstacle for Mustafa Kemal, and the impact this had on the exclusion process aimed at Çerkes Ethem by the national movement. Thirdly, this chapter will demonstrate how the regular–irregular army debate on the western front led to the elimination of Ethem from the national movement.

Struggle for power: Çerkes Ethem, Enver, Mustafa Kemal and Bolsheviks

Following the Mudros Armistice, the executive members of the CUP, including Talat, Enver and Cemal Paşa, left the empire for Germany to avoid court cases relating to their activities. The CUP leaders had already anticipated the Allied occupation of Anatolia and had taken precautions before the First World War ended. Indeed, they had arms and money hoarded in Anatolia. Enver Paşa also planned to go to the eastern Black Sea coast of Sochi in the North West Caucasus, to pass towards Baku where the Ottoman army was strong, to take the region under his control and build up resistance against the Allies, particularly the British. Although the foremost leaders of the CUP left the empire, its mid-ranking members, such as local governors, captains in the army and high-ranking military men, were all seeking out ways to preserve the empire from occupation.[4] The CUP and the Special Organization were the most highly organized structures in the empire at the time and therefore best placed to establish a resistance movement in Anatolia. Without their participation, resistance was not possible in the empire. The resistance movement was organized top–down[5] and the CUP used its organizational capabilities and the military bureaucracy to mobilize the first non-regular armed groups in the empire, such as those led by Çerkes Ethem (who was persuaded by another Circassian, Rauf (Orbay), to create a resistance group around Salihli against Greek forces).[6]

Enver Paşa was a military general with experience fighting guerrilla wars not only against Bulgarian and Macedonian bandits during the Balkan Wars of 1912–13, but also in Libya and the First World War. Irregular armed groups from the national movement were close to Enver Paşa because of their united struggle against enemy troops during the wars of the previous ten years, and all had broad experience of guerrilla warfare.[7] He formed a loyal group in the Special Organization from those who were closest to him; even the members of the Organization, as will be assessed below, backed him, although they fought for Ankara at the beginning of the resistance movement. After his arrival in Berlin from Istanbul in the winter of 1919, his objective was to go to Moscow to meet with the Bolsheviks. He survived six plane crashes, but he finally arrived in Moscow in August 1920.[8]

The leaders of the CUP were still viewed as significant figures in the Muslim world by the Russians – particularly Enver Paşa, who was also known as 'Seyfullah' by other Muslims (the 'sword of Islam'). To have the support of the CUP leaders was significant for the Bolsheviks since they sought to influence the broader Muslim world. The reason for this policy was that the majority of countries populated with Muslims, such as India, Afghanistan, Algeria, Tunisia, Morocco and Libya, were under colonial European rule (particularly British). Bolshevism, as an alternative ideology to capitalism, required the support of the 'oppressed' people of the world against the European powers. Although the Ottoman Empire had lost the war to the Allies, its leaders remained influential. The Bolsheviks were aiming to take advantage of this influence to use it against the Allies.

The Bolsheviks were also seen as important allies by the Ankara government. However, Ankara was not seen as a legitimate representative of Turkey by the Bolsheviks from the outset. The Bolsheviks did not take Ankara seriously due to the civil war and disorder in Anatolia. To change the situation with the Bolsheviks, Ankara took steps to forge closer relations with them. A delegation was sent by Ankara to visit them, consisting of Bekir Sami (Kunduh) (chairman), Yusuf Kemal (Tengirşenk), İbrahim Tali (Öngören), Osman Bey of Lazistan (MP) and Seyfi (Düzgören) Bey.[9] They reached Moscow's train station on 19 July 1920 after an almost two-month long journey. The representatives of the Ankara government were not welcomed according to the necessary diplomatic protocols in Russia; none of the members of the Russian Ministry of Foreign Affairs were waiting for them at the station in Moscow. Indeed, the representatives had to wait for about an hour at the station before they were taken to a place near the Kremlin Palace.[10] They then struggled to arrange meetings with their counterparts in Moscow over the following days. The Bolsheviks still considered meeting the CUP leaders, namely Talat, Cemal and particularly Enver Paşa, who had escaped to Berlin but who retained a good reputation in Bolshevik circles.[11] Indeed, the three Paşas had met with Trotsky, Lenin, Chicherin and Stalin (the leaders of the Bolshevik movement).[12] Enver Paşa did facilitate affairs, ensuring the representatives of the Ankara government were granted an official meeting with the Bolshevik leaders.

Enver Paşa's policy in this case is worth examining, to understand the differences between the two different wings of the nationalists; one was represented by him and the other by Mustafa Kemal. While Enver Paşa's aim was to form an Islamic resistance by gaining Bolshevik Russian support against British imperialism in Ottoman territories, Afghanistan, Iran and the Muslim world, Mustafa Kemal's only concern was for the Anatolian part of the remaining Ottoman territory. For his part, Enver Paşa thought that to succeed in his ambitions he would have to develop Islamic socialism.[13] He also expected that he would have to convince the Russians to bestow financial and military support to spread the idea of Islamic socialism in the region. It emerges that Enver Paşa attempted to demonstrate to the Russians just how close his views were to socialism when compared with those of Mustafa Kemal.[14]

Enver Paşa published an article titled 'Mesai' to map out the ideology and to strengthen his followers' positions inside the assembly in Ankara. Although 'Mesai' was inspired by Marxism, it is best described as a blending of socialist, corporatist, Islamic and nationalist ideas.[15] On the other hand, Akal claims that the CUP leaders supported Bolshevism for reasons that were more pragmatic and that their aim was not to create a Bolshevik-inspired state in Anatolia. However, it must be noted that Bolshevik terminology was spreading among the bureaucrats and the military in Anatolia, following the Bolshevik revolution. Despite the fact that there was limited network and communication among people at the time, due to the uncensored and moderate number of Bolshevik-inspired newspapers, such ideas did permeate in Anatolia. Açıksöz (Kastamonu), Albayrak (Erzurum), İstikbal (Trabzon), Öğüt (Afyon and Konya) and Yeni Adana (Adana) were some of the Bolshevik-oriented newspapers in Anatolia. What made the newspapers sympathetic to Bolshevik ideas was their shared enemy: the Western capitalists. Although the reasons behind the support for the Bolsheviks were pragmatic, a large number of articles were published in these newspapers favouring the Bolshevik ideology.[16]

Enver was relatively ambitious in his agenda and the Russians saw him as an important player, a force necessary to balance Mustafa Kemal, rather than an alternative to him. Enver had already left the empire in October 1918. Due to Mustafa Kemal's opposition to his return to Anatolia, he could not find any place in the new military or the political structures of the post-First-World-War period. The eastern front commander of the Ankara government, Kazım Karabekir, had already been warned not to allow Enver to enter the Turkish side of the border.[17] One reason for the Bolsheviks' support for Enver Paşa was that their support could create a division between the CUP leaders and the leaders of the Anatolian movement, allowing them to take advantage and expand their ideology further in Anatolia.[18] Enver Paşa was already working on plans to bring together areas that had been Ottoman pre-First World War under a new Ottoman confederation. He also planned to go to Anatolia in the spring of 1921 with numerous military divisions, provided by the Russians, under his command.[19] In a letter he sent to Halil Paşa in November 1920, he underlines that if the Russians would give him military troops consisting of Muslims, he would be willing to go to Anatolia to fight against the Greeks. He also emphasized that Şükrü (Yenibahçeli), Eşref (Kuşçubaşı) and Nail (Yenibahçeli) should create a group for him in Anatolia.[20] Enver Paşa also used one of his closest allies, Hacı Sami (Kuşçubaşı), to create the group.[21] He wrote to the centre of Islamic Unity in Istanbul, which was under his control, asking that they should also have contact with the Circassian brothers Ethem and Reşit, who were loyal to him.[22]

Enver Paşa was also effective at mobilizing bureaucrats, bringing politicians and paramilitary leaders to his side. The existing historiography does not direct attention towards his impact on the Anatolian resistance movement. Although he was mostly in Berlin and Moscow during the period 1919–21, he remained influential within the movement. Indeed, several of his closest allies were positioned in Eastern and Western Anatolia. In the east, Trabzon proved an important centre for Enverists,[23] the most prominent being Halil Paşa, Küçük Talat, Yenibahçeli Nail, Naim Cevat, Kazım Bey (Enver's brother-in-law), Seyfi, Ali Rıza and Yahya Kaptan.[24] The city afforded both sea and overland access to Russia through the Caucasus. Enverists used this opportunity not only to meet with Enver and Russian authorities but also to contact executive members of the North Caucasian Republic – something that would become one of the main differences between Enver and Mustafa Kemal in terms of their policy towards those in Bolshevik Russia and the North Caucasus. In the assembly, there were already forty MPs close to Enver Paşa.[25] He also had a close relationship with the left-wing opposition in Anatolia, and his influence over people disturbed Mustafa Kemal[26] since he did not want to share his authority over the movement with Enver Paşa. Ethem, Reşit and Eşref (the paramilitary group leaders) were also closer to Enver Paşa than Mustafa Kemal. They helped him to climb the career ladder in the army, and later to become commander in chief.[27] Moreover, it seems that one of the reasons for the conflict between Ethem and Mustafa Kemal was the relatively close relationship between Ethem and Enver Paşa.[28]

Enver Paşa and Dr Nazım made an agreement with Ali Fuat Paşa (representative of the Ankara government in the Turkish Embassy of Moscow). According to their agreement, Enver Paşa would not involve himself in the domestic problems of Anatolia. He would work outside Anatolia for Islamic unity and, together with the Russian communists, would battle the imperialists. However, they would not accept communism as their ideology and would never work against Turkey's interest.[29] In July 1921, however, Greek troops moved towards Ankara to put an end to the national movement by occupying its headquarters. They took Kütahya and Eskişehir, and came to Polatlı, just 50 km away from Ankara. It was here that Enver Paşa sent a letter to Mustafa Kemal blaming him for behaving like a dictator and for preventing him from coming to Anatolia. Enver wrote that when the time came he would move to Anatolia without considering Mustafa Kemal's thoughts and that if he were in Anatolia, there would be no conflict and division among the nationalists, as was already happening and could be seen with the Çerkes Ethem incident.[30] Enver met with Soviet foreign policy commissar Chicherin in Moscow on 28 July 1921,[31] later moving to Batum where he met with his own inner circle, consisting of Halil (Kut) Paşa, Küçük Talat, Dr Nazım and Hacı Sami (Kuşçubaşı), to discuss the actions they would take.[32] If the Ankara government under Mustafa Kemal's leadership did not succeed in halting the Greek advance towards Ankara in the Sakarya battle, Enver would come to Anatolia with major Muslim forces backed by the Bolsheviks.[33] Mustafa Kemal already grasped the severity of the situation, warning the eastern front commander of the army Kazım Karabekir to be vigilant against possible attempts to bring Enver to Anatolia.[34] However, with the success of the nationalists against Greek forces in the Sakarya battle, two birds were effectively killed with a single stone: both Ankara and Mustafa Kemal were saved while the Soviets accepted Mustafa Kemal's leadership and Enver lost his opportunity to return to Turkey and become the leader of the national movement.[35]

After the Battle of Sakarya, Enver turned his attention to Central Asia and to his aim of promoting Islamic unity and fighting against the British by mobilizing the Muslims of the region.[36] He asked Sami (Kuşçubaşı) to send his brother Eşref to him.[37] Enver probably thought it was wise to gather his inner circle around him in Central Asia after the inner circle had lost its battle against Mustafa Kemal in Anatolia, as a necessary part of mobilizing other Muslims to fight the British. However, he was unable to succeed in his aim and was killed in a battle against Russian forces on 4 August 1922 in what is now Tajikistan.

North Caucasian Republic: The split between Mustafa Kemal and Enver Paşa

After the February Revolution in Russia, the North Caucasian notables established a committee, comprised of socialists, wealthier landowners and liberals, to organize a congress to discuss the future of North Caucasia and its people.[38] The congress was held on 7 May 1917 and consisted of three hundred delegates: Circassians, Dagestanis, Abkhazis, Turkmens and Nogays.[39] The aim of the congress was to unite the different peoples of the North Caucasus under the ideals of 'liberty, equality and fraternity' (as espoused by the French Revolution) and under a federal–democratic state structure in Russia.[40] The Cossacks, who settled in the region after the indigenous population of the North Caucasus (the Circassians, Chechens, Abkhaz, Dagestanis and Karachays) were exiled by Russia during the nineteenth century, were already seeking self-governance. Although they attempted to work together with the Cossacks against the Bolsheviks, the alliance did not work and conflict soon emerged between the Chechen-Ingush and the Cossacks (over land disputes).[41] Due to the conflict, and the spread of Bolshevism in the region, the committee altered its status from that of a federal state under Russia, becoming a sovereign 'Provisional Government' on 15 November 1917.[42] Abdulmejid Chermoev was elected president, and independence was declared with the support of the Ottoman Porte on 11 May 1918.

The independence of this entity was another cause of controversy between Mustafa Kemal and Enver Paşa. Arguably, the different approaches the two men took provided a further incentive for Mustafa Kemal to pacify those close to Enver Paşa. Mustafa Kemal's policy was to secure Russian financial and military assistance for the Anatolian resistance campaign. He opposed any independent state in the Caucasus between Russia and Turkey. For him, any possible state in the Caucasus had the potential to prevent Russian aid arriving and could worsen the relationships between the two countries. It was also believed by some Special Organization analysts that it would not be possible to mobilize the Caucasian Muslims due to their very limited political aims.[43] Therefore, he chose not to support the existence of the North Caucasian Republic. However, Enver Paşa and the other prominent figures of the time, such as Rauf and Bekir Sami (Kunduh) Beys, did not agree with this policy. For them, a barrier between Russia and the Ottoman Empire was a crucial must-have. Enver also believed that in the post-First-World-War period, such a policy should be supported, to keep the Bolsheviks out of the Caucasus and cut the Armenians' connection with Russia if Enver could gain sufficient support from the Caucasian Muslims and Georgians.[44]

Mustafa Kemal believed that the Allies used the Caucasian nations (the Azeris, Armenians, Georgians and the people of the North Caucasus) to prevent Turkey from connecting with the Bolsheviks. For him, this was a ploy by the Allies to support the Caucasian republics, which would ultimately hamper the Anatolian movement's access to Syria, Iraq, Afghanistan and India. If Turkey worked with the Bolsheviks and helped them in the Caucasus, the doors of these regions would then be opened to Turkey.[45] He referred to the Caucasian states as a 'barrier' and expected that Turkey should fight to stop the Allies to establish the republics in the Caucasus.[46] Mustafa Kemal underlined the suggestion that if the Caucasian states were to act as a wedge between Turkey and Russia (in other words, if they are hostile to the Bolsheviks or if they became independent), then Turkey and Russia would need to work together against them.[47]

Meanwhile, some of those who would later be excluded from the national movement supported the proposal that there be an independent Caucasus federation in the Caucasus. Those espousing this view included Ali Fuat Paşa, Rauf Bey, Bekir Sami and Yusuf İzzet Paşa. According to Ali Fuat Paşa, the federation would be expected to consist of several autonomous states. However, due to flawed policies executed by the British, such a federation could not be established.[48] Rauf Bey had already worked to convince the Ottoman government that it should meet with the British to prevent the expansion of the Bolsheviks into the Caucasus. They could then safeguard the region against being swallowed up by the Bolshevik movement. However, Rauf's precondition was that their (the Ottoman Empire's) independence must be recognized by the British.[49] The 14th Corps commander, Yusuf İzzet Paşa, was also against the suggestion that the Allies build a Caucasian barrier in the Caucasus, because Bolshevism was an ideology, and, for him, to prevent an ideology by forming a physical barrier was not possible.[50] The 13th Corps commander, Ahmet Cevdet, also sent a telegram to Mustafa Kemal emphasizing that working with the British against the Bolsheviks would be better for both Turkey and the Islamic world. He underlined that Russia was already seen as an ancient enemy of the Ottoman Empire by the people and if the Bolsheviks were to sustain Tsarist Russia's policies, they would aim to occupy the east of Anatolia to reach the Turkish Mediterranean coast. Thus, on balance it might be better to reach an agreement with the British.[51]

At the end of 1920, when the North Caucasian Republic collapsed under Bolshevik attacks, the executive delegates and founders of the republic attempted to move to Turkey as they had been supported by the Ottoman Empire, particularly by Enver Paşa. However, the political situation also then altered in Turkey. Enver left the empire, which was occupied by the Allies and the Greek forces. Moreover, Mustafa Kemal came to power choosing not to share the same policies as Enver Paşa in terms of having a state in the North Caucasus between Bolshevik Russia and Turkey. Nevertheless, he had an ambivalent policy towards the North Caucasian Republic. On the one hand, he believed that if Turkey supported an independent state in the Caucasus, this would damage the relationship between the Bolsheviks and Turkey; moreover, Turkey would no longer receive military and financial support from the Bolsheviks. On the other hand, although he did not want to extend support to the North Caucasian Republic, he preferred not to end their relationship with the republic either, wanting to keep it as a possible ally against the Bolsheviks. The Ankara government tried to use Azerbaijan and North Caucasian Muslims to act as a buffer against Russia in case it subsequently insisted on making the Bitlis and Van regions part of Armenia.[52] On 23 December 1920, about twenty people, consisting of the president of the North Caucasian Republic, Pşimafo Kosof, a full colonel, three other lesser colonels, three lieutenants, two doctors, students and group of soldiers as representatives of the republic, moved to Trabzon from the North Caucasus.[53] Their demands were to extend their security measures in Turkey, to serve Turkey and to meet with the Ankara government.[54] However, despite the fact that Ankara was unwilling to abandon the committee entirely, they were still hankering for collaboration with the Russians in some fields. Russia was viewed as a saviour by Ankara, particularly Mustafa Kemal, in terms of military and financial support. Hence, the leaders of the committee were not allowed to gain an appointment with the Ankara government.[55] It can also be seen that Ankara pragmatically attempted to use the committee to strengthen its hand to bargain with the Russians. It was thereby demonstrated by Ankara that it could exert an influence on North Caucasia and its representatives.[56] Therefore, while Ankara might require financial and military aid, the Bolsheviks would know that Ankara was not powerless against them.

Green Army Society (*Yeşil Ordu Cemiyeti*)

The Green Army Society has been a controversial topic of discussion in historiography. The founders of the society, who included Mustafa Kemal, never sought to make the society an official one.⁵⁷ It remained a secret and unofficial organization. The ideology of the society developed out of the 1917 Bolshevik Revolution and aimed to mix Bolshevik ideology and Islam, offering an alternative to the existing Western capitalist one. The ideology was welcomed by a group of politicians and bureaucrats in Turkey since the country was already in a state of war at this time with the Western powers. The idea of the society resulted from the alliance between CUP members who still had connections to the three Paşas, Enver, Talat and Cemal, and leftists who wanted to become allied with Bolshevik Russia and Mustafa Kemal in the spring of 1920.⁵⁸ All the founding members of the society were MPs: Tokat MP Nazım, Hakkı Behiç, Adnan (Adıvar), İzmit MP Sırrı, İzmit MP Hamdi Namık, Muğla MP Yunus Nadi, Saruhan MP İbrahim Süreyya, Saruhan MP Çerkes Reşit, Eskişehir MP Hüsrev Sami, Eskişehir MP Eyüb Sabri, Kozan MP Dr Mustafa, Bursa MP Şeyh Servet and Afyon MP Mehmet Şükrü.⁵⁹ They set up the society and published the *New World* (*Yeni Dünya*) newspaper as an official publication.

The leftist members of the alliance believed that it was not possible for Ankara to succeed in defeating the Allies using its power alone. They believed that to create a union under the banner of socialism in the Muslim world would bring Muslims together against the imperialists. Moreover, Turkey would be a leader in this struggle, as it would not be alone in its fight against the Allies.⁶⁰ They also thought that they would protect the Muslims who were already under Russian occupation. This policy would benefit not only Green Army supporters but also the Bolsheviks, since they would only have to engage with Turkey or the Green Army to engage with the entire Muslim world.⁶¹ The centre of the society was Eskişehir,⁶² where there were labour groups that agreed with the ideology of the Green Army. There were also supporters of the society in the assembly in Ankara. It published a newspaper to spread its Islamic–Bolshevik ideas. The newspaper was called *Arkadaş* (*the Friend*), but the title later changed to *The Mobilized [Ones]*. Thereafter, it became *New World* (*Seyyare Yeni Dünya*), when Arif Oruç returned to Eskişehir from the western front on 6 September 1920.⁶³ In the earlier title, the word 'mobilized' referred to Ethem's 'mobilized forces' (*Kuva-yi Seyyare*).⁶⁴ The relationship between the two sides was critical to both. The Ankara government required a vast amount of financial and military equipment to continue its struggle against Greek troops backed by the British. Russia was also seeking a political ally against Western capitalist powers, particularly the British. The Bolsheviks did not like to see the British forces and Allies on its southern border, in the Black Sea region and in Istanbul; therefore, they supported the Anatolian resistance movement against the Greeks.

A huge amount of financial and military aid was given by the Bolsheviks to the Ankara government. In its first round of meetings with the Ankara government, Ankara demanded the Bolsheviks provide the following: 200 thousand rifles with 5 million bullets, 500 machine guns with 7.5 million bullets, military clothes and equipment for 100 thousand soldiers, 200 aircraft, 100 lorries and buses, 40 automobiles and some military experts in addition to other military equipment.[65] Responding to these demands, the first military and financial aid was sent in September 1920. According to Yusuf Kemal Bey's telegram from Trabzon, the train contained 1,000,000 golden rubles, one wagon for rifles, eight wagons for machine guns, in addition to three hundred thousand bullets, six thousand rifles, one hundred machine guns, and eight British artilleries.[66] It can be said that Mustafa Kemal's strategy of relying on Bolshevik financial and military aid was successful during the Turkish–Greek War. Up until the end of the war, Bolshevik financial aid amounted to 11 million golden rubles and 100 thousand Ottoman golden liras (equal to 90 million Ottoman liras).[67] It is worth mentioning that Turkey's budget was 63,000,000 Ottoman liras in 1920 and 79,000,000 Ottoman liras in 1921. This means that the Russian financial aid exceeded Turkey's annual budget in 1920 and 1921. Total military aid was 45,181 rifles, 9,520 bayonets, 52,599 ammunition chests, 310 machine guns and 166,910 cannon shells, along with other military equipment.[68] One can see the results of this aid: from the end of the First World War to the Turkish–Greek War, Russia represented the greatest threat to the Ottoman Empire; however, later it became its (Turkey's) best ally, thanks to the extensive military and financial assistance it extended to the nationalists of Anatolia.[69]

Mustafa Kemal was neither a communist nor did he believe in communist ideology. He had differences with the Bolsheviks in terms of culture and tradition, and he aimed to gain benefits from interactions with them to protect Anatolia from occupation, rather than to create a new Bolshevik state.[70] He routinely used communist rhetoric in speeches during the war to gain Russian support; as Russians were the enemy of Turkey's enemy, they were through this mutual enmity a friend of Turkey. However, Mustafa Kemal struggled to maintain control of Bolshevik support in Anatolia as the communists and their associations were becoming influential during this period. Small communist groups in Anatolia were assisted by the Bolsheviks, and of these, many members had been prisoners of war in Russia during the First World War.[71] Ankara was aware of the potential danger from the Russians gaining control over Anatolian communists, and therefore an official communist party was set up under the control of Mustafa Kemal in Ankara. The Communist Party of Turkey (*Türkiye Komünist Fırkası*) was established on 18 October 1920.[72] However, the Bolsheviks had never believed Ankara would make communism its official political ideology. They already recognized that Ankara was seeking Russian support out of pragmatism.

Also at this time, the influence of the Green Army organization gradually increased in Ankara and Mustafa Kemal lost control of it.[73] The organization favoured using irregular forces rather than regular troops for fighting. The success of Çerkes Ethem's irregular forces against both the Greeks and the anti-nationalist incidents solidified the suggestion that they use irregular forces. When Ethem was in Ankara, either before the suppression of the disorders in Yozgat or upon return from Yozgat, he joined the Green Army.[74] With the involvement of Ethem in the Green Army through his (at a minimum) three thousand irregular cavaliers, this became a very significant irregular armed political force at the time.[75] One of his military units began to be called the 'Bolshevik Battalion', having about three hundred soldiers and five lieutenants under its control.[76] Although Mustafa Kemal attempted to keep the society under his sway, he was unsuccessful, as it turned into an important centre of anti-Mustafa Kemal activity. At the outset, as noted in the preceding paragraph, it was endorsed by Mustafa Kemal with the aim of receiving Russian military and financial support. However, with Ethem's participation in the society, the political balance of power changed in Ankara. While the society increased its political influence and power, Ethem's participation as leader of the leading irregular armed group of the era showed that it was becoming an uncontrollable political group from the perspective of Mustafa Kemal.[77] He did not want to have to battle against powerful or armed political opponents in the assembly. As a result of Ethem's increasing political and military influence on Ankara, and over the Bolshevik-backed communists, Mustafa Kemal's authority was beginning to falter. Therefore, he closed down the society in the autumn of 1920.[78] Those who participated in the Green Army out of leftist sympathies (e.g. Eyüp Sabri, Adnan, Şeyh Servet, Hakkı Behiç, Nazım and Yunus) then established the 'People's Group' (*Halk Zümresi*) in the assembly, offering a left-wing alternative to Mustafa Kemal.[79] However, with the exclusion of Ethem from the nationalist core, the leftists in Ankara were silenced by Mustafa Kemal.[80]

The Struggle between *Kuva-yi Seyyare* and the Ankara government

Ethem lacked the political experience of Mustafa Kemal. He was the leader of a paramilitary group and more a man of arms than of politics. He had fought on many different fronts, spending over ten years in the army. Mustafa Kemal, when compared to Ethem, was educated in one of the best schools of the empire at the time, the Royal Military Academy. Although he fought in several wars for the Ottoman army, in North Africa, the Balkans, Anatolia and Syria, during the eight years up until 1918, he was never far removed from politics. Ever since the end of the First World War, he had been seeking out a role in the new cabinet of the Ottoman Empire, primarily to occupy the post of minister of war.[81] It is also claimed that the reason behind his move to the Pera Palace after the Moudros Armistice in October 1918 was his political desire to become involved in the new cabinet. Certainly, Pera Palace was well used by the commanders of the occupation forces and an important centre for those who were seeking political careers in the new post-First-World-War Ottoman political scene.[82] His experience and knowledge of politics were more significant than those of Ethem. Ethem, however, had some qualities that were difficult for Mustafa Kemal to match. Although he was a member of a Circassian immigrant family, which had come to Anatolia from the North Caucasus probably in the late 1860s, he had a large family providing him many local networks in Anatolia. His father was from Bandırma, west of Anatolia, one of the founders of the İzmir branch of the CUP and a member of a well-known wealthy local family, while his mother was from the north-western town in Anatolia, Düzce. Both places were settled by a significant number of Circassians.

Circassians lived as a closed community for a long time. As an immigrant/diaspora community, they preferred to marry within their own community, avoiding mixing with the different Anatolian communities. Marriages were an important factor in the survival of their networks and identity. They married young and built up internal community relations between the different regions of Anatolia. These marriages connected different Circassian communities around Anatolia. Another significant feature was their experience of war. They had fought many wars between the 1750s and the 1860s, principally against Russian forces who wanted to occupy the North Caucasus. Although they did not have a formal state structure in the North Caucasus, they had skilled fighters in their ranks. However, after many battles, they were ultimately defeated and were exiled to the Ottoman Empire from the Caucasus. Here, they had two options; either to begin their new lives as farmers, or to be recruited into the Ottoman army. The latter option was more preferable to many Circassians.

Ethem experienced many paramilitary wars in the Ottoman army in the years leading up to the end of the First World War. From the Balkan Wars to the First World War, Ethem had been active in the military. Furthermore, when Greek forces occupied Western Anatolia, he had been one of the first to fight against them and halt their advance into Anatolia. However, after a year and half of Greek occupation (beginning on 15 May 1919), in autumn 1920, Ankara took crucial steps to solidify its authority in terms of its military power and financing and to launch effective counter-attacks. With the military and financial backing of the Bolsheviks, military successes on the eastern and southern fronts of Anatolia against the Georgians and the Armenian forces ensued, and Ankara now had a force more prepared to act as a regular army than ever before. It did not need the irregular forces on the western front any longer. Ethem was also seen as the leader of the Anatolian branch of Mustafa Kemal's rival, Enver Paşa. From the beginning of the movement, Mustafa Kemal did not want to challenge Enver openly. However, after some prominent figures of the CUP, including Rauf Bey, İsmail Canbulat and Fethi Okyar, were arrested by British forces, no powerful political leaders against him remained. Although opposition groups in the assembly prevented him from creating an authoritarian single-man regime, other MPs supported Mustafa Kemal.[83] In this situation, Ethem was the only person in Anatolia to command a non-political but armed group, which could potentially create problems for Mustafa Kemal.

Ethem and his brother were continuously criticized as ruthless by their opponents. They had chosen to execute deserters and 'rebels' after only a short judicial process in a self-styled 'military court'. This policy led to an ambiguous relationship between Ankara and Ethem. On the one hand, Ankara supported Ethem, since he was resisting Greek forces, restoring order in the country and suppressing anti-nationalist movements.[84] However, the way in which Ethem implemented his policy was controversial from the perspective of some members of the assembly. Although Ankara did not oppose the use of violence to suppress disorder and anti-nationalist incidents or to implement its policies, the excessive use of violence by Ethem would be exploited by Ankara as one factor demonstrating the unamenable personality of Ethem.

The problem on the western front was that there was a power struggle underway. Until the regular army was militarily strengthened by Ankara, resistance against the Greek forces was overseen by irregular forces such as Ethem and Demirci Mehmet Efe.[85] These irregular forces set up lines of resistance against the Greek troops before the regular forces gained power. Although they were ruthless against those who rose against Ankara, they organized their forces effectively ensuring order. On the other hand, there were people in the army and assembly who represented state power and came to the stage very late. For example, İsmet (İnönü) and Fevzi (Çakmak) joined the Anatolian movement very late, at the end of April 1920. Their appointment to important positions by Mustafa Kemal, as can be seen from İsmet's appointment as commander of the western front, caused new problems. For those who were at the front from the very beginning of the occupation of Anatolia, such as Çerkes Ethem, it was not easy to accept serving under those who came to the front very late.

The beginning of the end: The Simav and Gediz battles

After Ethem suppressed the incident in Yozgat, he returned to the western front. In some areas of the western front, as with the people in Düzce,

Adapazarı and South Marmara, many had little sympathy for the nationalist forces. The nationalists were viewed as responsible for the continuation of war, high taxation and conscription. For example, in Simav, the nationalists faced stiff opposition from the populace. On 12 July 1920, Greek occupation forces began to march towards Kütahya. They did not face local resistance in the region, particularly in Simav, where people were opposed to the nationalist forces.[86] Ethem was appointed the commander of Kütahya and surrounding areas on 27 July 1920, and in Kütahya 400 prisoners were released and armed by him, and another 150 people joined his forces as volunteers.[87] He moved to Simav with 5,000 men, both cavalry and infantries with 4 canons and 14 machine guns.[88] In Simav, a group of local people worked with the Greek forces. Ethem tried to convince them to stop working for the Greek forces but his attempts failed. On 30 July 1920, Ethem entered the town and fought with the Greek sympathizers there.[89] On this occasion, fifty people were killed by Ethem's forces and another fifty were left wounded.[90]

He then moved on to the north of Demirci town. There, his forces confronted the Greek troops. Ethem attacked them using guerrilla tactics to weaken their position. Ali Fuat Paşa agreed with Ethem's use of guerrilla tactics as important to the nationalists,[91] since they were already aware that the nationalists did not have sufficient military force or supplies to sustain a longer engagement. Ethem's first attack was on 30/31 July 1920, and his forces were successful. Four days later, the Greeks launched a counter-offensive against Ethem's forces. Ethem's forces withdrew to the east of Demirci town on 5 August.[92] Then, in the early morning of 18 August, Ethem carried out a surprise raid against the Greeks who were then forced to the south of Demirci town.[93] The eventual fifteen-day-long confrontation between Ethem's forces and Greek troops resulted in a unit of the Greek army, which consisted of ten thousand men, losing its ability to sustain military operations.[94] According to Ali Fuat Paşa, Ethem had successfully proved that his forces were not only useful for resolving domestic problems and incidents, but could also be helpful to counter Greek forces via guerrilla tactics.[95] Ethem's forces were officially then referred to by the Ankara government as the 'First Mobile Forces' (*Birinci Kuva-yi Seyyare*), particularly after the *Kuva-yi Milliye* forces began participating with the regular forces, following a government decision on 18 September 1920.[96]

The Gediz Battle (24 October–12 November 1920) holds an important place in the history of the western front. The battle was between Greek forces and the Anatolian movement, which consisted of the *Kuva-yi Seyyare* and the regular army. For Ali Fuat Paşa, the Gediz raid was crucial from the perspective of the nationalists, in terms of cutting off the lines between Greek troops in Uşak and Bursa. Moreover, the raid was not costly for the nationalists, since the ammunition used during it had been obtained from the Italians.[97] Division 61, Division 11 and Ethem's forces were later moved towards Gediz. However, the raid proved instrumental for Mustafa Kemal and his close circle as he was able to strengthen his power over the front, and later Mustafa Kemal created his own narrative about the period in *Nutuk*. Nonetheless, the events that took place here were controversial and increased the disagreement between Mustafa Kemal and Ethem and his brothers Tevfik and Reşit. This was because Ali Fuat Paşa, Ethem, Mustafa Kemal and İsmet Bey were making plans on the western front to deal with Greek forces in Gediz. Mustafa Kemal and İsmet Bey were against attacking these forces for military reasons because they believed the army was not ready for such an attack. Although the attack could potentially be successful in the long term, due to a shortage of military equipment and a lack of a regular army, the army would ultimately not be able to resist a possible Greek counter-attack.[98] As a result of the battle, the Greeks had to deal with the Anatolian movement for the first time, and although the attack was largely an unorganized one, the Greek forces were forced to leave Gediz. Nevertheless, Ali Fuat Paşa, Ethem, his brothers, and the leaders of the regular army, İsmet and Refet Beys, then criticized one another for the unorganized nature of the attack.[99] Ethem argued that the regular army had not committed to fulfilling their duty. On the other hand, the commander of the western front, Ali Fuat Paşa, tried to find a middle way between the *Kuva-yi Seyyare* and the regular army, in order to reconcile them. However, his strategy did not work.

Although Mustafa Kemal did not criticize the Gediz raid at the time, later, when Ethem and Ankara had seen their relationship collapse, he went on to claim that Greek forces had not been defeated during the encounter. He argued that they merely withdrew from Gediz to avoid taking risks (because of foggy weather) and that the town was then taken by nationalist forces.[100] As a result of the battle, he concluded that Ali Fuat Paşa should be removed from the western front.[101] While aiming to control the western front, he coveted the loyalty of the commander at the front. Indeed, it was not possible for Mustafa Kemal to gain complete control over the front while Ali Fuat Paşa was in charge, since the latter was a leading military member of the Anatolian movement who had moved there before Mustafa Kemal. Mustafa Kemal favoured choosing a military man who would be loyal to his decisions and who would not challenge him. İsmet and Refet were the two appropriate candidates assigned for this job. However, the problem then was how to remove Ali Fuat Paşa from the front without creating additional difficulties.

In order to achieve control over military units and fronts, Mustafa Kemal used different strategies. Just as was seen in Chapter 2 in reference to the Anzavur Ahmed incident, loyalist Circassians and Pomaks also rose up against nationalist forces in the Gönen–Manyas region in early 1920. Yusuf İzzet Paşa,[102] who was the commander of the nationalist forces in the region, did not attack the group. Mustafa Kemal expressed his suspicions that Yusuf İzzet Paşa did not attack since they were also Circassians. On 6 January 1920, Mustafa Kemal asked Bekir Sami via telegram whether, during the Anzavur incident, contact was made between the Circassian bandit leaders, Çerkes Şevket and Şah İsmail, and Çerkes Ethem, Yusuf İzzet Paşa and Ahmet Fevzi Paşa. According to Mustafa Kemal, contact among the Circassians and associated support from military officers could be a potential cause of conflict between the Turks and Circassians.[103] As he did not wish to face further problems on this front, Mustafa Kemal invited Yusuf İzzet Paşa to Ankara to join the assembly, to become an MP. As head of the assembly, Mustafa Kemal could have removed Yusuf İzzet Paşa from the military unit. Instead, he took a different approach, inviting him to Ankara, thereby preventing any possible dispute either in the assembly or at the western front. Yusuf İzzet Paşa accepted Mustafa Kemal's offer, joining the assembly as an MP before he left the military unit.

In Ali Fuat Paşa's case, Mustafa Kemal employed a similar strategy to that used in the case of Yusuf İzzet Paşa's, instead of forcing him to leave the western front. Due to the developing relationships with the Bolshevik Russians, Ankara required a permanent ambassador in Moscow to maintain relations and ensure financial aid would be available at a certain level. Ali Fuat Paşa was selected by Mustafa Kemal as a Turkish ambassador to Moscow, claiming that he was a well-known general and an enemy of the British. He was expected to have a good effect on Moscow.[104] On 10 November, the Ankara government appointed Ali Fuat Paşa as ambassador to Moscow.[105]

However, the plan was carried out without Ali Fuat Paşa having ever been informed. Indeed, he was appointed ambassador to Moscow by Mustafa Kemal while still at the western front.[106] He was therefore invited by Mustafa Kemal to Ankara. Ali Fuat Paşa, without being aware of Mustafa Kemal's decision, came to Ankara where he was welcomed at the train station by him.[107] The decision was taken without any consultation. Ali Fuat Paşa was informed by Mustafa Kemal of the post at the train station, and he expressed his surprise at the decision. In his little-known memoirs *Bilinmeyen Hatıralar*, Ali Fuat Paşa claims that he already felt that an era of single-man rule had begun in Ankara. According to Ali Fuat Paşa, those who had recently come to Ankara – that is, those who came to Ankara after Istanbul had been occupied by the British on 16 March 1920 – helped Mustafa Kemal establish single-man rule in the country, by dividing up old friends.[108] It was obvious to Ali Fuat Paşa at this point that Mustafa Kemal's intention was to send him away from the front and Anatolia.

Mustafa Kemal also chose to send Ethem and his brothers to Moscow along with Ali Fuat Paşa. Ethem and his brothers had no diplomatic career backgrounds, which Mustafa Kemal already knew. They were men of arms rather than men of politics or diplomacy. Mustafa Kemal was aware of Ethem and his brothers' personalities and background. So we can question what his aim was in sending Ethem to Moscow. Possibly, to make him second secretary to Ali Fuat Paşa? Thus, it is apparent that his strategy was to eradicate potential problems efficiently by sending opponents abroad. However, Ethem and his brothers did not readily accept leaving the front. They had been at the front from the beginning of the Greek occupation in May 1919. At that time, İsmet (İnönü) had been in Istanbul, which was under de facto occupation from the British (November 1918);[109] meanwhile, Mustafa Kemal was occupied with local and regional congresses in the Black Sea region.

Mustafa Kemal determined that the western front would be divided into two parts: a western and southern one. While İsmet (İnönü) became commander of the western front, Refet (Bele) became commander of the southern one. According to his plan, Çerkes Ethem's *Kuva-yi Seyyare* would serve under the Kütahya branch of the western front. This meant the *Kuva-yi Seyyare*, with its irregular forces, would become a subunit of the regular army.[110] Ethem's older brother Tevfik disagreed with the decision made in Ankara and refused to serve under a regular military unit in Kütahya.[111] Ethem and his brothers, especially Tevfik, were also against the appointment of Refet Paşa (Bele) to the front. The reason for their opposition was that Ethem and Refet had personal problems from the time of the Yozgat/Çapanoğlu incident. If we recollect events, we can observe that after he had suppressed disorder in Yozgat, a group of armed Alevis from Yozgat then joined Ethem's forces at the western front.[112] However, Refet Paşa threatened the local Alevis of Yozgat after Ethem had quelled the unrest. This situation caused problems among Ethem's forces, with Alevi soldiers leaving the front and declaring that if they would not be pardoned for their activities in the Yozgat incident, there would be no reason for them to join the nationalist forces. For this reason, Ethem tried to send Refet Paşa to the military court in Eskişehir, alleging that he had caused the desertion of soldiers from the military front.[113] However, this created a further problem between Mustafa Kemal and Ethem, since Refet was the minister of interior in Mustafa Kemal's government. Consequently, Ethem's attempt was prevented by Mustafa Kemal.

At the beginning of the Anatolian movement, there was no proper working state structure in Anatolia. The central government, which was in Istanbul, was unable to rule the empire effectively. With the opening of the assembly in Ankara in April 1920, a central authority was finally beginning to re-emerge. Until the assembly opened, in the period between 1919 and 1920, Ethem was fighting against both the Greeks troops at the western front and suppressing the anti-nationalist movements in Central and Western Anatolia.[114] A single year had not passed since the opening of the assembly, which brought about an increase in Ankara's military and financial power, before a struggle began to emerge, which made irregular forces appear an unsustainable option for Mustafa Kemal. In November 1920, he no longer saw such a need for irregulars, as he had in the opening days of the assembly in April 1920. In late November, a new struggle began between Mustafa Kemal's and Ethem's circles, especially between İsmet and Tevfik, the latter of whom was responsible for the *Kuva-yi Seyyare* on behalf of Ethem. İsmet was the commander of the western front, and Ethem's brother, Tevfik, was his representative at the western front. İsmet tried to take control of Tevfik; however, Tevfik did not consent to accept İsmet as a senior commander. İsmet sent a detachment with a lieutenant colonel, who prepared notices against the leaders of the *Kuva-yi Seyyare*.[115] Tevfik sent them back to İsmet, declaring that he would no longer accept İsmet as a senior commander.[116] İsmet and Mustafa Kemal sought a way to control the *Kuva-yi Seyyare*, as they had other 'regular divisions', since Ethem and his irregular forces were becoming a threat to the Ankara government, interrupting the political business. İsmet demanded the official military reports of the *Kuva-yi Seyyare*, to regulate it.[117] İsmet also aimed to control the *Kuva-yi Seyyare* at the front and prevent their political intervention in the assembly. It was also declared that the *Kuva-yi Seyyare* should focus on enemy troops only, and nothing behind the front.[118] However, Tevfik opposed İsmet's plan to make the *Kuva-yi Seyyare* a regular force, emphasizing that their forces consisted of 'good-for-nothings' (*serseriler*), whom he believed would never be able to serve as a regular force since they were also illiterate. He suggested they should either continue as an irregular force or be disbanded.[119] He also refused to send military reports pertaining to his forces to İsmet in Kütahya, choosing to send reports directly to Mustafa Kemal in Ankara.

Bilecik Meetings

Ethem was invited by Mustafa Kemal to Ankara to meet with representatives of the Istanbul government.[120] However, it is worth noting that these meetings were in Bilecik, which was about 80 km from Eskişehir and 350 km from Ankara in the northwest of Anatolia. Ethem was in Kütahya at this time, which was also next to Eskişehir (about 75 km from Eskişehir and 350 km from Ankara). He also had to pass through Eskişehir to go to Ankara. The question raised here is, what was Mustafa Kemal planning to do with his invitation to Ankara before travelling to Bilecik for negotiations? Ethem was not accustomed to having regular diplomatic meetings as he was a paramilitary force leader. To solve the issues between İsmet and Tevfik, Mustafa Kemal moved to Eskişehir with Ethem, Reşit, Kazım, Kılıç Ali, Celal, Hakkı Behiç and Şükrü Beys. According to Kazım Özalp, when travelling on the train, Ethem had more armed people in his group than usual during the trip.[121] Some counter-measures were also taken against Ethem.[122] Mustafa Kemal brought fifty guards with him,[123] including Topal Osman ('Osman the cripple') his personal guard, who brought an extended armed group with him. Topal was one of Mustafa Kemal's best-known and most ruthless guards at the time. His presence on this journey is therefore significant. Ethem expected that Mustafa Kemal might try to organize an attack against him.[124] Indeed, in their memoirs, both Mustafa Kemal and Ethem accused one another of organizing an armed attack against the other.

When the train arrived at the station in Eskişehir, two officers greeted Ethem. The officers provided some information about the regular army's ongoing preparations in Eskişehir. They feared that some military units were being transferred to Eskişehir.[125] The plan, according to Ethem, was that he would be killed by Eskişehir–Bilecik on the train journey. The regular army units were being readied in Eskişehir to counter possible riots by the people of Eskişehir.[126] Ethem felt that the troop activity was directed against him personally, and he prepared a counter-attack at the Eskişehir station. He used his sickness as an excuse to leave the train, to rest in a house close to the station. Except for Mustafa Kemal, all the other members of the committee also left the train. However, due to suspicions over possible preparations by Ethem, Mustafa Kemal chose not to stay in the station, moving towards Bilecik with the train, without waiting for members of the committee to return.[127]

The lack of trust on both sides, described above, heightened expectation of an armed conflict in Eskişehir, when Mustafa Kemal and İsmet arrived there. On this occasion, Ethem left Eskişehir for Kütahya since he believed that he was not secure there. Diyarbakır MP Hacı Şükrü Bey, who was also on the train with Mustafa Kemal, went to Kütahya with Ethem Bey. He explained that in a secret session of the assembly, Ethem conveyed his suspicions about the Ankara government, citing the military mobilization in Eskişehir, as Battalion 61 had been moved there. Ethem thought that this was one component of preparations being made against him by Mustafa Kemal.[128] In his memoir, Ethem confirmed that he suspected military preparations were being made by Mustafa Kemal in Eskişehir and that this meant an assassination plot. When Mustafa Kemal returned from Bilecik, the MPs who came from Ankara with him came together and decided that Reşit, Ethem's older brother, would go with Kazım Bey to Kütahya to meet with Ethem.[129] Following the meeting in Kütahya, Ethem agreed with Kazım Bey to serve under him at the western front as an army commander. However, he spoke against Refet Bey's appointment to the Southern Front as commander there. From the perspective of Ankara, it was considered contrary to military discipline to change a military commander based on a paramilitary leader's opinion.[130]

Superficially, it appears that the disagreement between Tevfik Bey and İsmet Bey was on the grounds of military strategy and because Tevfik Bey refused to send reports about his military unit to İsmet Bey. However, we contend that the reason for the disagreement was not about military strategy at all. Tevfik Bey did not favour working under İsmet and Refet Beys. Indeed, he was not completely against the regular army, since he had already sent military reports to Ankara (to Mustafa Kemal). However, he had experienced problems with senior officers, İsmet and Refet Beys. The tension between Ethem Bey and the Ankara government thereby increased, as Mustafa Kemal, as head of the assembly, along with his close circle, had already decided to exclude Ethem from the armed groups, to pacify him, because he (and his brothers) could not be controlled. Mustafa Kemal would no longer work with them. Although Ethem had been useful for suppressing Anatolia's domestic incidents, during the critical period of resistance in the absence of a strong regular military, there were no longer important threats from Anatolia to the Ankara government. Now Ankara had enough military power for the regular army against the Greek forces on the western front, particularly after the war against the Armenian forces ended on the eastern front. Some of the regular forces were later transferred to the western front from the east. The resulting agreement with the Bolsheviks meant that Ankara would soon have sufficient financial and military power to strengthen its military. Mustafa Kemal no longer required the irregular forces at the western front. The irregulars were already creating threatened his power.

According to Mustafa Kemal, some MPs and bureaucrats directed too much attention towards Ethem in Ankara. Ethem's self-confidence had increased with the attention that was showered on him by the people,[131] encouraging the opponents of Mustafa Kemal to use Ethem against the former. They tried to balance Mustafa Kemal's power with that of Ethem. However, before Ethem came to the assembly, he had not been involved in any collusion. Despite the continued armed confrontation against Greek forces and the civil war in Anatolia, there was an extensive political struggle within the assembly. The composition of the political assembly was diverse; the assembly included ulema, bureaucrats, senior military officers and local notables. Thus, a great many different elements of society were represented in the assembly. This diversity made governing the assembly challenging, complicating the process of arriving at concrete decisions; MPs themselves were generally striving to save the empire and the sultanate from Greek and Allied occupation.

Nationalist officers successfully used bandits and irregular armed groups at the beginning of the resistance against Greek occupation. The nationalists did not see the crimes committed by the bandits and irregulars or the release of convicts from jails by irregular forces as problematic.[132] However, when the relationship between Ankara and Ethem became uneasy, Ankara began to find 'excuses' to justify its exclusion of Ethem from the front. Complaints were flowing in about Ethem and his brother Tevfik, specifically in relation to their discretionary hanging of anti-nationalists. Although Ethem and his brothers worked hand in glove with Ankara for more than six months, for the first time, on 24 December 1920, Ankara took complaints about Ethem's acts of insubordination seriously. These acts included his refusal to accept the verdicts of military tribunals and the authority of the central government.[133] Although the Ankara government also took harsh measurements and used independent courts to 'deal with' opposition, Mustafa Kemal criticized Ethem for hanging people after only a short trial, without recourse to independent courts for approval.[134] It is important to note that there was already a plan on paper to prove Ethem's disobedience to Ankara, and as Mustafa Kemal's political and military power grew, he increasingly believed that if the army could defeat Ethem's forces, then no one in Ankara would question his decisions or make his job difficult. On 27 December, the cabinet declared that Ethem and his brother Tevfik had violated the assembly's authority through their actions.[135]

From the end of November 1920 onwards, both sides increasingly expressed doubt about the activities of the other side. However, they chose not to display their distrust for each other. Kind language was used in the correspondence from both sides. However, intra-group correspondence demonstrates that the confidence between the two groups had already broken down. According to İsmet (who informed Ankara), Ethem was seeking to gather all irregular nationalist forces around his own troops so that he would be in a position to attempt to take control over the assembly with Bolshevist ideas.[136] İsmet's forces were also ready to attack Ethem's *Kuva-yi Seyyare*.[137] Mustafa Kemal argued in his reply that while the activities in the assembly were controlled, *Kuva-yi Seyyare* still had the ability to recruit people from the western front.

However, on 23 December, a group of MPs moved from Ankara to Kütahya to negotiate with Ethem regarding the problems between himself and Ankara.[138] Mustafa Kemal did not support the idea that a delegation should meet with Ethem. However, under pressure from MPs in the assembly, he agreed to send a council to Kütahya to meet with Ethem, in order to negotiate. The council reported on Ethem and Tevfik's demands, two of which were that Refet and Fahrettin Bey should be removed from the front and that the local government should pay for their expenses incurred at the front. Ethem and Tevfik, however, swore not to act against the regular forces if they did not attack them.[139]

After receiving the report, Mustafa Kemal thought that the members of the delegation had been arrested by Ethem and had been coerced into sending the reports. This was despite the fact that the reports did not include any unacceptable demands. The delegation did not think in the same way as Mustafa Kemal and İsmet. Their aim was only to try to reconcile the *Kuva-yi Seyyare* with Ankara. In the assembly, moreover, the majority of the MPs did not favour a military attack on the Circassian brothers. Mustafa Kemal expected the delegation to share his ideas. Without waiting for their return to Ankara, Mustafa Kemal chose to end the problem and fight Ethem. Despite his position as head of the assembly, Mustafa Kemal believed that he did not need to inform the assembly of an impending military attack. If the attack were to succeed he believed he would receive approval and that the assembly would agree as he already had sufficient evidence to convince its members.[140] The delegation was however disappointed by the approach taken by the cabinet regarding their reports and its reaction to their suggestions to solving the problems noted.[141]

Mustafa Kemal, in his own memoir, the *Nutuk*, added some documents at the end about the incident to push forward his own version of the story. The documents suggested that Mustafa Kemal was seeking a way to solve the problem without causing an armed conflict. Then, on 26 December 1920, Mustafa Kemal sent a telegram to İsmet informing him that he was thinking of explaining every point to the assembly. On December 28, he sent a telegram to the delegation, informing them that the problem would be spoken about at government level and that the decision would be taken by the government.[142] However, in one document dated 27 December 1920, not present in Mustafa Kemal's *Nutuk* but which can be found in the *Journal of Military History Documents* (an official journal of the Turkish Armed Forces), we see that Mustafa Kemal had sent a telegram to İsmet, arguing that he did not believe the problem could be resolved peacefully. Therefore, he explained his military plan to İsmet and Refet.[143] It is noteworthy that Mustafa Kemal supported a military attack but chose not to include the documents, thus showing his resolve to handle the problem alone using military power.

Two days later, during negotiations in the assembly sessions, Mustafa Kemal almost convinced the other MPs of the need for a military solution to the *Kuva-yi Seyyare* (30 December).[144] However, after the delegation had informed the MPs about their meetings with Ethem and his brothers, the MPs agreed they were not in favour of fighting the *Kuva-yi Seyyare*. Mustafa Kemal's willingness to use force against Ethem and his men was contrary to the general opinion of the MPs, which was to avoid 'spilling Muslim blood' ('*Müslüman kanı dökmek*') in the country.[145] As a result of negotiations in the assembly, and as a final offer to Ethem and his brothers, Mustafa Kemal informed Refet and İsmet that they should notify Ethem that if they were to leave the *Kuva-yi Seyyare* their lives would be guaranteed and the assembly would request a pardon in the courts.[146] A day after Mustafa Kemal's telegram to Refet and İsmet, Refet sent a telegram to Mustafa Kemal informing him that he was continuing his military preparations against the *Kuva-yi Seyyare*. He then prepared his unit and pushed some of his cavalry forward to facilitate the attack.[147]

It is worth pointing out that Ethem attempted to open a place for himself in the anti-nationalist camp. He stated to the members of the Istanbul government, such as Ali Kemal, that the country could not continue to pursue a war agenda any longer. It is significant to emphasize here, that, although Ethem was seen as no more than a leader of bandits, Ethem's position changed in response to circumstances. He was one of the first to organize local resistance against the Greeks in Western Anatolia, and many people were hanged by his forces, due to their opposition to the nationalist cause. However, after he began to fear that he would be excluded from the national movement, he adopted an anti-nationalist rhetoric.[148] Ethem sent a telegram to the assembly to protest the arrest of Istanbul government members by the Ankara government after the Bilecik meeting. He demanded their release and criticized the members of the Ankara government for increasing their own salaries.[149] It could be said that Ethem sent this telegram to Ankara to gain the support of the Istanbul government and the palace, since his relationship had already deteriorated with the Ankara government.

Celal Bey also mentioned in his assembly speech that when the delegation met Ethem and his brother in Kütahya, military equipment and soldiers belonging to the Ankara government had been moved to Kütahya from Eskişehir via train. This consignment concerned Ethem and his men, and indicated to them that it could mark the commencement of Ankara's military operation against them.[150] It was also emphasized in the speech that *Kuva-yi Seyyare* forces did not wish to fight against Ankara's forces. Meanwhile, the preparation continued among İsmet Paşa's unit in Kütahya. According to Celal Bey, İsmet Paşa was also concerned about the situation. However, he claimed that there was no option besides the military one if Ethem and his brothers chose not to leave the military units.[151] Celal also believed that both sides were exaggerating the situation for personal reasons. It is also important to mention that details concerning the end of the session were completely absent from the assembly records. Thus, it is not clear how the session concluded.[152]

After the meeting, İsmet Bey asked Ethem to leave his forces along with his brother Tevfik. He also stated that he had sufficient military forces to deploy against him.[153] In his reply, Ethem accused İsmet and Mustafa Kemal of selfishness. He also blamed his brother Reşit Bey, arguing that it was due to Reşit's naivety that İsmet and Mustafa Kemal had been given an opportunity to lead the nationalist cause, arguing that he would have fought them to prevent their emergence as leaders.[154] Mustafa Kemal planned that Refet Bey, the head of the Southern Front army, would attack the *Kuva-yi Seyyare* with all his forces, and would also begin a propaganda campaign to break the unity binding the *Kuva-yi Seyyare* units together.[155] Mustafa Kemal already thought that the *Kuva-yi Seyyare* might not wish to fight against the regular army. In this case, the southern and western front of the regular cavalries would then be expected to attack and pursue them.[156] İsmet Bey had been ordered by Mustafa Kemal to move to Kütahya in a coded telegram. İsmet informed Ethem that they should move to Gediz.[157] Ethem would then either remain in Kütahya and confront İsmet's forces, or he would move to Gediz as İsmet had told him, where he would be squeezed between İsmet's forces and the Greek troops. Ethem's aide de camp, Lieutenant Sami, claimed that Ethem's aim was to capture Ankara, to eliminate the assembly and to execute its executives and then reorganize the assembly and the army to fight against the Greeks.[158] When the military attack was carried out by the regular army, however, Ethem avoided joining in. He withdrew his troops to the Gediz region without resisting the incoming army.[159] He declared to the *Kuva-yi Seyyare* that there was no longer an opportunity for them to continue working together. They had three options: they could join the regular forces (Ankara) or the Greek forces, or live as bandits in the mountains.[160] Ethem did not force his troops to follow him. He himself preferred to go into hiding in the Greek-occupied zone.[161] It can be asserted that Ethem's decision to dissolve his forces prevented a civil war between his forces and Ankara. Kazım Özalp also states that after the military attack began, a group of officers and soldiers joined their side. Another group from Ethem's forces did not fight, choosing to go into the mountains.[162]

After Ethem withdrew to Gediz, the regular troops attacked them. His forces were caught in the crossfire between the regular army and Greek forces. He then demanded a ceasefire from the Greeks,[163] and after they agreed, Ethem attacked İsmet's regular forces. İsmet then withdrew to Kütahya from Gediz on 6 January 1921.[164] Ethem continued his attack on İsmet until the Greek forces began their attack. The Greek forces then moved towards Gediz. Around Gediz, Refet's regular forces, which had passed over the Greek troops, now attacked Ethem,[165] leading him to decide to defect to the Greeks. His plan was to scatter his unit; he would move into the mountains with fifty to sixty of his armed men. From there, he would move further inside Anatolia,[166] where eventually due to an illness he had to hide in a Circassian village (*Eski Manyas/ Soğuksu*), in a Turkish family's house around Susurluk.[167] Initially, Ethem did not favour joining the Greeks; however, when he was left with no option, he, along with his brothers Tevfik and Reşit, joined the Greeks.

After the military operation commenced against Ethem and his forces, Mustafa Kemal sought to justify the military attack. He blamed Ethem and his brothers for trying to establish a feudal structure (*Derebeylik*) under their control in the Kütahya, Afyon and Isparta regions.[168] He alleged that they also aimed to replace the assembly with a new one under their own control. Mustafa Kemal claimed that they then worked alone for their own benefit. Moreover, he claimed they had tried to influence the Bolsheviks, to organize a Bolshevik uprising in Eskişehir.[169] While demolishing Ethem and his brothers' reputation in nationalist circles, Mustafa Kemal utilized black propaganda in the assembly. He went further in his claims, arguing that Ethem and his brothers had tried to collaborate with the Bolsheviks, the Greeks, the Istanbul government and even the British.[170] However, only a month before this speech, Ethem had been in Ankara. Although the Ethem–Mustafa Kemal relationship had broken down, there had been attempts to seek a solution to the problems between Tevfik and İsmet at that time. However, now Ethem was simply declared a collaborator.

To cut off all ties between Ethem and his forces, a declaration was published by western front commanders calling on Ethem's irregular forces not to fight against the Ankara government forces; this call used Islamic rhetoric and referred to Ethem as having been 'Greekified'.[171] It was also ordered by the Ankara government's Ministry of War that, in response to Ethem's impact on the Circassians of the Tokat, Sivas, Kayseri regions, they should be observed closely by military intelligence to prevent possible support emerging from the region for Ethem.[172] In the same session, MPs voted to remove Reşit Bey from his deputyship in the assembly.[173] On 24 January 1921, Mustafa Kemal declared that Ethem had ceased to be of concern.[174]

The year 1920 has been described in this chapter as an especially difficult year for the Ankara government since domestic problems and the civil war in Anatolia had made it difficult for it to fight against Greek and Allied occupation forces. On the one hand, the regular army had not been as strong as the anti-nationalist forces. As we have seen, the Anzavur, Adapazarı-Düzce and Yozgat incidents seriously threatened Ankara's existence. On the other hand, Çerkes Ethem, as a leading irregular force leader at the time, had preserved Ankara from many disastrous outcomes. However, towards the end of the year, Ankara (or Mustafa Kemal) expanded its authority over the country both militarily and in terms of government policy. Order was restored in the areas surrounding Ankara, and Ethem was no longer as valuable as he had been previously. Thus, the time arrived for Mustafa Kemal and İsmet (İnönü) to ensure they had control over him. This situation provided an opening for the opposition to strengthen his military and political power, although Ethem had not strived for this. Ultimately, Mustafa Kemal and İsmet succeeded in their objective to exclude him from the nationalist cause, forcing him into the Greek-occupied zone by January 1921.

5

The Circassian Congress, bandits and the Gönen–Manyas deportations

The days following the exclusion of Çerkes Ethem from the national movement saw anti-nationalist Circassians take new steps to oppose the Kemalists in İzmir. They had collaborated with occupiers to establish a semi-autonomous structure within the Greek-occupied zone. The members of the group were not a monolithic bloc. They had already fought each other during the Düzce–Adapazarı and Anzavur incidents. However, now they had a common enemy in the Kemalists. Among the members of the group, there was a variety of people from different backgrounds. They included ex-members of the Ottoman Special Organization, bureaucrats, members of the Committee of Union and Progress (CUP) and of its opposition, the Liberal Entente, Ottoman officials and bandits. All were now members of the Association for the Strengthening of Near Eastern Circassians' Rights (ASNEC, *Şark-ı Karip Çerkesleri Temin-i Hukuk Cemiyeti*), and included participants from the Circassian Congress held in İzmir (October 1921).

In the year after the congress, the Ankara government exiled fourteen Circassian villages in the Gönen–Manyas region to central and eastern parts of Turkey. The reason for this exile was to regain control over the region. In the days following the defeat of Greek forces in Western Anatolia (final battles were fought between the 26 August and 9 September 1922), Circassian bandits seemed to remain the only, although a grave, threat to the Ankara government. It was against this backdrop that the government took the decision to exile fourteen Circassian villages, which was a collective punishment for them. They were exiled because of the presence of Circassian bandits in the region, and the government also intended to deport all other Circassian villages from the region, to cut off the supply of human resources. Some of the villages were evacuated because some of their inhabitants were known to have joined armed groups; yet not all the members of the civilian population supported these groups. The only 'crime' that they had committed, if it can be considered a 'crime' at all, was coming from the same villages as some of the bandits. Ankara proposed to end the alleged chaos in the region by removing the Circassian villages entirely from the region.

This chapter will examine the motivation behind those anti-nationalist Circassians establishing an association, seeking Greek support and declaring their independence from both the nationalist government of Ankara and the Ottoman government of Istanbul. This chapter will also study the armed Circassian opposition. As a response to noted declarations and opposition movements, a collective punishment for the Circassians was applied by the Ankara government. This involved deporting them from the Gönen–Manyas region to Central and Eastern Anatolia, something discussed in the third section of this chapter. This chapter argues that the tense Turkish–Greek War in Western Anatolia (1919–22) convinced the Ankara government that it would be nearly impossible for it to control the region, and thus it sought extremely harsh methods to deal with the Circassians. This culminated in four thousand deportations from the region. As a result of this overreaction and the associated collective punishment, many women, children and innocent people in the region became victims.

The emergence of the idea of autonomy and the Circassian Congress

A) Governorship of (Çule) İbrahim Hakkı in İzmit from April 1920 to June 1921

Çule İbrahim Hakkı Bey was an opponent of the CUP even during the pre-First-World-War period, having been implicated in the assassination of Mahmud Şevket Paşa in 1913.[1] Due to increasing pressure from the CUP, he had to leave the empire for Egypt, where he built a good relationship with the British, explaining why he was also known as İbrahim the English (İngiliz İbrahim).[2] With the signing of the Mudros Armistice (1918), he returned to the empire and was appointed as governor of İzmit by Damad Ferid Paşa. He remained in İzmit from April 1920 to June 1921. He was a CUP opponent, as were the majority of the bureaucrats in the post-First-World-War period, appointed by the Istanbul government. The division between the CUP and the Liberal Party stemmed from the pre-First-World-War period, when multiparty elections were first established in the empire. Later, in 1913, the CUP dominated in terms of its political power, carrying out a military coup in Istanbul. İbrahim later returned from Egypt after the First World War, when he was appointed governor of İzmit in 1920. From the beginning of the British and Greek occupation, İbrahim Hakkı had a warm relationship with the British. Indeed, a British officer in İzmit also considered him a friend.[3]

The idea of autonomy came to the fore for İbrahim Hakkı when the Ottoman Porte[4] lost control over the İzmit region in June 1921. The region was then taken over by the Ankara government's forces. From April 1920 to June 1921 Çule İbrahim Hakkı Bey was the governor of İzmit,[5] and his activities there disturbed even the Istanbul government. Due to his warm relationships with the British, the Istanbul government tried unsuccessfully on a number of occasions to remove him from power. Indeed, the Ministry of Interior of the Ottoman government even requested the permission of the British High Commissioner to remove İbrahim Hakkı from İzmit.[6] The commissioner declared that they were not against the decision taken by the Ottoman government on İbrahim Hakkı.[7] Abdülvahab Bey was appointed to the position.[8] However, he was not allowed to take the governorship of İzmit, since İbrahim Hakkı had already organized a paramilitary group to secure himself and the region under his governorship.[9] Although the British, on paper at least, allowed the Ottoman government to remove him from his position, the Ottoman government was not able to do so, or to bring him to Istanbul for trial; indeed all attempts made by the Porte resulted in failure.[10]

İbrahim Hakkı tried to create an autonomous structure to create a buffer zone between the Istanbul government and the Ankara government during his governorship. He opposed the actions of the Ankara government and did not allow its military units or supporters to live in this region. He pursued a policy that was not overly aggressive when trying to convince people to accept his anti-*Kuva-yi Milliye* move.[11] He acted, in fact, rather peacefully. At the same time, since the Istanbul government had no authority in the region, public security was constantly under threat from the presence of armed bands.

Even in mid-1919, he had been considering establishing his own armed group to ensure his security.[12] Later, at the end of 1920, after the Düzce–Adapazarı incidents, he formed an armed group consisting of Circassians who had been attacked by the nationalists during the incidents, and whose homes had been burnt down.[13] It appears that those Circassians who had suffered from the nationalist attacks were purposely selected by İbrahim in order to keep the region under his control by gaining their loyalty and support.

One of İbrahim Hakkı's local rivals was from the Maan family in the Adapazarı region. This was Maan Midhat, who described İbrahim Hakkı's policies as a kind of triple game in a letter to Sultan Vahidettin.[14] According to him, İbrahim Hakkı juggled three groups during his governorship. The first of these groups was the Circassians of the region. İbrahim Hakkı followed a deceptive policy of trying to convince those Circassians who believed that İbrahim Hakkı was implementing the decisions of the Ottoman Porte and the sultan during his governorship. However, he thereby strengthened his own authority in the region rather than that of the Ottoman government and the sultan. The second group was the British, who employed İbrahim Hakkı, since they believed that he had influence over the widespread anti-*Kuva-yi Milliye* movement led by the Circassians.[15] The final group was the Ottoman government, which was under British control by that time. Due to the occupation of Istanbul, the Porte was unable to take any precautions preventing İbrahim Hakkı from strengthening his authority in the region.[16] It is noteworthy that Maan Midhat claimed that the troubled relationship in the area between the Circassians and Turks would deteriorate because of İbrahim Hakkı's policies. However, the Porte and the sultan himself believed they could influence the Circassians, believing they would gain their support, since they still had an important place in their hearts and minds.[17]

After the nationalist forces attacked İzmit on 28 June 1921,[18] İbrahim Hakkı and his armed group left the city. However, they were unwelcome in Istanbul due to their activities during his governorship in the region. Some of them had attacked villages in İzmit along with Greek and Armenian bandits. Therefore, a group that included Maan Mustafa was arrested in Istanbul upon arrival.[19] It is still not clear whether İbrahim Hakkı remained in Istanbul or if he went straight to Midilli (Lesbos) in the Aegean Sea when he left İzmit along with Greek forces. However, one thing was obvious: his service as an

Ottoman governor finished when he left İzmit. A new stage had begun in his life, with his settlement in Midilli and collaboration with Greek forces. His aim was now to mobilize the Circassian population of Western Anatolia politically. His position changed from one of a loyal Circassian subject of the sultan to a Circassian activist/nationalist with the objective of establishing an autonomous structure in the Greek-occupied zone of Anatolia. To achieve this aim, he prepared several charters, a booklet focused on 'the Circassian nationalist movement in İzmit' under his governorship, and several proposals for the Circassian Congress while in Midilli.[20] As will be seen later in this chapter, this attempt affected the lives of hundreds of Circassians rather negatively.

İbrahim claims in his writings that April 1920 was the date on which the Circassian nationalist movement began. The movement had two important characteristics, its Islamic and Circassian identity. The Circassians were loyal to the caliph because they were Muslims. Their identity was also important, as it was necessary to retain their nationalist values against Turkish nationalism.[21] Moreover, according to this narrative, the Circassian fighters (mujahedeen, *mücahid*) were already fighting for the sultan/caliph against the Anatolian Turkish nationalists (*Kuva-yi Milliye*), who were recognized as rebels by the Istanbul government. The fighters kept Düzce, Bolu, Gerede, Safranbolu, Mederni, Hendek, Akyazı, Adapazarı, Sapanca, Kandıra, Karamürsel and Yalova.[22] İbrahim also claims that they did not fight alone; a number of other Muslim groups also joined them in the fight against Ankara. Because of his success organizing the anti-Ankara movement, İbrahim Hakkı was appointed as the official governor of İzmit on 25 April 1920 by the grand vizier Damad Ferid Paşa.[23]

The Circassian opposition was supported by Damad Ferid and Sultan Vahidettin. Both favoured signing a peace agreement with the Allies to avoid another war, since, according to them, people had had enough of war and the state had little power to sustain an armed struggle. For that reason, both agreed with the Circassian intention to fight against the nationalist forces.[24] However, the Ottoman Porte and the Ministry of War mostly consisted of supporters of the *Kuva-yi Milliye*. They tried to prevent Circassian attacks on the nationalists. Subsequently, Damad Ferid feared that the Circassian movement might represent a greater danger to the empire than Mustafa Kemal's movement.[25] For this reason, the only force under the sultan capable of fighting Mustafa Kemal was not given adequate support to fight against Ankara. The towns taken by Circassians were then retaken by Ankara.[26]

Although Istanbul was under British occupation, İbrahim Hakkı's relationships with the British made Istanbul government uncomfortable. He was rather close to the British and was not controlled by the Ottoman Porte. Several Ottoman governments attempted to remove İbrahim Hakkı from office. On 6 July 1920, Grand Vizier Damad Ferid Paşa tried to appoint former Antalya governor İhsan Adli Bey as the governor of İzmit; however, he failed to do so.[27] The successor to Damad Ferid, Tevfik Paşa, on 11 November 1920 assigned Abdülvahab Bey to İzmit to replace İbrahim Hakkı. However, Abdülvahab Bey was prevented from coming to İzmit by İbrahim Hakkı's men, as mentioned earlier in this chapter.[28] Abdülvahab reported that İbrahim Hakkı had a relatively warm relationship with the British and had some Circassian and Abkhazian military groups around him.[29] The Porte also applied to the British forces in Istanbul to remove him; however, the British did not.[30] Thus, İbrahim Hakkı was not just a governor of İzmit; he received British support and backing from groups of armed Circassians and Abkhazians, making him seem rather like a feudal lord. Although he was in İzmit, which is about 100 km from Istanbul, the Porte could not assert its authority over him.

Ibrahim claims that due to the rise of Turkish nationalism in Ankara, the Circassians supported the Istanbul government and the sultan. The Adapazarı–Düzce incidents were examples of this support. According to him, on 11 June 1920, the Circassian government (Hükümet-i Çerakkisiye) was set up in İzmit; it lasted until 27 June 1921.[31] When the Greeks had to leave İzmit in June 1921, İbrahim Hakkı and his supporters asked for help from the Ministry of Interior in Istanbul; however, help was not forthcoming. He used this situation to demonstrate the changing policy of the sultan, which was to not assist the Circassians, but to replace Islam with 'Turkishness' as the main ideology of the state.[32] However, İbrahim Hakkı already had been involved in prior disputes with the Istanbul government. As noted, his relationship with the government had deteriorated, and he had been unwilling to accept Istanbul's decision to replace him as governor ever since June 1920.[33] He sent the newly appointed governor of İzmit back to Istanbul. Although both İbrahim Hakkı and Istanbul were anti-nationalist, the stubborn behaviour of İbrahim Hakkı created many problems between him and Istanbul.

According to İbrahim Hakkı, it is also worth mentioning that the Istanbul government refused to help him and the anti-nationalist Circassians when the Ankara forces took on İzmit. They were assisted by Greek forces instead. The Greeks took them from İzmit to settle in Midilli. İbrahim Hakkı set up the Association for the Strengthening of Near Eastern Circassian Rights (ASNEC, *Şarkı Karip Çerkesleri Temin-i Hukuk Cemiyeti*) in July 1921. He prepared the charter of the association, which stated that every North Caucasian (Adige, Abkhaz, Oset, Laz, Chechen, Lezgian, Kumuk and others) had a right to be a member of the society.[34] He tried to show the Greeks that there was Circassian opposition to the *Kuva-yi Milliye* from the beginning and that this opposition came together around him.

The deteriorating situation between İbrahim Hakkı and the Istanbul government was arguably the trigger for the birth of ASNEC. At the beginning of the process, the reason for establishing the association was not one based on ideology or ethnicity. Ethnicity took an important role only later, after problems began with the Istanbul government. In his own writings, İbrahim Hakkı mentions that the Circassians had no problems living with an Ottoman identity[35] since the Ottoman identity was intentionally constructed as a political identity of the subjects of the empire. The Ottoman and Circassian identities did not clash, and 'Ottomanness' proved an umbrella identity for the subjects of the empire. Under this umbrella, every religious and ethnic group had its own identity. The Circassian identity was an ethnic and cultural one. However, according to İbrahim Hakkı, when the Ottomans began to follow the policy of Turkishness, the Circassians also began following their own way, triggering a need for Greek assistance.[36] Until the 'wrong people' came to power in the empire, the Circassians were very loyal to the Ottomans. Unfortunately, since they had to leave the Ottoman Empire due to the problems they had experienced during the previous two years, they began to establish their own nationalist organizations.[37] This led İbrahim Hakkı to begin to develop 'Circassianness' as a political identity. İbrahim Hakkı also intentionally exaggerated the nationalist spirit of the Anatolian movement. While there were nationalist MPs, bureaucrats and officers in the movement, the main reason for most people going to Ankara was to save the empire and the sultan/caliph from the occupation. The participants in the national movement and in the assembly in Ankara consisted of different ethnic and religious groups.

İbrahim Hakkı ignored these points to legitimize his own attempt to carve out a new political niche for himself.

Ibrahim Hakki argued that despite the fact that the sultan and some other groups in Istanbul opposed helping Ankara, the Porte/Ottoman Government supported Ankara. Consequently, he was the governor of İzmit, and the Circassians came together to support him. The Circassians had to defend themselves with the Greek forces against the *Kuva-yi Milliye*, because they encountered a lack of support from the Istanbul government.[38] They moved to Midilli to seek political asylum from the Greek government.[39] The Circassians had suffered for seven years from state pressure, ever since the assassination of Mahmut Şevket Paşa (11 June 1913) up until the *Kuva-yi Milliye* (1919).[40] It can be said that Ibrahim Hakkı aimed at creating a discourse that would see the Circassians as victims of the Ottoman state's policies over the preceding decade. This was partly true; however, not only the Circassians, but also other groups in the empire had been placed in a difficult situation by the conflict and the wars of the previous decade.

This period was already one of 'perception wars' between rival groups. İbrahim Hakkı joined in this, by declaring that the Istanbul government had altered its policy to accept Turkish nationalism. His aim was to strengthen his hand against criticism directed at his movement by the Istanbul government and other Circassians. Some Circassians took up important positions in the Ottoman army and bureaucracy. To prevent reactions from them, İbrahim Hakkı blamed the so-called nationalist policies of the Porte.

B) The Congress

The congress was an attempt by a group of notables who thought Greek occupation and British support would be permanent in the region. It was not possible for them to work with the Ankara government since their relationship with Ankara had already broken down. Due to their involvement in the Adapazarı–Düzce incidents and opposition to the *Kuva-yi Milliye*, they were facing the possibility of being sentenced to death by the Ankara government. The aim of the congress was to obtain Greek support. However, the congress was not expected to lead to a separatist movement among the Circassians of Turkey. There was no mass support from the majority of Circassians.[41] Rather, it can be characterized as a more limited political move by some notables in the Düzce–Adapazarı, Bilecik and Gönen–Manyas region. Other Circassians, including those who lived in the Black Sea region, Central Anatolia and South Anatolia did not participate in this congress, and they may have been entirely unaware of it.

When Ankara took İzmit from the Greek and British forces on 28 June 1921, İbrahim, as governor, had to leave the city. İbrahim aimed at creating an autonomous structure under Greek occupation and moved to Midilli to work with the Greeks. He prepared the first declaration of the ASNEC in Midilli for the Greek government. In this declaration, İbrahim Hakkı underlined that the Circassians had left the North Caucasus because of the Russian occupation of the region and settled in the Ottoman Empire in the 1850s and 1860s. They were more loyal to the Ottoman sultanate than even the Turks. In the empire, the Circassians took on important positions in the bureaucracy and military. However, when incompetent individuals came to power, the coexistence of different ethnic and religious groups within the empire was in danger. Like the other groups in the empire, the Circassians had now begun to carve out their own path.[42] Despite the Ottoman sultan's opposition, the Porte had allied with the Kemalists; therefore, İbrahim Hakkı claimed, the Circassians were gathering around him to fight the Kemalists.[43]

From this declaration, it seems that İbrahim Hakkı was trying to legitimize his movement by accusing the Porte of pursuing 'Turkishness' policies. He also used the historic exile of the Circassians[44] as an analogy to the current situation they faced. In the former case, the Circassians were massacred en masse and forced to leave the North Caucasus, where they had had their own principality and structures. However, in the Ottoman period the Circassians had lived for a long time as subjects of the sultan, equal to other groups. They were not treated by the Ottoman Porte in the same way as they had been by the Russian forces. However, İbrahim Hakkı now used the Circassian exile to reach into the emotions of the Circassians. He aimed to convince the Greeks that the Circassians fought against the Ankara government without mentioning all those who had supported the Ankara government.[45] The aim of İbrahim in preparing this declaration was to ensure that ASNEC would be recognized by the Greek government as legitimate.

Some Circassian local notables also supported the Greek–Circassian alliance proposed by İbrahim; there had been a previous agreement between several Circassian notables (*Beys*) and the Greek occupation forces. According to that agreement, İzmit, Bolu, Biga and the Bandırma region would be governed by both Greeks and Circassians together under British control.[46] Furthermore, the İzmit–Adapazarı region, it was argued in the agreement, would be retaken with the support of Circassians. The Greeks supported Çerkes Bekir and Ragıb[47] in pursuance of this aim. However, they did not succeed in recapturing the region from the nationalists.[48] Nevertheless, the intention was clear: anti-nationalist Circassians had tried to influence the Greeks by exaggerating their impact on Circassian society as a whole. They had declared to the Greeks that there were about five thousand Circassians under their influence. However, this did not accurately reflect reality.[49]

On the other hand, the activities of İbrahim Hakkı had been harshly criticized by leaders of the Society for Circassian Mutual Aid (*Çerkes Teavün Cemiyeti*), such as Müşir Fuad Paşa. He underlined that the society represented the Circassians, not İbrahim Hakkı; he also underscored that İbrahim Hakkı had been rejected by the society and was therefore to be considered 'shameless'. Ultimately, only three hundred to four hundred Circassians joined his movement, and the other Circassians paid little attention to his activities.[50] It is worth mentioning that Müşir Fuad considered İbrahim Hakkı, Ahmed Anzavur and Şah İsmail in the same category: as having no relations with 'Circassianness' (*Çerkeslik*). This was because their activities could not be linked with the remainder of the Circassian community who were loyal to their state and their people.[51] One can argue that Müşir Fuad Paşa attempted to simplify anti-nationalist Circassian activities by pointing out that a 'mere three hundred to four hundred people' were backing İbrahim Hakkı, ignoring the broken relationships of many Circassians with the Ankara government. He aimed to prove the anti-nationalist Circassians' marginalization. While only a small number of the hundreds of thousands of Circassians in Anatolia worked with the Greeks, one could argue that the majority of Circassians favoured Istanbul and the sultan/caliph and not the Ankara government, and so could easily be mobilized during this period, as seen in the Anzavur incident and the Adapazarı–Düzce incidents.

C) The declaration by Congress

Although the congress and the declaration were prepared by İbrahim Hakkı Bey, there was also an internal struggle among the anti-nationalist Circassians.[52]

This centred on who would lead the congress. One group supported Kazım Bey from Manyas/Yeniköy. Another group, which Takığ Şevket and his men dominated, supported Çerkes Ethem. The commander of the Bandırma branch of the Greek occupation forces unsuccessfully sought a middle way between the two. According to Özer, he asked for Ethem's help, but Ethem and his brother Reşid convinced Şevket not to interrupt the congress.[53] Although only a very small number of Circassians joined the group, the congress was known as 'the Circassian club' among the people.[54] The club did not only include the Circassians; it also consisted of other people working with the Greek and the British forces. Some Circassians – for example, those in Manyas (which was an important centre of the Circassian club) – opposed the club. Yusuf Bey, from Haydar village, Çerkes İsmail Bey and Hafız Ahmed Efendi, from Demirkapı, were all arrested by the Greeks and exiled to Greece due to their opposition.[55]

The majority of the participants of the Circassian Congress (24 October 1921) were from the Düzce–Adapazarı region. Three non-South Marmara-originating Circassian families dominated the congress. The families from Çule, Bağ and Maan were all residents of the East Marmara and west Black Sea regions (Düzce, İzmit, Adapazarı and Eskişehir) and were well-known families among the Circassians.[56] The most prominent figures at the Congress were (Pşevu) Reşit Bey (Çerkes Ethem's brother) and the old governor of İzmit, (Çule) İbrahim Hakkı (who was also the pre-eminent person of the association and at the congress). On 11 October 1921, twenty-four people came together as members of the congress in İzmir. The members then made a declaration (the participants of this congress were from the Greek-occupied zone of Anatolia). Although hundreds of different Circassian families lived in the region, only fifteen Circassian families were members of the congress. It is necessary to quote from the declaration at length:

> The authorities signed below are the representatives of the Circassian people of western Anatolia, which is today under the Greek occupational army, [and in particular of] Balıkesir, Bandırma, Erdek, Gönen, Biga, Kirmasti, Mihaliç [Karacabey], Bursa, İnegöl, Yenişehir, Aydın, Manisa, İzmir, Eskişehir, Kütahya, Afyonkarahisar as well as İzmit, Adapazarı, Hendek, Düzce, Bolu and their environs. They are also the founders of

'The Association for the Strengthening of Near Eastern Circassian Rights' [which is] sanctioned by the Greek government. This meeting, which is in the form of a congress, undertakes its national rights as a minority based on the national rights as determined by the national principles accepted and declared by the Great Powers at the end of the Great War. The representatives ask for their national demands with the declaration that the Circassians will seek refuge under the Allied Great Powers, who agreed among themselves to force Separatism, Violence, and Collaboration acceptance [of these rights] of the losing states, and its partners, in particular the Greek government.

The population of Circassians today residing in Anatolia is at the very least two million. Circassians defend and maintain their national traditions through language, customs, feelings and civilization. ... They are in the contemporary family of civilizations and are a part of the white race and the distinguished Aryan family. ...

Upon the collapse of the Arab government and upon the decision of the Egyptian government in Cairo, the Circassians were continuously in the governments that were established in the Arab lands, North Africa and Syria for three centuries. In the Caucasus, which is their national homeland, the Circassians formed a republic [which was] independent administratively and politically. They are the famous fighters [who] continuously fought for twenty years against the Russian Empire, under the administration and command of the well-known Sheikh Shamil (Şeyh Şamil), who saw the danger of the Russian invasion.

A population of two million Circassians from the northern and western Caucasus, which was composed of three million people, was suspicious of [Russian actions] and bit by bit emigrated to Turkey (at that time the Sublime Porte extended a protective invitation). The one million people that stayed in the North Caucasus have today grown to a population of three million according to Russian statistics.

According to calculations, the two million Circassians who immigrated to Turkey would have risen to a population of between three to six million. Unfortunately, today it is closer to two million. The reason why is this: It is extremely clear that there were tragedies in transport as a result of mismanagement, which is impossible for the Ottoman government to deny. As a result of being sacrificed to these catastrophes, the Circassians have been denied four million of its population.

Thirteen years before with the institution of constitutional rule, the Turkish administration became bereft of correct policies. Now filled with feelings [stemming] from Turkishism and Turanism, Turkish administrators followed at this unique moment in history a false policy of terrorism, by means of Turkification, towards the various Ottoman nationalities. With the destruction of the nationalities and the destruction of the vital security of non-Turks, the Circassians were stirred with a just grievance coming from a 'pure desire of self-preservation'. Because of these continuous calamities, Circassians have [moved towards] a national goal of self-preservation and commit themselves to armed resistance against the mass murder of the Circassian nation.

Because of this, Circassians have lost thousands of their precious children. Their property and animals have been stolen and their villages burned. In short, Circassians have been and continue to be in a state of defiance in this war despite being allotted no sanctuary and the destruction and seizure of their property. However, it is not [the case] that Circassians did not join the world war either as commanders or as soldiers with their farm animals. But like various other nations, they were forced by their feelings and by the law. Nevertheless a very small portion of Circassians joined the Anatolian revolutionaries (filled with false feelings) right after the ceasefire. Mustafa Kemal [says] his movement supports the foundation of the sultanate, yet the Kemalists are seen and understood as a movement against humanity and with false policies. Regretfully, a very small number of Circassians have entered into the service of this movement.

The Circassians in the Sublime Porte, who continue to support the caliphate, are especially working together with the Kemalists. Despite this self-sacrifice, [the Porte] still neglects the Circassians. After not seeing that they will be saved, the Circassians decided correctly and naturally to join the Greek army, which promises to preserve them, in the occupation zone. (There is no doubt that Albania and the Arab States similarly sought foreign saviours well before.) These Circassians, who have struggled for a year and a half and who have saved thousands of innocent Muslims and non-Muslims from mass murder, should be praised for their services.

The understanding Greek government, which is included in the highest levels of civilization and humanity among nations, recognizes no difference among Circassians, Armenians and especially Rum. It has provided for the welfare of Circassian immigrants and refugees in the form of substance and settlement.

It is fitting to remember, with thanks and with kind words, those who aid and extend trust to our countrymen taken as prisoners of war, those under the submission of Kemalist oppression and to the Circassian people living in areas under the administration of the military occupation since the days the Greek government set foot in Anatolia.

As a consequence of these kind actions, the Circassians hope and request that, because of their convictions, they be included in the understanding of civilization and their legal and human rights be defended. These things have been [discussed] face to face between the Circassians, and the Rum peoples.

The goals of this petition are:

A. Recognition of our national existence.
B. To make known that the secular Circassian nation lives in constant danger.
C. To advance the demand that the Circassians wish to live as an element of peace under Greek protection in order to protect the Circassians of the Near East from the sins of the Turkish administration. [This is in response to] the Ottoman government which was a warring and tumultuous element in Europe and the Near East, both within and without, which denied a competent, modern and civilized administration and which collapsed because of the mismanagement of the sultan over the last three hundred years. [This continued with] the constitutional government, which stood in the place of the Ottoman government, which insisted, under the extreme Turkists, that it did not recognize the human rights of non-Turks in Anatolia. This is an impossible denial of the truth according to the civilized world.

As a consequence, our congress requests a statement to the petitioners, who expect action with impatience, regarding the acceptance of our demands which are national [in nature] according to the Allied Great Powers and their partners.

1. The application of the laws regarding the guarantee of human rights to minorities to all Circassians, laws that were accepted and proposed among the states following the war and that was to be brought into the Near East.
2. The imposition of protection under the civilized Greek government [and] of the desired [fulfilment] of the predestined unity of the Circassian nation with the Rum nation, which has been agreed upon. The Greek government hopes by force to [further] the progress and development [of these two nations].

3. The rendering on an indemnity from the Turkish government to the Circassian nation for all the damages incurred ....
4. The participation of our representatives in the peace conference in order to negotiate our national demands.

The following individuals undersigned the document.

> Adapazarı representative – (Bag) Talustan Bey
> İzmit representative – (Çule) İbrahim Bey
> İzmit representative – (Çiyo) Kazım Bey
> Hendek representative – (Bag) Osman Bey
> Düzce representative – (Maan) Ali Bey
> Düzce representative – (Hamete) Ahmet Bey
> Kandıra and Karasu representative – (Maan) Şirin Bey
> Yalova–Karamürsel representative – (Ançok) Yakup Bey
> Bilecik representative – (Bag) Rifat Bey
> Eskişehir representative – (Bag) Kamil Bey
> Geyve representative – (Çule) Beslan Bey
> Bursa representative –Harunelreşit Efendi
> Biga representative – (Ançok) İsa Nuri Bey
> Gönen representative – (Lampez) Yakup Efendi
> Gönen representative –Hafız Sait Efendi of the Regional Committee
> Erdek representative – (Şahabel) Hasan Bey
> Bandırma representative – (Neçoku) Hasan Bey
> Bandırma representative – (Brau) Sait Bey
> Bandırma representative – (Berzek) Tahir Bey
> Balıkesir representative – (Bazadog) Sait Bey
> Manisa representative – (Pşev) Reşit Bey
> Aydın representative – (Kavaca) Hüseyin Bey
> Kütahya representative – (Açofit) Sami Bey.[57]

This declaration was sent by İbrahim Hakkı to the Greek government in Midilli. However, in the three months between July 1921 and October 1921, some changes were made to it. Thus, there are some differences between the first version of the declaration written by İbrahim Hakkı and the final version of it (as quoted above). In the first version of the declaration, it was mentioned that Circassians, Kurds and Turks, who were also in opposition to the Kemalists, would live peacefully in Western Anatolia. However, in the final edition, the reference to Turks and Kurds had disappeared. The only emphasis was on the Circassians, since the movement had transfigured to become an ethnic one. Another important emphasis was on the Circassians who had fought for Ankara. In the first edition, it was stressed that they had left Ankara, and returned to the Porte, sultan and Circassianness (Çerkeslik[58]). However, in the final version of the text, the words 'Porte' and 'Sultan' were excluded from the text and only Circassianness remained.[59]

The vice governor of Aydın province informed the Porte that a group of Circassians had come together at the seaside in İzmir (Kordon) in a coffee house (Kainfoti'nin kahvesi).[60] The gathering was organized by İbrahim Hakkı Bey. Although Ethem was not one of the signatories to the declaration, his brother Reşid and his men had participated in the meeting.[61] The decision was taken by the participants that they would not recognize the Ottoman government, but would recognize Greek rule instead. The vice governor did not take the meeting seriously since there were only twenty-five signatories who had been supposed to represent all the Circassians in the region.[62]

The other Circassians, or those still loyal to the sultan, then criticized the congress and its participants, defining them as 'good-for-nothings' (Serseriler). They underlined that the Circassians were still loyal to the caliph along with the Turks and that the congress and its participants in no way represented the Circassians. They also declared that those who participated in the Congress were simply a few people working for their own ends, with no intention to benefit the Circassians.[63] The majority of the loyal Circassians of the Ottoman Empire remained as either military men or bureaucrats. After the declaration by loyalist Circassians, two leading and two regular members of the Circassian Congress prepared an additional text. This text, which was signed by Talustan Bey, İbrahim Hakkı,[64] Mehmed Sami and Mehmed Said, drew an analogy between the movement of the Circassian Congress and the Arab independence movement. According to the text, during the First World War, the Arabs had sought the help of the Allies to protect their nation against increasing Ottoman burdens and atrocities. The Circassians now encountered the same problem and so sought Greek help.[65] They also criticized loyalist Circassians who remained silent as their fellow Circassians were being hanged by nationalist forces during clashes in İzmit and the surrounding areas.[66]

Circassian opposition in the Western Anatolia

Following the Turkish-Greek War, Ankara still had difficulty consolidating its authority in South Marmara. To gain control of the region Ankara employed very harsh policies against its opponents. Execution by shooting was commonplace during both the war and in the years that followed. On 5 September 1922, Ankara government forces advanced towards Gönen, where the nationalists were exposed, and opened fire on the Circassian and Christian districts in the town as a skirmish erupted between nationalists and local armed groups. However, it is noteworthy that despite ten hours of clashes in which 150 people from the local forces were killed and 170 others were taken hostage, only one person was killed on the nationalist side.[67]

Two approaches existed for the opponents of Ankara – one was to fight against the Kemalists to the end in collaboration with the Greeks, while the second was to leave the country, because there was no opportunity to sustain their way of life. Initially many chose the first option; however, ultimately they had to take the second as Ankara's power in the region grew. Some Circassians, such as Kirmastili Çerkes Davut, Osman Çavuş of Akhisar/Selendi, Anzavur's son Kadir and Kısıkça Çerkes Hasan Bey, believed that the Ankara government's policy was to wipe the Circassians from the region, and this led them to collaborate with Greek forces.[68] Irregular Circassian forces used Midilli Island as a staging ground to incite the people of the South Marmara against the Ankara government.

There were a number of different opposition groups in South Marmara at the time.[69] Although there were some intelligence reports on the activities and estimations of their numbers in the region, with one claiming that there were six thousand Circassian and Turkish anti-nationalists in the Kirmasti, Susurluk, Mihalliç and Gönen areas, it is very difficult to calculate the precise number of anti-nationalists.[70] Towards the end of the war, although Greek occupation forces were often suspicious of Circassians activities, they nonetheless attempted to use some of the anti-nationalist Circassians in South Marmara against the Ankara government to provide security in the region.[71] A number of Circassians colluded with the Greeks since they had already broken ties with Ankara, and their return to the nationalist cause was prevented by a decision taken by the cabinet in Ankara.[72] The decision also stipulated that they would be executed if arrested by government forces.⁷³ One could argue that both the Greeks and the British used armed groups to pressure Ankara during the Lausanne Peace Treaty negotiations held between Turkey and the Allies from November 1922 to July 1923.

Among the armed groups, the support for the British and the Greeks was vital because they had no opportunity to reconcile with the Ankara government. Some ex-CUP and *Teşkilat-ı Mahsusa* agents from among the anti-nationalist Circassians were seeking ways to start an insurgency to achieve their aims. One noteworthy example was a plan by Kuşçubaşı Eşref Bey. Eşref had split with the Ankara government and joined Ethem when Ethem had met with the Greek general in Dereköy/Susurluk on 28 January 1921.⁷⁴ Eşref's activities between February 1921 and April 1923 remain unclear. However, in April 1923 Eşref came to the stage in Midilli as the founder of the Anatolian Revolutionary Society (*Anadolu İhtilal Cemiyeti*). This society was established in Athens and then moved to Midilli in April 1923.⁷⁵ The aim of the society was to start an anti-nationalist uprising with the support of the British and the Greeks in Western Anatolia and to overthrow the Ankara government.⁷⁶ As with the other armed groups of the region, the majority of this group's members were Circassian. However, it should be emphasized that the intention behind recruiting members from this group was not to create a Circassian national aspiration; this was something that did not exist among the group's members. They benefitted from being Circassian in terms of easy network access and creation; however, one cannot say that they worked to advance the Circassianness (*Çerkeslik*) issue.

The driving force of the group was to oppose the Ankara government, because they feared that if that government were to take complete control over the region it would either execute them or force them from it. One of Eşref's aims was to create chaos in South Marmara and to overthrow the government. For this aim, a declaration was prepared for the military in order to convince the soldiers not to fight against them for the Ankara government.⁷⁷ The declaration would be circulated in Istanbul with the support of the people, and at some houses and via centres of the Anatolian Revolutionary Society, which he hoped would open in Istanbul.⁷⁸ The evidence shows that Eşref preferred to avoid fighting with the Turkish security forces, choosing instead to convince them to rise up with him against the Ankara government.

To this end, he utilized his networks in Istanbul, İzmir, Thrace and Anatolia. He met with the different opposition groups to solidify the opposition movements in Western Anatolia. These included representatives of the İzmir Rum Association, Taşnak Party, Pontus Association (Agop Pargasiyan and Virnat Beys), various British intelligence officers and others like Çerkes Mustafa, Çerkes Kazım, Cemaleddin and Hayreddin Beys.[79] The core of the organization comprised Çerkes Ragıb, Çerkes Hurşid, Çerkes Osman in Sakız Island, Gürcü Muharrem and Çerkes İsmail in Athens.[80] With this help, Eşref attempted to mobilize the Circassians of South Marmara against the Ankara government. He also approached local Circassian notables in the districts of Bandırma, Gönen and Manyas; however, as had happened when he was working for the nationalists in February 1920 in Adapazarı, the local notables paid little attention to his activities.[81] He had no impact on the local notables of Bandırma, Gönen and Manyas.

The Anatolian Revolutionary Society also tried to mobilize the anti-nationalists in Istanbul and issued copies of a declaration prepared by the society to promote their ideas among anti-nationalist circles in Istanbul.[82] Rahmi Bey (Evranos), the well-known former governor of İzmir, whose son had been kidnapped by Çerkes Ethem in 1919, was the main personality involved on the Istanbul branch of the committee. He mentioned that their aim was to overthrow Mustafa Kemal and to return the Ottoman sultan to Istanbul.[83] Eşref and Reşid were also active in Athens and the various Greek islands. Ankara monitored their activities through officials in Athens. Furthermore, Ankara planned to place one of their agents in the group to pose as an anti-nationalist to gather information.[84] The group later moved the headquarters of the committee to Bucharest under Hoca Vasfi's control.

Çerkes Ethem, his brothers, Eşref, Anzavurzade Kadir and some other Circassians were known to gather in a pub in Athens sometimes.[85] Kadir would be sent to the Ayvalık coast with four thousand Circassians living on Sakız island (Chios). This group also planned the assassinations of leading figures in the national movement, such as Mustafa Kemal, İsmet, Fevzi, Nureddin and Refet Paşas.[86] Nevertheless, one should be cautious and note that some of the correspondents sent by the Turkish military services exaggerated the activities of Çerkes Ethem and the other Circassian dissidents in Greece. For example, it was mentioned in one report that four thousand Circassians living in Sakız might join Kadri's military attack against the Ankara government.[87] These four thousand Circassians were later settled in three villages in Athens and Thessalonica with their wives and children. The numbers referred to in the correspondence should most likely be viewed as hyperbole. According to other correspondence relating to the same report, Ethem, Reşid, Tevfik, and Eşref were expected to organize an attack against the Ankara government with twenty thousand Circassians and eight thousand Greek volunteers.[88] It can be said that if anyone had twenty thousand armed people under his/her control at the time in South Marmara, he/she could easily set up his/her own state. It seems likely that the report was a huge exaggeration.

Other active groups during this period, in the Biga–Gönen–Manyas areas, can also be listed: the *Teğmen Mehmet Ali çetesi* (Sub-lieutenant Mehmet Ali's Gang) in Manyas; the *Kel Ali çetesi* (Ali the Bald) in Gönen; and, lastly, the one led by *Kanlı Mustafa*, (Mustafa the Bloody) in Biga.[89] Mehmet Ali's group became depleted in Dikili following a battle with Ankara's forces. After this Mehmet Ali and (Takığ) Çerkes Şevket[90] took control of the group. In December 1922, he was active in the Aegean Islands and tried to pass over to Western Anatolia. Although he had people in his group from different towns of Anatolia, Şevket also attempted to mobilize the Circassians of the region to sustain his anti-nationalist activities.[91] From the shores of Dikili in the Aegean Sea, north of İzmir towards the north east of the region to Düzce in the coast of Black Sea, there were a huge number of Circassian settlements. While they were seen as loyal subjects of the empire in the late Ottoman period and were settled near the capital by the Ottoman government, with the emergence of the 'new Turkey' they were now viewed as a threat. With this suspicion came the deportation of Circassians from South Marmara and the Adapazarı regions. The Circassians' loyalty to the Ottoman state and armed opposition to a group of them against the nationalists were seen as problems by Ankara. With the declaration of the end of the Ottoman state by the Ankara government (after the abolition of the Ottoman sultanate on 1 November 1922), the armed Circassian groups became more active in the region than ever before. In the post-Turkish Greek War period, the only armed threat to Ankara was from these armed groups. The Circassians of the region clearly did not favour the Ankara government, as seen during the Anzavur incident and as reflected in documents on the incident, but they also did not support an armed struggle against them in the post-Turkish-Greek-War era.

The intelligence services of the Ankara government informed the nationalist leaders that Çerkes Şevket was planning to attack from Athens with twenty-five armed men, and that he was moving towards Edremit and Ayvalık in Western Anatolia via the Aegean Islands.[92] His aim was to reach the Manyas, Kazdağı and Bozdağ areas to prepare the people there for further uprisings – largely by gaining the support of local Circassians.[93] Şevket argued that with the participation of local Circassians the group would be able to start an uprising that would then lead to a broader insurrection against the nationalist government.[94] The group came ashore between İzmir Foça and Dikili in a two-staged landing, on 18 and 20 December 1922 under Şevket's leadership.[95] The group also aimed to assassinate leading figures of the Ankara government. However, after a skirmish in the town of Kaplanköy between Şevket's group and nationalists, two individuals from Şevket's group were killed and nine captured by nationalist forces. Seven of these were questioned by the nationalists on the activities of the group.[96] Although a leading member of the group was a Circassian, it also consisted of Turks. Eight people were Circassian, from Manyas, while others were from İzmir, Ayvalık, Antalya, Afyonkarahisar and Konya.[97] Their names were Şevket, Kadir (son of Mehmet), gendarme lieutenant Mehmed Ali, Harun Çavuş, Arab Hamdi, Abdül, Yusuf Efendi, Yusuf, Mehmed Çavuş, Mehmed Efendi (son of Mustafa), Bekir, Kadri, Bayram, Vapur İbrahim, İbrahim (son of Tahir), Mustafa, Mehmed and Tahsin. There are too many details about the members of the group, ranging from their ethnicity and age to what clothes they had on them at the moment.[98] Another report, a western front (Garp Cephesi) report, mentions that Arab Hamdi and his gang was told by Şevket that their aim was to raise the Circassians of Manyas in order to remove Ankara (Kemalists) from power and bring back the sultanate and Vahidettin.[99]

The nationalists took further precautions following this event, fearing that those who could not be captured would move to the Manyas region (eight of those captured were from Manyas).[100] Thus, the government's attention was turned towards Manyas. It is also important to mention that, for Ankara, both the South Marmara and Adapazari regions were under threat. Even in Adapazari, there was a threat of an anti-nationalist raid led by Şevket's group.[101] This fear was because of the high population of Circassians, which meant that Şevket's group could take action in the region. This made the Ankara government paranoid about the Circassians in the region, who they thought could rise against the Ankara government. The First Army Command sent warnings to commanders in İzmit and Adapazarı that the Circassians should be observed closely but secretly by military intelligence. Due to the activities of the armed groups in the region, they should also be kept under strict control.[102] If anyone in the region worked with armed Circassians, then the military authorities should be informed.[103] The Circassian Association of Istanbul (Çerkes Teavün Cemiyeti) was also monitored by representatives of the Ankara government. As a consequence of Anzavurzade Kadir's presence in Istanbul, the Ankara government suspected that he was attempting to contact members of other associations and the Circassians in İzmit-Adapazarı.[104]

Ankara took a harsh measure, and it led to the suffering of the local people who did not have any connection with the armed groups. Due to the increasing possibility of an attack and assassination attempts from Şevket's group, it was demanded by the second army in Edremit Gulf from Ankara that a Circassian village, Yeniköy, should be removed from the region since it was on the coast and it was not far from Midilli Island. The village had thirty-one houses, and it was located at the southwest of the Edremit Gulf.[105] It was decided by the Ministry of General Health and Social Benefit that members of fifteen houses of the village would be sent to Konya and the members of the other sixteen houses to Niğde.[106] It is also noteworthy that the head of ministers Rauf (Orbay) Bey insisted that the deportations should be under the control of a local authority (*mutasarrıf*), and the process should be done in groups of three householders. It could be argued that Rauf Bey aimed to protect the villagers by giving control to a civil servant to prevent any possible catastrophe.[107]

In this context, Şevket's family members were harassed after he became involved in anti-nationalist activity in South Marmara, where he was branded a 'traitor' by the government. He, however, took revenge punishing those who claimed this, especially those who caused trouble to his family.[108] He hid in Söğütlü village,[109] close to Gönen. However, a few days later, a villager from Söğütlü informed the gendarme of his whereabouts. The gendarme carried out military operations, and he was killed on 7 June 1923.[110] His aunt and his aunt's husband were arrested. His aunt was punished with a ten-year sentence.[111] Şevket's killing by nationalist forces caused indignation among the Circassian residents of the area. The government then became concerned about an uprising in the region, since the majority of Şevket's group was from the Gönen and Manyas region.[112]

Moreover, a second group came to the region from the port of Dalyan, which was close to the other Circassian settlements in South Marmara. The Circassian members of this group were not from the Gönen–Manyas region,[113] and the group itself was centred in Greece.[114] Their leader was Ali, and they had prepared a manifesto against the Ankara government. Another important group was led by Mustafa 'the bloody'. Anzavur's son, Kadir, was a member of this group. They tried to come to Biga through the British-occupied zone of Çanakkale. However, they were attacked by nationalist forces around Biga, and some were killed, including Kadir. The remainder of the group were captured. Between 70 and 150 people were active in the band, 15 of whose members were Circassian.[115]

Gönen–Manyas deportations

Ankara's main policy when trying to halt the activities of the gangs was to destroy their sources of recruitment and financing. The Circassians were targeted by the Ankara government, which had tried to wipe their political and economic presence from the region in order to take effective control over the area and to cease bandit activity.[116] When Anzavur came to the region bringing an uprising against the Ankara government in the early 1920s, he was supported by people from several villages: Muratlar,[117] Keçeler, Bayramiç, Üçpınar, Karalar Çiftliği, Çerkes Keçidere, Karaağaçalan, Ayvalıdere, Hacı Menteş, Sızı Hasanbey, Çerkes Çalı Oba and Asmalıdere (Muhacir–Türk).[118] Anzavur was not only supported by the Circassians of the region, but also by Turks and other groups sympathetic to the anti-nationalist movement.[119] Ankara hoped that by employing the security-centred policy, the birthplace of banditry in Western Anatolia would be destroyed. This policy brought about a collective punishment for many civilian Circassians in the region. Without differentiating between whether individuals supported the gangs or not, the Circassian villagers and the Circassians in otherwise ethnically mixed villages were exiled to Central and Eastern Anatolia. It should also be noted here that it was argued by some witnesses to the incident that in order for the new state to develop an idea of a Turkish nation, a Turkish national grudge directed towards the Circassians proved useful, while also punishing their formerly close relationship with the sultanate.[120]

Conversely, it can be argued that the anti-nationalist Circassians were stuck between the Greek forces and Ankara. Ankara had already concluded that they would have no place in South Marmara. Kuşçubaşı Eşref and Çerkes Ethem (although the latter was in Germany at the time), through his close connections with Çerkes Şevket and in view of Şevket's presence in the region, led the nationalists to believe that Ethem too was active in the region. Their groups were clearly seen as security threats by the Ankara government, which believed that Eşref and Ethem would attempt to raise the Circassians of Biga and the Karesi regions against Ankara.[121] On 7 May 1923, the Ankara government cabinet declared via a government order (*Kararname*) that anyone who informed the government of the activities of the Eşref and Ethem groups would be awarded 200 Turkish liras. Alternatively, those who supported these armed groups would have their villages erased from the region, and they would be deported to other parts of Anatolia.[122] It should be underscored that this government order was announced a month before the Gönen–Manyas deportations were carried out. It can also be argued that the removal of the thirteen Circassian villages from the region were based on this same government order. Ankara saw the Circassians as a security problem, whether they backed the anti-nationalist movement in the region or not. For Ankara, being a Circassian from the region meant one was a potential rebel. Therefore, the government punished these individuals collectively without differentiating the innocent from the bandits.[123] If armed groups clashed with the army, the army would consider it reasonable to fire on the entire village. Due to the extraordinary situation in the region, the government took harsh decisions. Policies of intimidation from the government engendered fear among the Circassian residents of the region.[124] They were encountering collective punishment carried out by the government. Without distinguishing criminals from the innocent, and not sparing the women and children, the government chose to exile all the residents of entire villages.

Takığ Şevket's village Mürvetler was the first village to be deported en masse by the government. This occurred in December 1922. In addition, thirteen other Circassian villages were deported to East and Central Anatolia. Fetgerey also suggests the populations of the fourteen villages were exiled to Central and Eastern Anatolia because of their perceived links with the Anatolian Revolutionary Association.[125] The exiled villages included those in Gönen: Üçpeykar (Üçpınar) on 28 May 1923,[126] Muratlar on 5 June 1923; Sızı on 9 June 1923; Keçideresi on 13 June 1923; Keçeler on 17 June 1923. The exiled villages of Manyas included Kızıl Kilise on 7 June; Yeniköy on 7 June; Dumye on 7 June; Ilıca on 11 June; Karaçalılık on 13 June; Bolağaç on 13 June; Değirmenboğazı on 21 June; Hacıosman on 21 June. The total number of exiled people was 3,500–4,000.[127] If any of the Circassians were married to a Turkish person, they would also be exiled.[128] In total, the fourteen villages had developed around 40,000 acres of land. The land was extremely fertile in this region, and every village had also comprised of about a thousand animals (horses, cows, oxen and sheep).[129] The exiling of the fourteen villages not only led to the economic destruction of the Circassians, but also accelerated their assimilation process, by weakening them as a community in terms of their identity and culture.

After the exile had begun, some nationalist Circassians, that is, those who had fought alongside the nationalists, were also exiled.[130] Bekir Sami (Günsav), who was also from the Manyas region, and one of the first persons to organize the national movement in Western Anatolia (but who then split with Mustafa Kemal) wrote two letters to Mustafa Kemal and Kazım Paşa to prevent the deportation of innocent Circassians, and those who had fought alongside the nationalists during the Turkish–Greek War. He underlined that there were many Circassians in the national movement from the Manyas region and that the government should be more careful when deporting Circassians, emphasizing also that they should not be killed.[131] The impact that these letters had is unclear, although subsequently the Ministry of Defence issued a declaration stipulating that the relatives of those who had fought with the nationalists would not be exiled.[132] It is clear that not all the residents of the villages were anti-Ankara. Esat Bey from Dereköy, for example, was the head of the Association of Defence of Rights of Gönen (Gönen Müdafa-yı Hukuk Cemiyeti), and he had fought for the nationalists during wartime. When martial law was declared in Gönen by the nationalists on 20 June 1920, he was appointed as the head of a paramilitary unit that consisted of about three hundred men and worked for the *Kuva-yi Milliye*. Later, he was killed in a clash by anti-nationalists while serving in the unit.[133]

The conditions under which the villages were exiled were extremely cruel. For instance, the residents of Dereköy were forced to walk to Bandırma, a journey of three days. They gathered in Bandırma in an area akin to an open-air prison. After ten to fifteen days, they were then packed like sardines on wagons used to transport animals. Those from Dereköy were sent to Kayseri.[134] Another twenty-eight villages (ten were from Gönen villages and eighteen from Manyas) were also informed by the government that they would be exiled.[135] Only two were fully populated by Circassians. The remaining twenty-six villages were mixed, with Turks and others. However, only the Circassian populations of these villages were to be exiled. The Circassian residents of the villages sold their houses and land for low prices since they would be exiled in a matter of days. However, the government changed its course and halted the second round of exiles.[136]

The Gönen–Manyas exiles did not result in any massacres, as seen in the case of Dersim in the mid-1930s and the Armenian *tehcir* of 1915. However, although few people died or were killed during this exile, the incident remains etched in the memory of those descended from the exiles of the Gönen–Manyas region.

The notion of autonomy was not welcomed by the Circassians. Only a group of Circassians who had already had problems with the Ankara government used the idea of autonomy to ensure their place in Anatolia in a Greek-occupied zone. Those who backed the Circassian Congress had already fought against the Ankara government from early 1920 onwards. They could imagine what punishment was in store for them once the Ankara government had finished fighting on other fronts. However, although the majority of Circassians did not support the Congress, they did not back the Ankara government either. The Congress was nevertheless unsuccessful in achieving its goals. With the defeat of the Greek forces, prominent figures of the Congress and the opposition more generally left Anatolia. However, in South Marmara, the unrest, which was created by armed Circassians and their groups, continued. The security of the region greatly concerned the Ankara government. Meanwhile, negotiations in the Lausanne were ongoing between Ankara and the Allies. The lack of security in the region could be viewed as a disadvantage to Ankara in these negotiations, and it was thus seen as necessary that the chaos cease as quickly as possible. To this end, Ankara made a decision that was detrimental to the local Circassians in the region: they were deported without due regard for who was a criminal and who was simply an innocent bystander. Ankara thus chose not only to terminate the bandit activities of the Circassians, but also to punish the Circassian residents of the Gönen–Manyas region indiscriminately, by exiling them to Central and Eastern Anatolia.

6

The 150'ers, Circassians and the Turkish state 1924–38

After the Circassian 'golden age' in the Ottoman Empire, under the CUP, from 1908 to 1913, there followed a period of political turmoil and war, and finally the creation of the Turkish nation-state. The Circassians then saw their rights becoming increasingly restricted, similar to other religious and ethnic groups in the country, such as Muslims, Christians, Jews and Kurds, in the early republican period. Their position in Turkey contrasted unfavourably with that of the Circassian minorities in surrounding states; for example, in Jordan they had more privileges than some of the other groups due to their role in the founding of the country and due to the special responsibilities they had as guards of the king; and in Israel, the state had given them full support to protect their identity.[1] Meanwhile, in Turkey, the assimilationist policies of the early republican period meant that the Circassians faced the threat of losing their ethnic identities. Unlike the Kurdish identity, which is not only a cultural identity but a political one also, the Circassian identity in Turkey today is far from being a political identity. Although some protests and demonstrations have recently been organized to address the issue of mother-tongue rights, for the protection of Circassian identity, and to form a party for the 2015 general elections, the majority of Circassian groups' protests and demonstrations are still targeted at Russia. It should also be emphasized that Circassian activism cannot successfully reach the wider audience of Circassians in Turkey. At present, disunity within activist groups and organizations and internal struggles between these groups and organizations are the main reasons for this limited mobilization of Circassian society in Turkey.

It is also important to underline that the ambivalent policy of the Turkish state towards the Circassians is another factor preventing a better understanding of their situation in Turkey in the early republican period and its aftermath. On the one hand, the state prohibited the expression of Circassian identity in public spaces and banned the language. On the other hand, Circassian refugees arriving into Turkey in the 1920s after the Bolshevik Russian expansion into the North Caucasus were used by several departments of state, from the Ministry of Foreign Affairs to the intelligence services, in order to strengthen Turkey's position against Soviet Russia.[2] As part of this policy, a number of Circassians and North Caucasian emigrants were employed in Turkish intelligence, and by military and police departments, particularly during the Democratic Party's reign in the 1950s.[3]

In view of the above, it can be stated that because of the rapprochement between the Turkish state and North Caucasian emigrants and the recruitment of them into the intelligence, military and police forces, the Circassians gained some freedoms. They were the first group, along with the Azeris, permitted by the state to open a cultural association in the republican period (in 1946).[4] After the elimination of the threat posed in the early republican period by some groups of Circassians, both inside and outside Turkey, and following reconciliation, the Circassians had relatively better conditions compared with other non-Turkish groups. They no longer seemed to pose a threat to the state as much as they had in the early republican period. The Cold War period partnership against Soviet Russia also positively predisposed the state to change its policies towards them. Moreover, as an external community who had settled in Anatolia only one hundred years before, they were not expected to be likely to demand an independent political structure in Anatolia.[5]

In the post-Turkish War of Independence period (1922), armed opposition was seen as more dangerous for Ankara than any political opposition. Therefore, regular armed Circassians of Adapazarı–Düzce and South Marmara were declared personae non gratae and were placed on a list prepared in April 1924. The opposition of Circassians abroad on the one hand was a threat to Ankara, since they still had the capability to organize assassination attempts and uprisings in Anatolia. On the other hand, although they insisted on opposing Mustafa Kemal and the Kemalists, towards the 1930s they lost their capability to carry out armed activities and affect developments inside Turkey. However, the continuity of their opposition in the 1930s became useful for the Ankara government, as it ensured greater support from the people for Mustafa Kemal, the cult character of the regime.

In the single-party period, even the existence of a Circassian identity was ignored by the state.[6] Indeed, one of the reasons why the Circassians were oppressed in the early republican era was because they were seen as the remnants of the *ancient regime* by the republican elites. As Ahmet Kuru has extensively studied, the ancient regime represented the Ottoman Empire and its values in the republican context of Turkey.[7] Circassians, as the single biggest opponents to the Ankara government in the early 1920s, were associated with the Ottoman past of Turkey, and one group of them represented the CUP's opposition to the Kemalists in the early republican era. At this time, as Charles King argues, even God had been nationalized;[8] the intention was then to assimilate the Circassians into the new nation to prevent them from expressing their identity, which meant a ban on using their mother tongue in public. Until the Democrat Party came to power in 1950, after which the Circassians and the state reconciled, the Turkish state viewed them with suspicion.

This chapter will focus on the anti-nationalist activities of a group of Circassians from 1924 to 1938, and on the Turkish state's treatment of the Circassians in the early republican period. In 1921 with the exclusion of Ethem from the nationalist cause, the Circassian opposition increased its activities against Ankara, particularly towards Mustafa Kemal and his circle. This opposition continued until 1938, when members of the list of personae non gratae (the *Yüzellikler*), the so-called 150'ers, were pardoned by the state. Those who stood against the nationalists, such as the organizers of the Adapazarı–Düzce incidents, and those who were excluded from the nationalists by the Ankara government, such as Çerkes Ethem and Kuşçubaşı Eşref, came together against the Kemalist movement. Although they had previously encountered problems among each other, they now had a common enemy in the Kemalists. Çerkes Ethem, Tevfik, Reşit, Kuşçubaşı Eşref, his brother Çerkes Sami, Çule İbrahim Hakkı, Maan Mustafa, a group of Circassians and Abkhazians from the Western Anatolia region and some Muslims of Anatolia provided the impetus behind this opposition. This opposition first appeared in the Greek-occupied zone of Western Anatolia, after which time it continued outside Turkey, as members of the group were deported by the Turkish government (having been declared personae non gratae in 1924). This chapter will first focus on how the list of personae non gratae was prepared by the Grand Assembly of Turkey, and the motivation for including eighty-six Circassian people[9] on the list. Secondly, it will focus on the anti-Kemalist activities of those Circassians on the list, such as assassination attempts and the organization of uprisings, and discuss how in response, their anti-Kemalist and more so anti-Mustafa Kemal activities were used by the Turkish state to strengthen support for Mustafa Kemal. Thirdly, the chapter will study a policy from the Turkish state directed towards the Circassians to involve them in the nation-building process by restricting the expression of their Circassian identity, as it will be seen in Keriman Halis's case, and language in public.

Making the list of 'traitors'

Anti-Ankara activities reached a highpoint in South Marmara in the post-Turkish–Greek War period between 1922 and 1923 (during the Lausanne negotiations). The groups of armed Circassians settled on the Greek island of Midilli in the Aegean Sea after the war, as mentioned in the last chapter. The anti-Ankara Circassians exacerbated the state of disorder that prevailed in Turkey. Although the state took harsh measures to prevent this, by deporting the Circassians to Central and Eastern Anatolia without differentiating between criminals and innocents in the spring and summer of 1923, gaining absolute control of the region took time. On the other hand, the punishment of the participants in the Circassian Congress, and that of other anti-Kemalist Circassians was not yet complete. The government took a further step to punish its wartime opponents.

At the Lausanne Conference, the Allies forced the Ankara government to declare an amnesty for those who had opposed it during the Turkish War of Independence (1919–22). The state pardon was to be extended to all members of the Istanbul government, and all anti-nationalist bandits, with the exception of 150 named individuals. Permission to create a list of these 150 individuals was given to the Ankara government by the Allies at the conference agreement. However, the decision about who should be on the list proved difficult for Ankara, since after almost two years of civil war and four years of occupation in Anatolia, many people could have been added, from Western to Eastern Anatolia, and from members of the Istanbul government to bureaucrats (including the significant number of bureaucrats, officials and officers who had worked under Allied rule). The decision-making process was the subject of enormous discussion in the assembly in Ankara, which examined who should be put on the list.

As a result of the discussion, 450 people were decided upon by the assembly. The final version of the list included 150 people, decided by executives in Ankara. When one looks at the list, it emerges that a significant number of those on it were local people and very few were important bureaucrats and political figures. The Ottoman family had already been deported by Ankara and the sultanate was abolished when the list was being prepared by the cabinet and the parliament in April 1924. Therefore, no one was added to the list from the Ottoman family. The criteria for the list were unclear. It can be seen that the participants of the Anzavur, Adapazarı–Düzce incidents, Circassian Congress and local Circassians of the South Marmara (Gönen–Manyas regions) were on the list. At least eighty-six names on the list were Circassians, the majority being local people and villagers. This prompts the question: why was the Ankara government mainly fearful of a group of Circassians?

Although the representatives of Turkey negotiated in Lausanne with the Allies to attain only a limited amnesty for those who had opposed it during the Turkish–Greek war, their demands were not accepted by the Allies, whose aim was to protect the minority groups and their wartime supporters.[10] At the end of the Lausanne negotiations, the Ankara government had to accept that only 150 people would be punished, and a pardon had to be issued for the rest. In the official Turkish historiography, only these 150'ers were to be considered 'traitors'. However, the reality was much more complex than the official historiography suggests. Thousands of people who we know about from the official documents, newspaper records and assembly sessions' records were anti-nationalist activists during the war, ranging from local bandits to the civil servants, military officials and politicians. Istanbul and the rest of the country were de facto occupied by the Allies immediately following the Mudros Armistice in November 1918.

Although the French and Italian occupation did not last long, the British and Greek occupation continued until November 1922 in Western Anatolia, Istanbul and parts of Eastern Thrace. During these long four years, occupation forces worked with hundreds of Ottoman officials to restore order in Anatolia. One can claim that the Allies were not seen only as occupiers by some local people and officials. For them, the Allies would be the new rulers of Western Anatolia, since the people of Anatolia were already tired of war, having experienced more than ten years of it, since the disastrous times in North Africa, the Balkans and Anatolia. In the post-First-World-War period, the Anatolian movement was not taken seriously initially by the Istanbul government and the local people. The nationalists were considered a continuation of the CUP, which was seen by the people as the cause of the current disastrous situation being encountered by the empire. Therefore, to admit the existence of the Allied occupation meant the termination of a long war, offering an alternative to launching an adventure against the Allied-supported Greeks with limited military power. However, history reveals that the latter circumstance was not simply an adventure. The nationalists won the war, both against their internal rival and the Greeks. Now the time had arrived for their opponents to pay the price.

The personae non gratae list was prepared during a closed session of the assembly in April 1924. After two separate sessions to debate the issue, the MPs declared the names of the 'traitors'. It was claimed by the assembly that the 150'ers had not recognized the assembly and its authority. The legal basis for their punishment was the High Treason Law of 29 April 1920 (*Hıyanet-ı Vataniye Kanunu*). According to the article, those who did not recognize the authority of the assembly were deemed to have committed high treason.[11] To determine the members to be added to the list the assembly held a secret session on 16 April 1924. The demands for the session came from the minister of interior, Ahmet Ferit (Tek) Bey.[12] On the day on which the issue of the 150'ers was discussed in the Lausanne negotiations, the Ministry of the Interior and the General Directorate of Security (*Emniyeti Umumiyye Müdüriyeti*) were already preparing the list. They demanded the names of those who had been involved in anti-nationalist activities during the Turkish–Greek War, and from towns that had either been occupied by the Allies and Greeks or involved in the incidents against Ankara. As a result of this process, six hundred names were determined by the ministry and the General Directorate of Security.[13] It could be understood from Ahmet Bey's speech that the classification of the list had already been completed by the ministers in a cabinet session. The list was classified by groups, such as Vahidettin's Entourage, the cabinet members who signed the Sèvres Peace Agreement, members of the Ottoman cabinet who organized the *Kuva-yi İnzibatiye* forces, and its high-ranking military generals, Çerkes Ethem and his close circle, members of the Circassian Congress, the leading bandits, and the organizers of the three committees: the committee of caliphate; the committee of Anatolia; and the committee of the revolution.[14] Furthermore, those who had committed high treason, some members of the local administration, the military, police and journalists were also on the list, presented under separate categories.[15] The final category was that of 'other people' (*diğer eşhas*). Akçoraoğlu Yusuf of Istanbul proposed the list should be prepared based on the principles which the assembly should decide (i.e. who was a traitor). However, the minister of the interior, Ferit Bey, responded by saying that those 'people who were in the category of "other people" are bandits etc. Would you like any other principle?'[16] None of the members of the Ottoman family were included on the list, since they had already been deported from Turkey after the law calling for 'the abolishing of the caliphate and deportation of the Ottoman family from the Republic of Turkey' was issued on 3 March 1924. With this law, every single member of the family, son-in-laws and people whose mothers were related to the family were deported. Their Turkish citizenships were revoked, and they were banned from entering Turkey.[17]

Ferit Bey explained in the closed session that they had prepared four different lists. The first one included 150 names, the second one included 300, the third one included those who were to lose their citizenship, and the fourth one included all 600 names. That is, he emphasized that they had 600 names on the lists in total.[18] The discussion continued during the session. İhsan Bey of Cebelibereket and Mazhar Bey of Aydın claimed that if they tried to find every single person working against Ankara, then the list would consist of thousands of people.[19] The cabinet considered that when the list was prepared not only those who had committed a crime against Ankara would be in the list, but also those who still had the potential to pose a threat to Ankara. Ferit Bey gave the example of the forty-two people who had already been sentenced to death for high treason. They still had the potential to challenge Ankara's authority in the region and to cause chaos.[20]

One could also observe that the majority of the list consisted of local people. Ankara did not consider the Ottoman bureaucrats and military men to be as threatening as those who had the potential to rise up in the regions. Therefore, it is apparent that the chaotic situation in the Gönen–Manyas region and Circassian Congress was the most discomforting concern for

Ankara. Those involved in the local anti-nationalist movement were also a threat since they were expected to continue their anti-nationalist activities and had the potential to mobilize more people. Under the title 'other people' (*diğer eşhas*), there were more than thirty local people from the Gönen and Manyas region. The majority of the names on this list were Circassian. The names were mentioned along with those from other villages, such as Mustafa Remzi of Düzakçı village. Although some of the villages had a mixed Turkish and Georgian population, the majority were populated by Circassians and Ankara punished the Circassians due to their post-First-World-War activities and their participation in the Anzavur incident. Although some participants' names were already mentioned during the session, a few were moved from the list later on since some political figures were put on the list. Some of the participants in the Anzavur incident were already sentenced to receive capital punishment. However, the Lausanne agreement did not allow Ankara to execute these individuals. Either they had to be pardoned, or they must be added to the list of the so-called 150'ers. However, Ankara found a third way to punish them. Those who were not resident in Turkey at the time were accused of working for a foreign army. A group of those included on the list simply had their Turkish citizenship revoked since they had already left the country for Greece due to a fear of execution and had reportedly worked for the Greek army. This decision by the cabinet resulted in ensuring that just 150 names remained on the list.[21]

However, a criticism came from Ali Sururi Bey of Karahisari Şarki, who underlined that the list did not consist of political figures, but rather of members of the Liberal Entente (*Hürriyet ve İtilaf Fırkası*). It was comprised of bandits who could not harm the general public.[22] At the end of the discussion over whether political figures should be on the list or not, Hulusi Bey of Karesi articulated that any Circassian named on it would be equal to a battalion of soldiers.[23] Therefore, they should be added to the list and not the political and intellectual opponents of Ankara. Fikret Bey of Ertuğrul also opposed the current list, as it consisted of individuals who were not deemed capable politically. He argued that this was a matter of security and that intellectual and political figures should be added to the list.[24] It was also questioned during the session as to why even a single Armenian or Rum (Anatolian Greek) was not named in the list, with some MPs, such as Saraçoğlu Şükrü of İzmir, arguing that some Armenians and Rums had betrayed the state.[25] However, the Lausanne Treaty stated that no non-Muslims, Armenians, Rums or Jews should be included in the list, even if they were involved in anti-nationalist activities during the Turkish–Greek War.[26] Thus, to avoid further problems with the Allies, the Kemalist government chose not to include any Armenians or Rums in the list.

It can be understood from the session records that many MPs were not wholly aware of the details of the discussion regarding the potential members of the list. The minister of interior, Ferit Bey, apparently stated the names one by one while the MPs were talking, yelling and shouting. When the turn came to name the participants of the Circassian Congress, Ferit Bey called the names using their Circassian family names, such as Lampad Yakup. Interestingly, despite being a member of the cabinet partly responsible for deciding who would be on the list, he did not know what these Circassian family names meant. He explained to the assembly that the Circassians used Greek names and that these family names were Greek names.[27] This assumption is mostly likely to have been based on a belief that the Circassians were heavily pro-Greek.

It is also worth mentioning that not all anti-nationalists who posed a threat to the Ankara government appeared on the list. For example, the members of the Çapanoğlu family were not added, despite the uprising organized by them in Yozgat being one of the most vicious to have taken place in the summer of 1920. If nationalist forces, especially the forces of Çerkes Ethem, had not succeeded in gaining control over the region and thus suppressing the uprising, it could have spread towards Ankara, the heart of the national movement. When Çerkes Ethem took control of the region and set up a military court, dozens of people were executed and order was restored in favour of Ankara. However, Ethem was one of the names highest up the list and no member of the Çapanoğlu family was present there.[28]

Ankara had declared Ethem a traitor on the basis that he went to the Greek-ruled region after his split with Ankara. It was risky for Ankara to simply drop his citizenship and prevent his return to Turkey based on this alleged 'betrayal', since Ankara was not be able to prove Ethem had ever served in the Greek army. If Ethem worked for the Greek occupation forces, Ankara could apply the citizenship law and article 1044 (*Tabiyet-i Osmaniyye Kanunnamesi*), whereby a citizen who had worked for any other army rather than the Ottoman army could have their citizenship revoked without any other explanation. Therefore, placing Ethem on the list of personae non gratae provided a greater guarantee that he would be neutralized than would have been possible using article 1044. Clearly, a political motive, that is to prevent Ethem's return to Ankara, was the reason why he appeared on the list.[29] Just a year after Ethem was excluded from the national movement (1922), the situation regarding him and the other oppositionists (the Circassians, Abkhazians and Eşref Bey) was already being discussed by members of the Ministry of War and the Cabinet in Ankara. In regard to their pardon, the Ministry of War asked the Cabinet whether they would be free to come to Anatolia or not. However, on 22 January 1922, the Cabinet declared that they would not be allowed to come to Anatolia.[30] Ankara insisted that they should be kept far away from Anatolia.

When looking at the situation objectively, one can also claim that there were no substantial ideological differences between the Kemalists and some of the 150'ers. Some of those on the list had once been affiliated with the CUP in its early years (as had the majority of the Kemalists in the post-1908 period). After the constitutional revolution of 1908, the CUP did not take power directly. Rather it remained behind the scenes, acting as a check on power (*Denetleme İktidarı*) until the assassination of Mahmut Şevket Paşa on 11 June 1913.[31] However, with the growing authority of the CUP, some members broke away from it. They were the victims of the repressive policies of the CUP towards the military and bureaucracy. They lost their jobs, were retired or sent into exile on the periphery as punishment. The CUP turned its back on ideas associated with the second constitutional period, relating to 'justice, equality, and liberty'. The post-First-World-War struggle between the nationalists and anti-nationalists in the post-1908 constitutional revolution period deepened the division between the CUP and the Liberal Entente, which was established in November 1911 after some policies of the CUP in the post-revolution were judged unappealing to them. Some Liberal Entente members – namely, Rıza Nur, Ali Kemal, Mevlanzade Rıfat, Nureddin Feruh and Sadık Bey – were required to leave the empire after the CUP's coup d'état on 23 January 1913 in response to increased pressure from the CUP.[32] Furthermore, after the assassination of Mahmut Şevket Paşa on 11 June 1913, some CUP opponents were dismissed from their jobs and others were arrested. Hundreds of people were sent into political exile.[33]

For those suffering under CUP rule, the post-First-World-War period offered an opportunity for the CUP to pay the price of its repressive policies of the past. It was a time to take revenge. The members of the Liberal Entente completely opposed the national movement since its members had come from the CUP. As one of these, Mustafa Sabri Efendi made it clear that they would rather live under the Allies' or infidel *gavur* rule than that of the CUP.[34] After the CUP leadership left Turkey in 1918, the members of the Liberal Entente came to power and pursued their policy of non-resistance against the Allies. For them, the Ottoman state did not have any power to continue its armed resistance. The only way to protect the state from disintegration was to conclude a peace agreement with the Allies. However, the nationalists defeated Greek forces in 1922, in addition to their long-time opponents of the Liberal Entente, due to their anti-nationalist activities during the Turkish–Greek War of 1919–22, and were added to the list of 'traitors' in April 1924 by the Turkish Grand National Assembly. Their names were Gümülcineli İsmail Hakkı Bey, Rıza Tevfik (Bölükbaşı), Mustafa Sabri Efendi, Konyalı Zeynel Abidin Efendi[35] and İzmit governor (Çule) İbrahim Hakkı.

The Names

The Ministry of Interior decided upon 149 names and the owner of *Köylü* newspaper Refet Bey was later added to the list making 150 names as declared in the official newspaper of the government *Resmi Ceride* on 7 January 1925. The names were arranged into nine groups as follows:

Vahidettin's Attendants

1. Kiraz Hamdi
2. Commander of the Special Attendants' Unit Zeki
3. Prosecutor of State Treasure Kayserili Şaban Ağa
4. Tütüncübaşı Şükrü
5. Head of the Aides de camp
6. Colonel Aide de camp Tahir
7. First Aide de camp Avni
8. Former Director of State Treasure Refik

Those who signed the Sèvres Agreement and Cabinet Members who took a role in the *Kuva-yi İnzibatiyye*[36]

9. Former Şeyhülislam Mustafa Sabri
10. Former Minister of Justice Ali Rüşdi
11. Former Minister of Agriculture and Trade Cemal
12. Former Minister of Navy Cakacı Hamdi
13. Former Minister of Education Rumbeyoğlu Fahreddin
14. Former Minister of Agriculture and Trade Kirilhançerci Remzi

The members of the Council who signed the Sèvres Agreement

15. Former Minister of Education Hadi
16. Former Head of *Şurayı Devlet* Rıza Tevfik
17. Former Bern Ambassador Reşid Halis

Those involved in *Kuva-yi İnzibatiyye*

18. The General Commander of *Kuva-yi İnzibatiyye* Süleyman Şefik
19. Aide de camp Cavalry Lieutenant Tahsin
20. Commander in *Kuva-yi İnzibatiyye* Colonel Ahmed Refik
21. *Kuva-yi İnzibatiyye* machine gun commander and the aide de camp of Damad Ferid Paşa Tarık Mümtaz
22. Commander in *Kuva-yi İnzibatiyye* Ali Nadir Paşa
23. *Kuva-yi İnzibatiyye* member Colonel Fettah
24. *Kuva-yi İnzibatiyye* member Çopur Hakkı
25. Former Governor of Bursa Gümülcineli İsmail
26. From *Ayan* Konyalı Zeynelabidin
27. Former Governor of Cebelibereket Fanizade Mesud
28. The Head of the Liberal Entente Colonel Sadık
29. Former Governor of Malatya Halil Rahmi (Bedirhani)
30. Former Governor of Manisa Giritli Hüsnü
31. Former Head of Military Tribunal Nemrud Mustafa
32. The Mayor of Uşak Hulusi
33. Former governor of Adapazarı Traitor Mustafa
34. Former Mufti of Tekirdağ Hafız Ahmed
35. Former Governor of Afyonkarahisar Sabit
36. Former Governor of Gaziantep Celal Kadri
37. The General Secretary of Liberal Entente Adanalı Zeynel Abidin

38. Former Minister of Foundations Vasfi Hoca
39. Former Governor of Harput Ali Galib
40. Former Vice Governor of Bursa Aziz Nuri
41. Former Muftu of Bursa Ömer Fevzi
42. Former Adviser of Qadı of İzmir Ahmet Asım
43. Former Istanbul Guardian Natık
44. Former Minister of Interior Adil
45. Former Minister of İnterior Mehmed Ali
46. Former Governor of Edirne and Vice Mayor of Istanbul Salim
47. Kütahya governor (during Greek Occupation) Hocarasizde İbrahim
48. Governor of Adana Abdurrahman
49. Former MP of Karahisarşarki Ömer Fevzi
50. Lieutenant (Torturer) Adil
51. Lieutenant (Torturer) Refik
52. Former Governor of Kırkağaç Şerif
53. Former Governor of Çanakkale Mahmud Mahir
54. Former Commander of Istanbul Emin
55. Governor of Kilis Sadullah Sami
56. Former Governor of Bolu Osman Nuri

Edhem and his Friends (*Edhem ve Avanesi*)

57. Çerkes Edhem
58. Edhem's brother Reşid
59. Edhem's brother Tevfik
60. Kuçşubaşı Eşref
61. Kuşçubaşı Eşref's brother Hacı Sami
62. Former Commander of Akhisar İzmirli Küçük Ethem
63. Düzceli Mehmed's son Sami Açofit
64. Burhaniyeli Halil İbrahim
65. Susurluk/Demirkapılı Hacı Ahmed

Those who participated in the Circassian Congress

66. Bağ Osman from Hendek/Sünbüllü village
67. Former Governor of İzmit İbrahim Hakkı
68. Beraev Said
69. Berzek Tahir

70. Maan Şirin from Adapazarı/Harmantepe village
71. Kocakömeroğlu Hüseyin Söke Ereğli/ Tekeli village
72. Bağ Kemal from Adapazarı/Talustanbey village
73. Hamta Ahmed
74. Maan Ali
75. Harunelreşid from Kirmasti/Karaorman village
76. Eskişehirli Sefer Hoca
77. Bigalı Nuri Bey's son Ali
78. Kemal from Adapazarı/Şahinbey village
79. Lampat Yakub from Gönen/Tuzakçı village
80. Kompat Hafız Said from Gönen/Bayramiç village
81. Retired Colonel Ahmed from Gönen/Keçe village
82. Bizedurug Said, a lawyer in İzmir
83. Şamlı Ahmed Nuri

Police

84. Former Police Director of Istanbul Tahsin
85. Former Vice Police Director of Istanbul Kemal
86. General Chief of Police Vice Director Ispartalı Kemal
87. Former Director of the First Branch of Istanbul Police Directory Şerif
88. Former Head Officer of the First Branch of Istanbul Police Directory Said
89. Former Officer in Arnavutköy Hacı Kemal
90. Chief Police Officer Namık
91. Police Chief of Şişli District Nedim
92. Police Director of Edirne and Governor of Yalova Fuad
93. Former Police Director of Adana Yolgeçenli Yusuf
94. Former Officer in Unkapanı Sakallı Cemil
95. Former Officer in Büyükdere Mazlum
96. Former Second Police Chief of Beyoğlu Fuad

Journalists

97. Member of the Liberal Entente and owner of *Serbesti* Newspaper Mevlanzade Rıfat
98. Owner of *Türkçe* Istanbul Newspaper Sait Monla
99. Owner of *Müsavet* Newspaper in İzmir İzmirli Hafız İsmail

100. Former Director of *Post and Telegraph*, and Owner of *Aydede* Newspaper Refik Halid
101. Owner of *Adalet* Newspaper in Bandırma Bahriyeli Ali Sami
102. Owner of *Temin* Newspaper in Edirne and Hakikat Newspaper in Selanik Neyir Mustafa
103. Former Correspondent of *Köylü* Newspaper Ferid
104. Owner of *Alemdar* Newspaper Refik Cevad
105. Pehlivan Kadri from Alemdar Newspaper
106. Owner of *Ferda* Newspaper in Adana Fanizade Ali İlmi
107. Owner of *İrşad* Newspaper in Balıkesir Trabzonlu Ömer Fevzi
108. Owner of *Doğruyol* Newspaper in Aleppo Hasan Sadık
109. Owner and Director of *Köylü* Newspaper İzmirli Refet

Other People

110. Tarsuslu Kemalpaşazade Selami
111. Tarsuslu Kemalpaşazade Kemal
112. Süleymaniyeli Kürd Hakkı
113. Son of Mustafa Sabri İbrahim Sabri
114. Manufacturer Bursalı Cemil
115. Spy for English well-known Çerkes Ragıb
116. Haçinli Kazak Hasan who worked for the French Army
117. Leader of bandit Süngülü Çerkes Davud
118. Major Çerkes Bekir
119. Necib, Brother-in-law of manufacturer Bursalı Cemil
120. Inspector Ahmed Hulusi
121. Madanoğlu Mustafa from Uşak
122. Yusufoğlu Remzi Tuzakçı village of Gönen
123. Hacı Kasımoğlu Zühtü Bayramiç village of Gönen
124. Kocakuzuk Osmanoğlu Şakir Balcı village of Gönen
125. Koç Ali, son of Koç Memed, Muradlar village of Gönen
126. Aziz, son of Mehmed, Ayvacık village of Gönen
127. Osman, son of Balcılı Ahmed Keçeler village of Gönen
128. Molla Süleymanoğlu İzzet İldiz village of Susurluk
129. Kara Kazım, son of Hüseyin, Muradlar village of Gönen
130. Arap Mahmut, son of Bekir, Balcı village of Gönen

131. Guardian Yusuf, Rüstem village of Gönen
132. Eyüb, son of Ömeri Balcı village of Gönen
133. İbrahim Çavuş, son of Talustan, Küçükler village of Gönen
134. İbrahim, son of Topallılı Şerif, Balcı village of Gönen
135. İdris, son of Topal Ömer, Keçeler village of Gönen
136. İsmail, son of Kurh, Bolağaç village of Gönen
137. Canbolat, son of Muhtar Hacı Bey, Keçeler village of Gönen
138. İshak, son of Yusuf, Kayapınar village of Marmara
139. Sabit, son of Ali Bey, Kızık village of Manyas
140. Selin, son of Deli Hasan, Balcı village of Gönen
141. Osman, son of Makinacı Mehmed, Çerkes town of Gönen
142. Kemal, son of Kadir, Değirmenboğazı village of Manyas
143. Galib, son of Hüseyin, Keçeler village of Gönen
144. Salih, son of Çerkes Said, Hacı Yakub village of Manyas
145. İsmail, brother of slain Şevket, Hacı Yakub village of Manyas
146. Deli Kasım, son of Abdullah, Keçeler village of Gönen
147. Kemal, son of Corporal Hasan, Çerkes town of Gönen
148. Kazım Efe, son of Kadir, and brother of Kemal, Değirmenboğazı village of Manyas
149. Yallaçoğlu Kemal, Kızık village of Gönen
150. Tuğuğlu Mehmed Ağa, Keçeler village of Gönen.[37]

The people on the list were not deprived of their Turkish citizenship when the law was first passed. At this time, only their entrance to Turkey was restricted. However, later on, on 28 May 1927 with law number of 1064, they had their Turkish citizenship revoked by the assembly, losing their citizenship rights.[38] The government also forced them to sell their property. Government declaration (*Kararname*) number 880 was signed by the Cabinet on 10 September 1927, indicating that the 150'ers had to sell their properties. They were given only nine months to do so.[39] For those who had died before 1927, their families were authorized to bury them inside Turkey. However, after the law was passed depriving them of citizenship, even their corpses were not allowed to pass back over the Turkish border.[40]

Military courts were another tool used by the state in this period to strengthen the government's authority over people. This topic is not part of this book and further research is required on the role of the military courts, but a brief note is needed. The new Turkish state relied on the military courts to intimidate as well as sentence wartime criminals and its opponents, thereby creating a new ideal for the model 'loyal citizen'. The assembly also passed laws to punish civil and military servants for their wartime activities. The names of the military servants expelled from the military were released in the official newspaper on 7 April 1924.[41] In relation to civil servants, another law was passed on 26 May 1926 (*Mücadele-i Milliye'ye İştirak Etmeyen Memurin Hakkında Kanun*); Law number 398. It was published in the official newspaper on 14 June 1926.[42] As many as 1,250 of the 3,150 civil servants whose files were investigated were expelled from their jobs; they also lost their retirement rights. This list consisted of three hundred members of the Association of Friends of the English (*İngiliz Muhipleri Cemiyeti*), and another three hundred were sentenced to death, including journalists who had voiced unfavourable opinions.[43] Their problems with the state continued until 1952.[44] The people on the lists at least secured certain rights, yet the court was used as an important tool of the regime during the early republican period to punish any opposition. There were also some trials based on an article in the so-called 'punishment law' that criminalized anyone insulting Turkishness, the government, the army, the president, the assembly, the republic or the justice system (*Türklüğü, Hükümeti, Orduyu, Reisi Cumhuru, Meclisi, Cumhuriyeti, Adliyeyi Tahkir (hakaret, aşşağılama)*). There are no details regarding how fair the trial process was and few details about the cases in the archive documents; only briefly were the legal grounds for the trials mentioned in the documents. The courts had to request permission from the Turkish Grand National Assembly (TGNA) by 1938, and the TGNA was the only authority allowed to give permission to sentence people accused of insulting the state, the president and other aforementioned republican units. The records of the trials started in 1926 and ended in 1938, when a change in the law was proposed by Prime Minister Celal Bayar to shorten the long bureaucratic process and to accredit the local courts to handle cases from 10 March 1938.[45] From 1926 to 1938, the courts investigated 1,027 separate cases. The average application number was about five hundred per year from 1933 to 1937.[46] Almost half of the applicants were allowed by the assembly to bring the case to the courts. For the pre-1938 cases, there was a legal obligation imposed on the Ministry of Justice to ask permission from the assembly to allow prosecutors to investigate the alleged insults. However, 1938 onwards, it is not possible to establish how many cases were investigated or how many people were sentenced by the local courts, since these records are not yet open to researchers or they do not exist in the republican archives.

Anti-Kemalist activities of the 150'ers

When the war was won by the Ankara government forces, opposition groups left the region. From 1922 to 1938, the opposition attempted to organize an anti-Ankara movement in different countries and cities. Prominent among these were Western Thrace, Thessalonica, the Aegean Islands, particularly Limnos (Midilli), Aleppo and Damascus/Syria, Amman/Jordan and Iraq. In exile, some of the 150'ers followed a similar path to the Young Turks, opposing Abdülhamid II. Their aim was to create chaos in Turkey and then overthrow the government. They were able to work with other anti-Ankara groups of the period, such as the Armenian Tashnaksutyun and Kurdish groups, just as the Young Turks had done prior to the 1908 revolution.

Before the Lausanne agreement, which was signed in July 1923, hundreds of anti-Kemalists had already moved to Western Thrace and the Aegean Islands.[47] The anti-nationalist Circassians left the region with the Greek forces. Of note, several thousand Circassians went with Çule İbrahim Hakkı and asked the British to resettle them. However, the British forces could not easily find a suitable place for resettlement. At the time India, Palestine, North Iraq and Greece were among the options examined.[48] İbrahim Hakkı wrote to the British ambassador in Athens to try and convince him that due to their work under England against the Kemalists, the Turks now hated them, and they should be sent to Cyprus for safety.[49] As a result of these correspondences, they were settled in three villages in Greece – one established close to Thessalonica, and another two near Athens. A group were later put on the list of the 150'ers. More than a thousand people lived in the three villages until they were pardoned by the Turkish state in 1938. Some of these Circassians settled in Western Thrace, especially around Gümülcine (Komotini in Greek), such as Hafız Reşad Efendi, becoming key symbols in the anti-Kemalist movement in Western Thrace. Hafız Reşad published several newspapers and Islamic magazines, continuing his opposition until his death in 1981.[50] The archival sources are very limited concerning the activities of these people and the 150'ers in Western Thrace and Gümülcine, in particular. Neither the Greek National archives nor the Foreign Ministry archives of Turkey have permitted researchers access to their records to review the activities of these people in Greece. However, it is unthinkable that hundreds of anti-Kemalists people could live in Greece without the express permission of Greek authorities, so there must have been some records kept regarding the relationships between the Greek authorities and the anti-Kemalists. In addition, it can be argued that the Turkish government would have certainly followed the activities of the 150'ers. Although police records do exist on these people, they have not been opened to researchers by the authorities of the Turkish Republican Archives; furthermore, the Ministry of Foreign Affairs also has records on them. Some of the Turkish consulate employees were assigned to track them.[51] However, these records have not yet been opened to researchers.

Although the Lausanne Peace Treaty was signed in 1924, a kind of cold war endured between Turkey and Greece until 1928.[52] Greece supported the anti-Kemalists and the wartime activities of those people who left Turkey due to their actions against the Kemalists. In the years following the deportation of the 150'ers from Turkey, Greece was at the centre of the anti-Kemalist activities. There were four different anti-Kemalist groups in Greece: the groups of Hacı (Çerkes) Sami, Çerkes (Çule) İbrahim Hakkı, Nigehban-ı Hukuk and Çerkes Ethem. Ethem's group consisted of Reşid, Tevfik, Major Kürt Abdullah, Captain Ethem, Çerkes Kazım, Lieutenant Kemal and Sabri.[53] Çerkes Ethem did not remain quiet in Greece awaiting pardon by the Kemalists. Indeed, contrary to existing historiography, Çerkes Ethem remained undaunted in his attempts to challenge Ankara during his lifetime. He sought a way to put an end to the Kemalist regime and take revenge on Mustafa Kemal. On 4 April 1925, Ethem, Sami and Mevlanzade Rifat moved to Baghdad using Greek passports to negotiate with Sheikh Tahir, a local sheikh there.[54] According to police reports, Ethem was in Beirut and Syria in the June–July 1925 period with Mevlanzade Rifat.[55] However, he was forced to leave Syria due to pressure from French forces. He then moved to Aleppo. In Aleppo, Ethem contacted Artufi and another local citizen. He sent both to the Urfa region in Turkey.[56] According to some reports, he and Mevlanzade Rifat were paid 500 English liras by the British forces, and Vehip Paşa claimed that the application process had been completed for Ethem's stay in Syria in November 1928.[57]

Ethem had already communicated with Kurdish groups and tribes in the north of Iraq. Over the next four years, Ethem attempted to create a Circassian-dominated opposition group against the Kemalists. He sought out Circassians from Egypt, Jordan, Syria and those who had settled in Greece.[58] In Amman, Jordan, Çerkes Ömer Hikmet, who was the director of the court, Kabartay Mehmet Taş, a member of the Amman Assembly, Kabartay Sait Mufti and Muhtar İsmail were all key supporters of Ethem in Jordan.[59] They would meet in cafes in Amman and Hemdan. In Cairo, Reşid met with Tevfik, Çerkes Haydar and the director of Camii Al Azhar Çerkes Abdülhamid.[60] Based on the reports from the national police archive, Halıcı argues that in 1929 Çerkes Reşid, Tarık Mümtaz and a group of Circassians organized a meeting in Cairo.[61] They printed stamps and created a flag to symbolize their movement. The colour of the flag was green and it had the Islamic declaration of faith (*Kelimeyi Şehadet*) printed on it.[62] It is also claimed by the national police that some Circassians from Greece and Damascus were also expected to participate in the uprising in the Dersim region, in March 1927, along with Kurdish groups.[63] Ethem's own writings reveal that he followed a pro-Kurdish policy in that period, voicing complaints about the cruel (*zalimane*) policies of the Ankara government towards the Kurds.[64] However, there are few sources describing his activities with the Kurdish groups in this era, aside from a few police reports.

The exiled members of the Ottoman family and some of the 150'ers also contacted one another through letters. The elderly Şehzade Mahmud Şevket Bey, a grandson of Sultan Abdülaziz, contacted the former minister of the interior Mehmed Ali (number 45). They went on to establish an anti-Kemalist newspaper, and worked to demolish the Kemalist regime.[65] Şehzade Mahmud wrote in one of his letters that they had no issues with all the Kemalists; rather he only hated Mustafa Kemal and his friends.[66] They also mentioned Amman in their correspondence. In one of his letters, on 2 January 1932, Mahmud Şevket asked Mehmed Ali how they might communicate with those who were in Amman, as this was where Çerkes Ethem had stayed for a long time. In the next letter, he mentioned that due to ongoing smuggling along the Turkish border with Syria and the Black Sea, it was easy to enter Turkey.[67] He told

Mehmed Ali Bey to ask Çerkes Ethem to prepare some Circassians as an armed force. He also asked that the Kurdish leaders and Armenians (komites) prepare for an uprising.⁶⁸ Kazım (number 148 on the list) from Bandırma/ Değirmenboğaz, organized correspondence between Çerkes Ethem and a Şehzade.⁶⁹ Ethem used 'Alelhas' as a nickname when writing letters.⁷⁰ He requested financial support from one of the Şehzades, probably Ömer Faruk Osman, the son of the last caliph Abdülmecid Efendi. He further stated that they should work for a revolution, which would save the people of Anatolia from oppression. After the revolution, they should establish a democratic system, which did not necessarily have to be a republic.⁷¹

Taking revenge: The insurgency and assassination attempts by the 150'ers

The first assassination attempt was organized by a group in June 1926. They planned to assassinate Mustafa Kemal during his trip to İzmir. However, on 15 June 1926, the attempt was reported to the governor of İzmir and prevented.⁷² Dozens of people were detained and the attempt became an opportunity for Mustafa Kemal to wipe out both his political and armed opponents. In August 1926, Kuşçubaşı Eşref wrote a letter to Refet Bey (probably to Refet Bele). In it, he accused the Ankara government on the basis that some nationalists had also been executed by Ankara due to personal problems rather than for their role in the İzmir assassination attempt.⁷³ He was upset by the Ankara government's policies, in that the attempt was used to silence the people. He also observed that several groups could resist Ankara, such as the Kurdists (*Kürtçü*), Assassins (*Suikastçiler*) and İttihadists (*İttihadcılar*).⁷⁴ The Kuşçubaşı brothers, Eşref and Hacı Sami,⁷⁵ were all close to Enver Paşa, (particularly Sami, who was Enver's right hand-man in his last days). Kamil Erdaha claims that due to the power struggle between Enver Paşa and Mustafa Kemal during the Turkish War of Independence, the Kuşçubaşı brothers and especially Hacı Sami expressed feelings of enmity towards Mustafa Kemal, since he did not allow Enver to return to Anatolia.⁷⁶ Shortly after this rejection, Enver was killed by Bolshevik forces near Dushanbe, Tajikistan, in 1922. After an unsuccessful assassination attempt in İzmir in 1926, Mustafa Kemal tried to root out and silence the opposition, and spread his absolute authority throughout the country. Those sentenced by the court to be executed included Dr Nazım and İsmail Canbolat while other important figures from the nationalist struggle, such as Kazım Karabekir and Ali Fuat Cebesoy, were detained by the regime. It can be claimed that Ankara had rid itself of prominent figures in the Liberal Party by adding them to the list of 150'ers. With the İzmir Assassination trial, the remaining leaders of the CUP were executed, and its political opponents were detained and imprisoned. The silencing of the opposition was complete with these two cases. One can speculate that this affected Hacı Sami and Eşref, in that they further saw a need to carry out an assassination against Mustafa Kemal, and to raise up the people of Anatolia for an insurgency.

Sami, his brother Ahmet and three other Circassians, Hakkı,[77] Düzceli Mecid[78] and Sökeli Mecid,[79] came to the Kalamaki Dock of Kuşadası from the Sisam island of Greece, which is about 20 miles from the Kalamaki Dock, on 17 August 1927.[80] Their plan was to follow a route from Kuşadası to Çine, Madran, Salihli, Akhisar, Kütahya and Afyon and to arrive in Ayaş (Ankara) by 15 September 1927, where they would plant a bomb on the railway, with the purpose of exploding it when Mustafa Kemal, his ministers and MPs took a train from Istanbul to Ankara. However, almost eight days after they reached Kuşadası they were seen by the nomads around the Madran Mountain on 24 August 1927. The nomads complained to the local gendarme forces about these strangers. They told the local people that they were tiger hunters and came to the region for tiger hunting.[81] Based on the complaints of the nomads, gendarme forces came to the region and a skirmish erupted between Sami, his retinues and the gendarmes. Sami and his brother Ahmed resisted until the end, but were killed by the gendarmes; the rest of the group, Hakkı, Düzceli Mecid and Sökeli Mecid, were captured and brought first to İzmir and then to Istanbul for trial on 30 August 1927.[82] The reason for holding the trial in Istanbul appears to have been to use the case to intimidate residents who might still not be loyal to the republican regime, since the city had been the capital of the Ottoman state for more than 450 years, and the anti-nationalist movement was very active there during the Turkish–Greek War. It should also be noted that after Mustafa Kemal left Istanbul on 16 May 1919 to go to Anatolia, he returned only on 1 July 1927, as Istanbul was not thought to be a secure place for many years. This explains why when an opportunity arose the regime grasped it to consolidate its power and show its strength to the people of the city.

Some people were also arrested in the investigation,[83] starting with Sami's younger brother Mekki[84] and his relatives Ahmed, Halil and Rasuh Bey, and Atıf Bey, an ex-military commander of İzmit, who was arrested for his relationship with the group's members.[85] With the exception of Hakkı, Düzceli Mecid, Sökeli Mecid and Mekki, many others were released. The suspects would be tried under various articles of the penal code, including article 126 which stated that those who fought against the Turkish Republic would be executed; article 146, stating that those who incited disorder could be punished with execution; and article 156, which proclaimed that those who carried out an assassination or an attempted assassination of the president would be executed.[86] The trial began on 5 November 1927. According to Hakkı's statement in court, Vehip Paşa and the old governor İzmir and CUP member Rahmi Bey had also supported the insurgency.[87] Vehip Paşa was in Romania and was to return to Anatolia to help the Kurds start an uprising in the Dersim region.[88] The plan was to travel to Anatolia immediately after the old CUP members were executed for their alleged involvement in the İzmir conspiracy of 1926. However, due to a lack of money and Sami's illness they had to postpone their plan.[89] They were armed, had rifles, bombs and about 250 bullets per person; they also carried some food, bandages and some tincture of iodine in their bag to treat any possible wounds.[90] They walked in the night and slept and hid in the morning, over a period of eight days beginning from 17 August 1927. Kuşçubaşı Eşref was also going to join them, bringing dynamite (after Sami was killed by the gendarme forces Eşref chose not to come to Anatolia). If they could succeed in the assassination of Mustafa Kemal, they would publish a declaration on behalf of the sultan (probably Abdülmecid Efendi or Vahidettin) all over the country, even in Trabzon, and an insurgency would be launched. Then the sultan and the members of CUP would be able to return to Anatolia.[91] Hakkı also emphasized that if Sami had not already organized people in Anatolia to support him, he would not have become involved in the situation in the region.

It was also underlined several times by the newspaper that Çerkes Ethem and Reşid were also behind the group, supporting Sami and his retinues to carry out their plan, although none of the suspects mentioned this.[92] It is also noteworthy, as it helps to explain the negative approach to the Circassians in the early republican period, that the head of the court asked Hakkı whether he had fought against the *Kuva-yi Milliye*. Hakkı said that he had fought, but, that everyone else had also fought:

> Hakkı: I fought but it was like everyone else.
> Head of court: How? Was there anyone else who fought against Kuva-yi Milliye other than Circassians?
> Hakkı: Of course, who organized those rebellions, only Circassians?[93]

The suspects were not represented in court by a lawyer and were questioned directly by the court, and their trial lasted only two days. At the end of the second day, the prosecutor declared his indictment that Hakkı, Sökeli Mecid and Düzceli Mecid were to be sentenced to death for their attempt to assassinate the president, their involvement in armed activities against the Republic of Turkey and their attempt to change the constitutional order. Eşref and his relative Mustafa were given life sentences in absentia due to their involvement in the Çerkes Sami group and their attempt to assassinate the president and change the constitutional order. However, Mekki, Sami's younger brother, was found innocent and released by the court.[94] The National Assembly approved the execution of Hakkı, Sökeli Mecid and Düzceli Mecid on 12 January 1928.[95]

The group was accused of attempting to assassinate Mustafa Kemal; however, they were captured on Madran Mountain, which is more than 700 miles away from Ayaş, Ankara. Despite their lack of opportunity to carry out an assassination attempt, they were sentenced to death for their supposed intent. Eşref and Mustafa were also sentenced to death for their involvement in the preparation of the uprising, even though they were not in the court to be questioned.[96] Hakkı, Düzeli Mecid and Sökeli Mecid were executed on 18 January 1928, in Eminönü square, Istanbul. The regime clearly used this trial to intimidate its opponents by executing the three in the heart of Istanbul in front of hundreds of people. It can be said that the state's propaganda tool and newspapers comparing with the later incidents were not used enough. As will be seen in the discussion that follows on the assassination attempt in 1935, the state saw it as an opportunity to attack the leader and the regime.

Another assassination attempt was allegedly organized by Ethem in 1935.[97] A Circassian man, Yahya[98] was arrested by the police forces. According to the subsequent investigation, he and another four Circassians organized an assassination attack against Atatürk on the orders of Çerkes Ethem and his brother Reşid. Urfa MP Ali Saip (Ursavaş)[99] was also involved, providing material support to the assassins. A man named Üzeyir, the brother of one of the assassins,[100] had complained about the group, which then led to the arrest of Yahya and the other members of the group. According to the prosecutor, Kuşçubaşı Eşref came to Syria and met with Ethem, where the men planned the assassination attempt together. Eşref said that he started (his own) history with the sword and he would finish it with the sword.[101] The prosecutor used the correspondence between several of the 150'ers, including Ethem, Maan Mustafa and Eşref, and the activities of Yahya as evidence of the planned assassination attempt. In the letters, although there was evidence suggesting that they had some plans to come Turkey, there was no convincing proof on when and how they would come to Turkey and with what connections they would succeed in their aim. It is impossible to know what motivation the prosecutor had when using the correspondences as evidence in the trial.

Yahya had gone to Syria to make money in order to marry a girl from his own hometown. He stayed in Syria for a few months with the Circassians and then crossed the border and went to Jordan where he met with Ethem in Amman, and was asked about Turkey and its political and military situation. Ethem also told him that he would join the Kurds and they would rise against Ankara, in an uprising that would be more organized than the Sheikh Said one in 1924.[102] Six months later, at the end of summer 1935, Ethem sent Yahya to Turkey and told him that Ali Saib (Ursavaş), Maraşlı İdris and Şemseddin Bey of Çokak town would help him. This statement was made by Yahya during the police investigation before the trial; however, in court he denied the latter part of the statement concerning his meeting with Ethem. He told the court that the statement about Ethem had been made under torture. It appeared that the prosecutor was looking for a motive behind Yahya's going to Syria and exaggerated the situation, despite the fact that he went there to make money to marry a girl from his hometown and to find his relatives in Syria. In Syria and Amman, his relatives and some other Circassians helped him by giving him a job and providing accommodation for him. The prosecutor found the relationships to be strange and unbelievable coincidences, and made the situation the basis of his investigations.[103] However, it appears that the prosecutor had fabricated a story based on Yahya's journey to Syria. Due to his lack of knowledge of Circassian networks and traditional customs, the prosecutor misinterpreted the situation. In Circassian tradition and customs one is not allowed to ask a guest who comes to your home or village, how long he is going to stay; one is only expected to feed his guest and provide him with accommodation.[104]

Hamdi and his friends, Yakub and Aziz, later designated assassins by the prosecutor, stayed in Üzeyir's house. Later, Üzeyir went to the local court and declared that he had some enemies and that those enemies would slander him. He said he was scared by his friends' anti-Atatürk talk. It seems that he took this move as a precautionary measure, since he had hosted Hamdi and his friends in his house and these people were seen to be working on anti-state activities.[105] However, Üzeyir's brother Arif confessed that he also saw the people and heard from Çerkes Ethem's brother Reşid in Jordan that a group of people would be sent by them and that they had told him that he should inform his brother Üzeyir, who should ask Ali Saib (Ursavaş) to conceal the group.[106] Ali Saib was a very close friend of Üzeyir.[107] The distance between their farms was about eighteen hours by foot.[108] Üzeyir claimed that Ali Saib had corresponded with Ethem, and that he himself had given a letter to Ali Saib from Ethem.[109] Yahya also supplied the names of Ali Saib and the local governor of Çokak town, Şemseddin Bey, to the prosecutor for their involvement in the alleged assassination.[110] Ali Saib's immunity was lifted by the assembly on 18 October 1935; he himself also voted to revoke his immunity.[111] In his speech to the assembly, Ali Saib underlined that he loved Atatürk and that it would be impossible for him to work with someone like Çerkes Ethem to kill Atatürk who 'created' (*yarattı*–meaning like God). Regarding the discussion about his ethnic identity, which was claimed to be Kurdish or Circassian, Ali Saip emphasized that he was pure Turkish and that only Turkish blood flowed in his veins.

It is important to note that this case was transformed into another opportunity for the Kemalists and the press. The Kemalists used the case to strengthen collectivization among their supporters by mobilizing thousands to curse the traitors who had attempted to assassinate their divine leader. Student unions, bars and people's houses organized protests around the country from east to west, including among Armenians, Jews and Assyrians. Many groups condemned the attempt, prayed for the president and sent telegrams to the presidential palace expressing their support for Atatürk.[112] Two large demonstrations were organized in Ankara and Istanbul on 22 October and 23 October 1935 and thousands of people joined them. This was turned into a nationwide event and exploited by the regime.

For more than a week, the news of the alleged assassination attempt was in the newspaper headlines. The telegrams sent to Atatürk were published by the newspapers every day. On the other hand, the press used very negative, discriminative and humiliating language. Before the trial started, *Cumhuiryet* had already condemned Çerkes Ethem and his brother, labelling them villainous '*alçak*'[113] *Son Posta* called him as a Circassian Monster (*Çerkes Canavarı Ethem*).[114] According to *Cumhuriyet*, the French colonial administration and the Circassians of Syria were working against Turkey.[115] The members of the Circassian community in Syria and Jordan were accused of assisting the assassins, and according to *Son Posta* the documents proving the assassination attempt were captured by the Syrian regime.[116] Those who were detained were called cursed people (*melun*) by the newspaper. *Cumhuriyet* also declared, 'An assassination on Atatürk is an assassination on the fatherland and the republic, an assassination on Atatürk is an assassination on the nation and Turkishness, an assassination on Atatürk is an assassination on history and the future, an assassination on Atatürk is an assassination against humanity and civilization.'[117] Another absurd approach was taken by the *Son Posta* newspaper; it was claimed by *Son Posta* based on a Greek newspaper that Italians were behind the assassination attempt,[118] and the newspaper further claimed that the attempt was also an act of states which did not want Turkey to progress and which were jealous of Turkey. The newspaper published this news without providing any source for this claim.[119]

Çerkes Ethem and his brother Reşid were arrested in Amman, Jordan, due to increasing pressure from Turkey over their involvement in the assassination attempt; however, they were then released on bail. Ethem's other brother Tevfik, Kazım İsmail and Edib Kemal were also arrested in Haifa.[120] Ankara warned the French colonial administration about the activities of Ethem and his co-conspirators, and officially requested the French rulers to deport them (Ethem and Reşid).[121] The trial began on 9 January 1936 in Ankara, and there were nine suspects in court: Yahya, Üzeyir, Arif, Şemsettin, Şaban, İsmail, İdris, Aziz and Ali Saib. The allegation of the prosecutor, Baha Arıkan, was that they had set up an armed group to assassinate Atatürk.[122] The language

Figure 1 *Cumhuriyet* newspaper 19 October 1935. 'Cursed Assassins Under Justice! Villainous Çerkes Ethem!'

he used was simplistic, and he attempted to incriminate the suspects using small pieces of evidence. For example, when giving his statement about Yahya, he said that because Yahya was a deserter and had been imprisoned before, he was capable of doing any kind of viciousness.[123] However, in the days following the opening of the trial, some members of the court were still not convinced that there had been an actual attempt to assassinate Atatürk. The prosecutor was not happy with the suggestion voiced by some officials that the entire case was a conspiracy, and he explained in a very demagogic

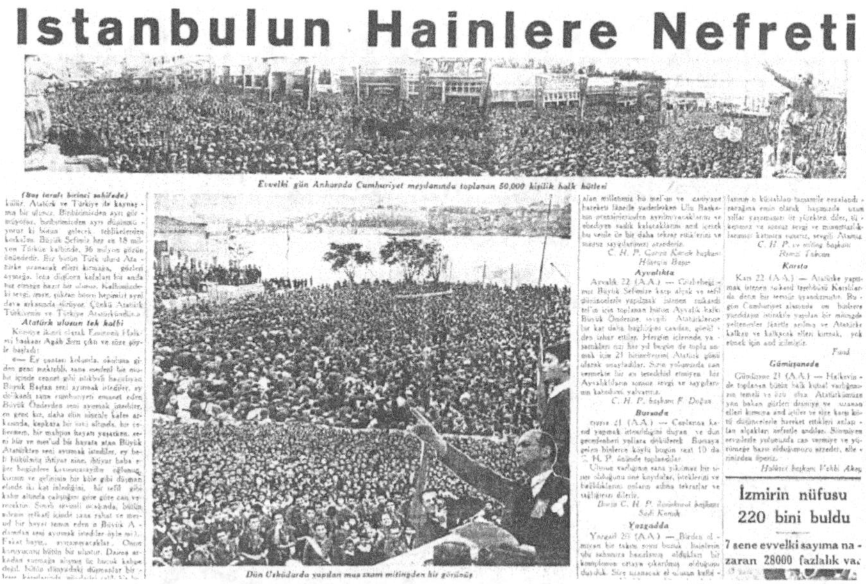

Istanbulun Hainlere Nefreti

Evvelki gün Ankarada Cumhuriyet meydanında toplanan 50,000 kişilik halk kütlesi

Dün Üsküdarda yapılan muazzam mitingden bir görünüş

İzmirin nüfusu 220 bini buldu

7 sene evvelki sayıma nazaran 28000 fazlalık var

Figure 2 *Cumhuriyet* newspaper 24 October 1935. 'Istanbul's Hatred for the Traitors!'

way that the people had not only attempted to take Atatürk's life but also that of the entire Turkish nation, since Atatürk was the soul and representative of the seventeen million people.[124] However, when it came to proving the assassination attempt, the prosecutor was not able to convince the members of the court. At the end of a long judicial process, the trial ended in the acquittal of all the suspects, on 17 February 1936. The reason for the acquittal was a lack of evidence and some suspects' testimony that they had suffered torture at the hands of the police; for instance, one of the suspects Arif told the court that the head of Ankara Police tortured them,[125] and he had therefore agreed with whatever the police had told them to do during the police interrogation. However, during the trial, they did not accept the claims, and at the end of the trial were acquitted.[126]

The trial findings suggest that Ethem and his close circle had always intended to come back to Turkey and overthrow the government and Atatürk. However, over time they had lost their ability to mobilize the people and had insufficient opportunity to gain support either inside or outside of Turkey so as to succeed in realizing their aims. The final serious attempt was carried out by Çerkes Sami in 1927, but he paid for it with his life. Although the Greek government had used them against Turkey for a long time, it was forced by

Figure 3 *Cumhuriyet* newspaper 23 October 1935. 'Villains are being Cursed!'

the Turkish government to deport them from Greece. Towards the end of the 1920s, Ethem and his close circle were no longer allowed to stay in Greece, and any financial support previously extended to them was taken away by the Greek government. As relations improved between the two governments, the Greeks lost their desire to use Ethem and others. On 30 October 1930, Turkey signed

Figure 4 Minorities (Armenians and Jews) made demonstrations for Atatürk! *Son Posta*, 28 October 1935.

Suikast Maznunları
Muhakeme 12 Saat Sürdü, Hüküm Gece 9 da Bildirildi
Maznunlar Kararı Dinlerken Sapsarı İdiler, Neticeyi Anlayınca İçlerinde Sevinçten Ağlıyanlar Oldu

Heyeti Hâkime Maznunların İddia Edilen Suçları İşlediklerine Kanaat Getiremediği Esbabı Mucibesile Hepsinin Beraatine Karar Verdi

Dün beraet eden maznunlar bir arada

Figure 5 Assassination suspects, *Son Posta*, 18 February 1936.

a friendship agreement with Greece. Turkey then demanded the deportation of the 150'ers who had settled in Western Thrace among the Turkish minority in the region. Mustafa Sabri, Gümülcineli İsmail, Aziz Nuri, Sefer Hoca of Eskişehir, İbrahim Sabri, Number 124 Remzi, Number 136 İdris and Number 146 Kasım were deported by the Greek government.[127] Ethem and a group of anti-Kemalists then went to the Middle East to continue their opposition. Although Ethem and his close circle did not have sufficient support to carry out an insurgency and overthrow Atatürk, the idea did not die. It seems that they talked about this topic until the end of their lives, and Turkish Intelligence Services supposed that they posed a potential threat to Atatürk.

The final trial, which took place in 1935, was established by a prosecutor based on exaggerated Turkish Intelligence Service reports; therefore, the court could not find any evidence to sentence the suspects for the assassination attempt. It is worth mentioning here that the language used by the press had dramatically changed by the end of the trial, when the suspects were acquitted by the court. They were called cursed people (*melun*) throughout the trial from their arrest to the end. However, although the press had labelled them guilty before the court made its decision, at the end of the trial, the press addressed its stance, referring to them as merely suspects.[128] The only benefit the regime gained from this trial was that the alleged attempt was turned into a national event; from the east to the west of Turkey, every group either cursed or felt it necessary to be seen to curse those who had allegedly attempted to assassinate their president. Atatürk once more strengthened his position as the symbol of the nation and, either willingly or reluctantly, people came together around him and his statues and in city centres to curse those who attempted to assassinate him.

The single-party period: Reform or repression?

The Kemalists believed that the society should be 'homogeneous' and that the 'religious, social and ethnic identities' should not be visible in the public.[129] A top–down approach adopted that the society should be changed by the direct intervention of the Kemalists who have the right to decide to what clothes people should wear, what music people should listen and what form of religion (Islam) people should believe.[130] With this perspective the Kemalist elites aimed to 'modernize/civilize' the society. Gradually, following the declaration of republic they increased their authority and control on the people, and the nation-building and centralization process was accelerated.

In the Ottoman political system, the lack of ethnic hierarchy protected the ethnic identities from an assertive single ethnic identity's dominance.[131] Hierarchy was based on the religion. The implementation of secularization policies reduced the influence of the role of Islam in the late Ottoman administration, and the abolishment of the caliphate by the republican elites virtually ended the role of Islam in the state.[132] The eradication of the caliphate, which was the guarantor of the existence of several ethnic groups and provider of unity for the Muslims,[133] was a sign of the total elimination of Ottoman multi-ethnic political structure. Although during the Turkish War of Independence the nationalists assured that they would be respectful to 'social and ethnic' norms of all the Muslims,[134] the state following its victory gradually began to deny the existence of non-Turkish Muslim groups in Anatolia. Assimilationist (Turkification) policies were applied. With this, the state hoped that all the Muslim groups would be assimilated in to the Turkish identity.

The Turkish nation-building project was to create 'a modern, central and secular nation state'; by doing this it excluded 'religion, tradition and the periphery'.[135] Moreover, with the law that was passed in 1926, it was made clear that being a member of the Turkish race was a greater privilege than being a state employee.[136] In the 1930s it was publicly announced by some state agency that being of Turkish race was necessary to be accepted for some positions (in the military) and schools in the state.[137] For the assimilation process, the settlement law was also used as an instrument for the demographic redesign of Anatolia.

On 21 July 1934, the settlement law was declared. The law was very detailed and pursued by the Ministry of Interior. According to the law, for the settlements, Turkey was divided into three regions. The first region was left for the people who had Turkish culture (Türk kültürlü) and the second region was prepared for those who adopt Turkish culture, which meant that the region was left for those who had assimilated into Turkish culture. The third region was places which had to be left or kept as empty due to health, financial, cultural, political and military reasons.[138] It is worth emphasizing that the refugee law gave more opportunity to those who were from the Turkish race; however, the settlement law was based on being linked to the Turkish culture. Although race occupied a place in the policies of the state in the early republican period from time to time and policy to policy, it was based on a nation state ideology.[139]

Abolishing the caliphate in March 1924 created a huge disappointment among the religious and Kurdish people.[140] It can be said that the caliphate was like a uniting structure among the Muslims of the state. Kemalist elites did not want to keep the caliphate in the new Turkey since it was like a reminder of the Ottoman past and in the new context of the state the religion (Islam) would not have any role in political life. The establishment of Turkish nation state and the reforms disengaged the 'periphery of the Kurds' from the political centre of the state.[141] As a result of this process Kurdish identity was eliminated from the state discourse. The disengagement between the Kurds and the state and disappointment also led to revolts and rebellions against the regime. Kurds were also seen as the remnants of the Ottoman past by the republican regime since any confrontation against the regime ensured its politicians and bureaucrats remembered the Ottoman era.[142] The regime saw the Kurdish resistance to the centralizations and assimilationist policies of the state as a premodern tribal people's act against the civilization which was provided by the Turkish state.[143]

During the nation-building process the Turkish state used different tools to shape the state and the society. The general inspectorships (Umumi Müfettişlikler) played a significant role in this case. Although they were set up in the time of Abdulhamid II, they re-emerged in the republican era in 1927. The aim of the state by opening the inspectorships again was to create a link between the centre and the periphery by skipping the long bureaucratic process. The general inspectorships consisted of four offices which were established in the south-east of Anatolia, the east of Anatolia, the Black Sea region and in Thrace. The inspectors informed the state centre on a wide range of topics, from agriculture, economy, security, military transportation and border issues to culture, health, trade and smuggling. The Kurdish issue, public and border security and improvement of state facilities were the main areas on which the state focused via inspectorships. It was hoped that the centre through the inspectorships could improve its ties with the periphery and could develop the regions, some of which were heavily underdeveloped.

The ideological approach of the regime was adopted by the inspectorships. The regime's sensitivity on the ban of calling Ezan (call to prayer) in Arabic and prohibition of Kurdish language were pursued by the first inspectorship.[144] In Diyarbakır, hocas were warned again to not call Ezan in Arabic and in Hakkari a group of people who were reading mevlid in Kurdish were captured by the security forces and sent to the court for punishment.[145] The existence of the Kurdish identity was seen as a problem, and it was described by the first inspectorship as 'Kurdishness Issue' (Kürtlük Meselesi). In the report, the inspector first wanted to be sure Ankara would accept the existence of the issue. It was suggested that those who expressed their displeasure at their removal from their villages and houses and pursued armed opposition to the state should be moved by Ankara to Western Turkey.[146] To make the Kurdish pupils familiar with Turkish culture (or to assimilate them) in boarding schools, the children could be picked up from their homes and registered in schools by local rulers, who could use administrative force on the families if they resisted.[147]

In order to eliminate Kurdish identity, the state took some precautions. The Turkish population was to be settled around the railway, sheikhs and agas (tribe leaders who were large land owners) were to be moved to Western Turkey, nomad tribes were to be forced to settle in one place, local and 'Kurdified' (Kürtleşmiş) people were not to be employed, and those who were Turkish, knew Turkish and called themselves Turkish were to be employed as headmen and tax collectors.[148] Furthermore, the state would apply the law against those who spoke any language other than Turkish.[149]

It was also mentioned on the report that Dersim region, which was described as a centre of banditry and Kurdishness, became a peaceful place and it could be called as 'not separated, conquered part of Turkish Republic' after the military operations to the region.[150] According to general inspectorship meeting report, in the first inspectorship region in eight cities the Kurdish population was about 60 per cent, in the third inspectorship in eight cities Kurdish population was about 19 per cent, in the fourth inspectorship population of Kurds was about 56 per cent.[151]

Some of the mostly Kurdish spoken regions and centres of the rebellions were kept under close observation, Palu of Elazığ and Maden of Bingöl.[152] Furthermore, the government took some extra measures to prevent the usage of the Kurdish language. It was suggested by the fourth general inspectorship that the teachers from the Bingöl region should be prevented from working in their own region since they would speak in Kurdish and Zaza (Zazaca) with the pupils in the classroom. It was thought by the inspectorship that allowing teachers to work in their own region would suggest that the government was encouraging the use of the Kurdish language. In order to prevent this impression, the inspectorship wanted the teachers from the Bingöl region to be sent to the western part of Turkey and the teachers from the west of Turkey to be employed in the region.[153]

A) Anti-Kemalist Circassians abroad, and Circassians in Turkey

From the archival resources, it emerges that the Turkish state was wary of the anti-Kemalist Circassians, punishing some and monitoring others. On the one hand, Ankara castigated those anti-Kemalist Circassians who had either moved themselves or had been deported by the Ankara government outside of Turkey in the post-Turkish–Greek War period, removing citizenship from some and prohibiting their return to Turkey. On the other hand, they remained closely monitored by the Turkish Consulates. For instance, a group of Circassians from Predromos village of Karaferya in Greece participated in a celebration of Greek Independence Day in Thessalonica in 25 March 1937.[154] This was considered peculiar by the Turkish consul, since they had been brought to Thessalonica from their own village, some sixty kilometres away, to celebrate independence. He elaborated that they had been removed intentionally by the local Greek rulers and the military. He was irritated by their attitude and therefore insisted that the local Greek governor should receive a warning from the Turkish authorities over this matter.[155]

Hakuç Çerkes Canbolat was from Uzuntarla village of İzmit. He served as a battalion commander and established a bandit group in Midilli at the end of the Turkish–Greek War. After the war, Canbolat moved to Greece, where he became the local governor (*Muhtar*) of Muradlı village of Gümülcine.[156] On 18 April 1925, Canbolat had his Turkish citizenship revoked by the cabinet, since he had worked for the Greek government as a local governor.[157] Çerkes İsmail was another such example. He was a bandit, from Karabacak village of Boğazlıyan, Yozgat, and born in 1889. He had escaped from Turkey to Syria where he worked as an officer in the Circassian unit.[158] İsmail also had his citizenship revoked on 24 July 1930 for violation of the article forbidding Turkish citizens from working in another army without obtaining permission from the government.[159] Çerkes Ethem and his nephew Arslan also suffered the same fate. The cabinet decided that due to their desertion and service for another country their citizenship would be removed. However, in the government order, which was signed by President Mustafa Kemal and the members of the Cabinet, no details were given about Ethem and Arslan's desertion, their activities or under what foreign country they served.[160]

Some changes were made to citizenship law on 23 May 1927. This was named law 1041 (*Şeraiti Muayyeneyi Haiz Olmayan Osmanlı Tebaasının*

Türk Vatandaşlığından İskatı Hakkında Kanun).[161] With this law, an increase in the deprivation of citizenship can be seen. Çerkes Neguç Yusuf Suad from Cedidiye/Düzce saw their citizenship revoked on 3 October 1928 based on this law.[162] Hapaç Çerkes İzzet of Esma Hanım village of Düzce witnessed the same, due to his absence in the Turkish–Greek War and his activities in the post-war period on 3 December 1933.[163] Çerkes Ali Haydar of Esma Hanım village of Düzce participated in the anti-nationalists uprising in Düzce in 1920, leaving Turkey for Bulgaria, where he published the *Dostluk* newspaper against the Kemalist regime. Although he was not on the list of the 150'ers, he did not return to Turkey until 1938. After the amnesty was declared, Ankara softened its policy towards the anti-nationalists. Ali Haydar came to Edirne in 1938 to apply for his return to Turkey. The cabinet determined that he would be allowed to return, but because of his suspicious behaviour, Ali Haydar had to stay in Amasya.[164]

It should be underlined here that due to the activities of the anti-nationalist Circassians, the Circassians of Syria were also monitored by the Turkish Embassy. The Circassian Union was established in Quneytra, with a branch in Damascus. The union concentrated on political matters and charity work.[165] The officers of the Circassian regiment of Syria were also members of the society. Some anti-Kemalist Circassians, such as Nuri Canbolat contacted these Circassians.[166] The activities of this society were viewed seriously by the Turkish government; the president, prime minister, chief of the General Staff, head of the Intelligence Service, and the general secretary of the Republican Party were all informed about the activities of this union, by the Aleppo Consulate of the Ministry of Foreign Affairs of Turkey.[167] The assassination attempt and exaggerations of the activities of some Circassians outside of Turkey such as Çerkes Ethem led to increased pressure on the Circassians by the state in the early republican period.[168] Although Ankara pressurized the Circassians, much as it did other groups in Anatolia, it did not attempt to deport or send the Circassians from Turkey back to the North Caucasus. Moreover, Ankara opposed moves from outside to encourage the Circassians to move to the North Caucasus. A Circassian student in the Al Azhar mosque in Cairo, Yusuf bin Ahmed, prepared a declaration to encourage the Circassians to return to their homeland in the North Caucasus. This declaration was labelled dangerous by the Ankara government and it was banned from circulation inside Turkey.[169]

B) Restrictions on the Circassian identity and language; and the case of the First Miss World from Turkey, Keriman Halis

It is worthy of mention that non-Turks were not permitted to express their ethnic identities in public in the early republican period. One example of this is the case of Circassian 'beauty queen' of Turkey and subsequently the World in 1932, Keriman Halis. Keriman was born and raised in Istanbul in 1913; she was from the Bijnau family who were Circassians.[170] She participated in the Miss Turkey Competition in 1932, after the competition was first organized by *Cumhuriyet* newspaper in 1929.[171] The regime used the organization for several reasons: to emphasize its modernist ideology and show the world that Turkey was a modern country, as well as showing how the Turkish race was beautiful, and how the republican regime had liberated women from 'backward Ottoman male dominant' culture. From 1929 to 1932, three Miss Turkey winners were sent abroad to participate in the Miss World Organization, although none of them could win any titles. In 1932, Keriman Halis was chosen as Miss Turkey and sent to Belgium for the Miss World competition, where at the end of voting the majority of the members of the jury voted for her, and she was chosen as Miss World.

When she gained the title of Miss World, this presented a good opportunity for the republican media and politicians to promote the success of the regime as liberating women and giving them the rights they deserved. Thirty thousand telegrams were sent to Keriman Halis by people to celebrate her success.[172] Her success also suited Mustafa Kemal; he made a statement to the effect that he already knew that the Turkish race was historically one of the most beautiful races in the world; therefore, he found the result entirely understandable. He congratulated both the *Cumhuriyet* and Keriman Halis for showing the whole world the beauty of the Turkish race.[173] It is also ironic that although Keriman Halis was born and raised in Istanbul, her family was originally from the Hacıosman village of Manyas, a Circassian village whose residents were deported by the Ankara government in 1923 for the anti-Kemalist activities of a group of Circassians in the region, as explained in the previous chapter. Despite this, Keriman Halis became the symbol of the modern Turkish race and state, being used by the regime as the 'new face of the modern Turkish woman'.

After she became Miss World, she was in the headlines of the newspapers for more than a month in Turkey. The approach taken by the newspapers is worth emphasizing. One headline in *Cumhuriyet* read 'Turkish Beauty Conquered the

World' (Türk Güzeli Dünyayı Fethetti). Keriman Halis went to France from Belgium, where she was welcomed and a dinner given in her honour by her French hosts. The republican press used this situation to increase nationalist sentiment after the mayor of Deauville/France spoke positively about Turkey. To Turkey's press, Keriman Halis was not only a Miss World, but also a symbol for use on the international stage.[174] Her rejection of a prince's offer of marriage and the British Press's references to her becoming Miss World were also reported in the headlines of the Turkish press in a very interesting way; for them it symbolized 'the east defeating the west for the first time' (İlk defa Şark Garbi mağlup etti). Furthermore, most probably the newspaper exaggerated the situation since Keriman Halis had told the *Cumhuriyet* she had rejected

Figure 6 *Cumhuriyet* newspaper 1 August 1932. 'Miss Turkey Keriman was Chosen as Miss World'

the offer since she would like to marry someone from her own race, which meant someone from the Turkish race.[175] *Akşam* newspaper was upset that the European media did not pay enough attention to the Turkish Miss World since she was representing Turkey. An inferiority complex was clearly at play in *Akşam* blaming the European media for their approach. The newspaper believed that Keriman changed the image of the Turkish woman who was represented in the Western media as someone who lies down on a couch (sedir), eats rose jam (gül reçeli), wears loose trousers (şalvar), fat and barefoot.[176]

When she returned to Turkey, Keriman Halis was welcomed by hundreds of people at Sirkeci train station in Istanbul on 31 August 1932. She was invited to other cities in Turkey and abroad. She travelled around Turkey and visited Egypt on 30 March 1933; however, on this visit something unpredictable happened, of which the Turkish regime did not approve. Although the national media and state propaganda attempted to show her to the world as the progressive face of the Turkish women, race and the revolution, when she visited Egypt it emerged that she was not of Turkish descent but was actually Circassian. At a dinner given in her honour in Cairo she met with a group of Circassians by chance. In the ensuing conversation, she told them that she was

Figure 7 *Cumhuriyet* newspaper 4 August 1932. 'Turkish Girl who Conquered the World!'

Figure 8 *Cumhuriyet* newspaper 3 August 1932. 'The Turkish Girl Who Became Miss World!'

also Circassian. However, her Circassian origins had never been mentioned in public before, as she had always been presented as representing the beauty of the Turkish race and the modern Western face of the Turkish people by the Republican regime. *Al Ahram* newspaper, based in Egypt, published the news of her encounter with the Circassians in Egypt, and her Circassian identity became known to the public.

Figure 9 *Cumhuriyet* newspaper 31 August 1932. 'Thousands of People welcomed Miss World!'

Although Keriman Halis denied the truth of the story in her interview with *Yenigün* magazine (probably fearing further problems with the Turkish regime), she was banned from future public engagements and from attending public events by the republican regime.[177] The *Cumhuriyet* newspaper archives reveal that although there were hundreds of articles and dozens of headlines and pictures about Keriman Halis before she went to Egypt (from 1 August 1932 to 30 March 1933), after her return from Egypt to Turkey on 19 May 1933, there was just a single very small news item on page 3 with no picture, and no welcome ceremony was organized for her.[178] After her visit to Egypt, there was barely any news about her in the media, since the regime did not want her brought to the attention of the public.[179]

During the early Republican era, the Circassians had faced restrictions and pressure from the state. The language issue was a focal point of the struggle between the state and the Circassians. The state aimed to create a unified identity and an official language that had to be Turkish. In rural areas, teachers and officials aimed to control and prevent the expression of non-Turkish mother tongues, but their efforts were unsuccessful. However, despite its limitation in the rural context, in the city centres, the state was very well organized and able to prohibit the publication of materials related to the Circassian language, culture and history, and the use of Circassian in public places. The author Çerkes Mehmed Bey applied to the government and the assembly to register two books on Circassians for copyright. However, his books were categorized as harmful publications (muzır neşriyat) by the government, due to their content. The government determined that the publications would be prohibited and withdrawn from circulation on 1 November 1926.[180] Another example was the Latin alphabet form of the Circassian language, which was prepared and published in Syria, but not allowed by the government within Turkish borders. It was seen as dangerous and officially prohibited by government orders on 9 June 1932.[181]

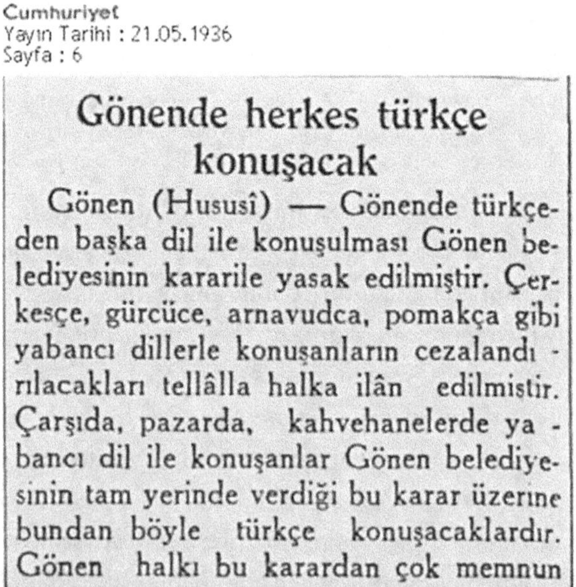

Cumhuriyet
Yayın Tarihi : 21.05.1936
Sayfa : 6

Gönende herkes türkçe konuşacak

Gönen (Hususî) — Gönende türkçeden başka dil ile konuşulması Gönen belediyesinin kararile yasak edilmiştir. Çerkesçe, gürcüce, arnavudca, pomakça gibi yabancı dillerle konuşanların cezalandırılacakları tellâlla halka ilân edilmiştir. Çarşıda, pazarda, kahvehanelerde yabancı dil ile konuşanlar Gönen belediyesinin tam yerinde verdiği bu karar üzerine bundan böyle türkçe konuşacaklardır. Gönen halkı bu karardan çok memnun olmuştur.

Figure 10 It was declared via the *Cumhuriyet* newspaper that the local municipality of Gönen banned speaking in languages other than Turkish. 'In Gönen Everyone will Speak Turkish' 21 May 1936, *Cumhuriyet*.

The declaration of an amnesty for the 150'ers

In 1938, the suggestion that there should be an amnesty for those involved in the activities against the Turkish state came to the forefront of political debate. It was thought that the Turkish Revolution had been successful, and that it would no longer be possible for the 150'ers to become involved in any activities against the Turkish state, since half of them had already died and the other half were not in a position to take further action. The government's proposal of an amnesty was made to reduce the hardship of the family members of the 150'ers.[182] In addition, the people on the list were not able to harm the republican regime or its leaders any longer. They had lost their influence and access to networks that would have allowed them to mobilize the masses against the regime. The majority were ageing, and thus unable to involve themselves in any armed activities against the state or the Kemalists. Only a few still posed a threat to Ankara, and they were not allowed to come back to Turkey; for example Çerkes Ethem, his brother Reşid and Sadullah Sami (number 55 on the list).[183] There was a long discussion in the assembly over the amnesty. Some MPs were completely against it. Emin Sazak of Eskişehir spoke expressing surprise that Celal Bayar's government would pardon the 150'ers.[184] He emphasized that he would like to have seen these people killed, as Ali Kemal had been, that is by lynching; and that he would like to kill them by scratching out their flesh.[185]

Despite the opposition voiced, an amnesty was declared by the government. It was issued for three different categories of people. The first group was the 150'ers. According to the law, these people would still have limited citizenship rights. They were not allowed to receive any salary for their previous service under the Ottoman government, and could not work in the Turkish government for the next eight years; they could work as journalists, but the law did not allow them to become owners or editors of a newspaper.[186] The second group were those sentenced according to the rules of the special council (*Heyeti Mahsusa Kararları*); they would have full citizenship rights, except for in a few areas. They were not permitted to work in government service for the next two years.[187] The final group were those sentenced in the *İstiklal Mahkemeleri* (Independent Tribunal). Twenty-five of these were still in prison. They were pardoned and were to have full citizenship.[188] The minister of justice, Şükrü Saraçoğlu, demanded from MPs that, although he had noted the long discussion and reaction against the 150'ers, they consider their families and children since they had not committed any crimes against the state but rather were victims of their fathers or husbands' mistakes.

Thus, although the Kemalist regime labelled the 150'ers as traitors to the state and did not forgive the members of the list until 1938, after the amnesty was declared in 1938, some of their descendants faced no discrimination by the state. They were able to take on roles as bureaucrats, high-ranking military officers and diplomats. Rıza Tevfik's grandson Deniz Bölükbaşı was a diplomat and an MP from Nationalist Act Party (MHP); Mustafa Madanoğlu's son Cemal Madanoğlu was a general in the Turkish army; Ahmet Refik Bey's (number 20) son was a general director of the state-owned Turkish tobacco and alcoholic beverages company 'TEKEL'; (number 11) Cemal (Keşmir)'s son Halit Nazmi was the minister of finance for the CHP between 1946–48; and, (number 14) Remzi Paşa's son, Şevket Mocan was an MP for the Democrat Party.[189] Therefore, it is possible to claim that once the regime had secured its position, the Kemalists no longer viewed the descendants of the 150'ers as a threat to the state. Moreover, those who no longer had any problems with the regime, even if their fathers and grandfathers had once been 'traitors' for the state, were permitted to hold high bureaucratic and even military positions.

Despite this, a small group of 150'ers continued to be involved in anti-Kemalist activities. Although Ankara was working on the idea of pardoning the 150'ers in 1938, on 5 April 1938, the Turkish government, through its Jerusalem consulate demanded from the king of Jordan, Emir Abdullah, that Ethem and Reşid should end their anti-Atatürk activities.[190] İhsan Tunalı, the Turkish Consul in Jerusalem was sent to Jordan by Ankara to demand from King Abdullah that Ethem should stay in Amman without involving himself in any anti-Ankara activities. Abdullah guaranteed that Ethem would stay in Amman, and that he would come under the observation of both the Jordanian authorities and local Circassians. If he became involved in any activities against Turkey, the king assured him, then all the Circassians would be deported from Jordan.[191] Nevertheless, they established anti-Ankara organizations, including the *Türkiye-Anadolu Yıldırım Komitesi* (Turkey-Anatolia Thunderbolt Committee), in 1938. Celadet Bedirhani, Kürt Emin Broski, Kürt Rifat, Ali Haydar Hoca, Çerkes Reşit, Ethem and his close circle convened the committee.¹⁹² The aim of the organization was to overthrow the Kemalist regime and to establish a state that would provide freedom and equality to its citizens. The religion of the state would be Islam. Turkish written in Arabic script would be the official language. The system of government was to be decided by the assembly.¹⁹³ In May 1941, Ethem attempted to move to Damascus from Amman. However, he was thwarted by the French authorities. Following a demand from Ankara and Amman, Ethem and his friend Emin were arrested for a short time.¹⁹⁴ Later, Ethem went to Aleppo and met with some Circassians there. They included Selahattin Tamuh, Hasan, Çerkes İsmail from Istanbul and some others.¹⁹⁵ After the Second World War started, the meeting focused on the possible German occupation of the Caucasus where Russia was in charge. The Germans promised that if they could occupy the Caucasus, then the Circassians, Georgians and Azerbaijanis would have their own government under a federal state. The main idea of the meeting was to create propaganda to encourage the Circassians of Turkey and Syria to fight with the Germans against Russia for their own government there.¹⁹⁶

It has to be emphasized that in Turkish historiography Ethem has always been portrayed as having rejected the pardon of the Turkish state, since he considered himself not guilty, and did not involve himself in any activities against Atatürk and Kemalists. Moreover, he rejected the idea of returning to Turkey even after the 150'ers had been pardoned. However, the records disprove this. After the amnesty was declared, the Turkish government informed its consulates that Ethem and Reşid should not be permitted Turkish passports and visas. On 11 June 1942, the National Police Directorate asked the prime minister to strip the brothers of their Turkish citizenship.¹⁹⁷ Although this did not happen, Ethem was refused permission to come to Turkey. He applied to the Turkish consulate twice; the first time in 1942 and then again in 1947. Despite his having been pardoned by the state after the amnesty law was passed, he was refused entry to Turkey due to his continued activities against the regime.¹⁹⁸ Among Ethem's brothers, Tevfik was the first person to come to Turkey after the law was passed. However, he faced financial problems: although his family had a mill, two houses and about 580 acres of land in Balıkesir, legal problems meant that he had difficulties reclaiming these assets.¹⁹⁹ After Ethem's death, and Democrat Party came to power, Reşid's son asked President Celal Bayar to allow his father's return to Turkey in 1950. The Ankara governorship allowed

Reşid to return to Turkey on 13 June 1950.[200] Reşid came back to Turkey on 2 September 1950, and settled in his son Hakkı Burcu's house in the Bandırma district of Balıkesir[201]; Reşid died there in September 1951.

The list of 150'ers was prepared to ensure there would be no prospect of armed opposition to the new Turkish state. Therefore, many political names were not included on the list. Some of those, still judged to have the capacity to oversee an armed struggle, such as Çerkes Ethem and the Kuşçubaşı brothers were put on the list, and continued to be very active abroad. Their aim was to start an insurgency in Turkey, overthrowing the government and Mustafa Kemal. They had plans to do so for some time, but only in 1927 did Çerkes Sami's attempt come to fruition. The outcome of the attempt was that Sami and his brother Ahmed were killed, and three others were hanged based on the decision of the Istanbul court's decision. This was the last serious attempt by the 150'ers to oppose the Kemalists and Mustafa Kemal. The attempts also represented an opportunity for the republican regime to gather its citizens around the cult character of the republic, Mustafa Kemal. Citizens clustered together to practise rituals and curse those who had acted against their leader and the republic. These rituals were akin to religious ones. Keriman Halis's becoming Miss World was viewed as a significant opportunity for the republican regime, since she was the true face of modern, liberated face of Turkish woman, which the regime wanted to show the world. Large events were organized to promote and celebrate her success both inside and outside of Turkey. However, when her Circassian origin was made public, she was hidden from public view and her name disappeared from the headlines. From being seen as a model for the new Turkish woman, and the face of the modern republic, she became an undesirable image, due to her ethnic origin. Her case shows that a narrow mindset existed among the early republican policy makers, as they sought to create a homogenous nation from among the very different religious and ethnic groups that remained at the end of the empire. Although Keriman Halis did not suffer from state repression to the extent that anti-Kemalist Circassian military men did, her case still reflects the fact that the Kemalist state had no sympathy for expressions of Circassian identity in the early republican period. When someone committed the error of displaying their non-Turkish ethnic identity in public, as Keriman Halis did, they were banned from public view and lost the praise of the regime.

7

Conclusion

This book aimed at highlighting the transformation of the Ottoman Empire by detailing its progress from empire to nation state through the lens of the paramilitary and political activities of the Circassians from 1918 to 1938. It focused not only on the history of Circassians in Turkey, but also on the major breakpoints of modern Ottoman–Turkish history, including the creation of the Turkish nation state in the post-First-World-War era, by providing a case study of the Circassians. It proposed to demonstrate how one loyal group of subjects in the Ottoman Empire, the Circassians, were forcibly turned into 'loyal Turkish citizens' of the new republic. Some of the dictatorial policies of the early republican rulers denied the different identities of the people, demanding they adopt a Turkish identity. The Circassians were forced to assimilate as the use of non-Turkish languages and other expressions of their identity in public places became prohibited.

The late Ottoman period witnessed breaking points in the empire's history. At the beginning of the second constitutional period in 1908, political matters were excessively discussed within the elite circles of the empire. After a relatively free atmosphere, following the loss of Bosnia, the occupation of Tripolitania by the Italians and the Balkan Wars, the political split gradually became more distinctive. Political divisions increased between the two main political groups, namely the Committee of Union and Progress (CUP) and the Liberal Entente (*Hürriyet ve İtilaf*). Although these differences were sometimes rather superficial, both groups harshly attacked and accused one another over the political decisions taken when the other was in power. In 1913, with the coup against the Sublime Porte and the CUP's taking control over the empire, the opposition was either silenced by force or left the empire. The positions taken by the CUP and Liberal Entente members in the post-First-World-War era were based on the pre-war division between the CUP and the Liberal Entente. This also affected the political atmosphere within the empire. When civil war broke out during the post-First-World-War period between the Istanbul and Ankara governments in 1920 and 1921, those supporting the nationalist cause were close to the CUP and those who supported the Ottoman Porte and the palace were former supporters of the Liberal Entente. The CUP did not have mass support behind it since it was seen by the common people as responsible for the disastrous results of the wars fought in the last decade between 1911 and 1919. Its image in public was already very poor, and it was subject to growing dissent against it.

Like other groups within the empire, the Circassians participated in the civil war on both sides, with some individuals playing significant roles. Anzavur Ahmed and the Adapazarı–Düzce incidents were the first threats that were believed to represent a challenge to the nationalist cause, with the potential to spread anti-nationalist sentiment to Ankara, the nationalist stronghold. The South Marmara and Adapazarı–Düzce Circassians opposed the nationalists due to their ties with the Ottoman Porte and their reaction to the wartime policies of the CUP. Ankara was protected by Çerkes Ethem in the Anzavur, Adapazarı–Düzce, and Çapanoğlu incidents, and he became a nationalist figure as a result. However, the growing power of Ethem caused problems between him and his brothers and between him and the executives of the nationalist cause, Mustafa Kemal, İsmet (İnönü) and Refet (Bele). Ethem was a useful paramilitary fighter from the perspective of Ankara, as his forces had preserved Ankara three times from palpable threats. However, the regular army in Ankara was slowly becoming stronger as soldiers and military equipment were transferred from the eastern front, and Bolshevik military and financial support poured in to strengthen the regular army. Following his disagreements with the nationalists, however, Ethem was excluded from the nationalist circle at the end of December 1920.

Ever since the Anzavur and Adapazarı–Düzce incidents, a group of Circassians in Western Anatolia opposed the nationalists. With the exclusion of Ethem and the expansion of the nationalists into the İzmit region in 1921, a group of Circassians altered their pro-Istanbul policy to collaborate with Greek forces. Under Çule İbrahim Hakkı's leadership, they aimed to create a form of Circassian nationalism that would distinguish them from both the

Istanbul and Ankara governments. They declared autonomy in the Greek-occupied city of İzmir via a congress. However, their call for autonomy was supported by only a very small group of Circassians, certainly not the majority. This act was done by a very small, third group of Circassians in Anatolia, positioned ideologically alongside the nationalist (pro-Ankara) and loyalist (pro-Istanbul) camps.

In the post-Turkish-Greek War period (1922–23), the Ankara government was unable to gain control over the South Marmara region. Armed Circassian groups were the main security threat to the Ankara government at this time. Some of those close to Çerkes Ethem, such as Takığ Şevket, and some other opponents of Ankara, such as Kuşçubaşı Eşref, aimed at creating chaos and insurgency in the region to achieve their ultimate aim of overthrowing the Ankara government and Mustafa Kemal. During 1923, the group continued its opposition from the Greek islands in the Aegean Sea. Chaos was widespread in Western Anatolia because of the activities of the Circassians and other groups. Considering the significant Circassian population in the region, proportionally a very limited number joined them. However, Ankara took the radical decision to deport the Circassians in the region to eastern and central parts of Anatolia. This was a decision that took the form of a collective punishment for thousands. Although they were allowed to come back to their homes a few years later, the catastrophic impact of the deportation is still felt.

Furthermore, Ankara took its revenge not only by deporting entire villages, but also by preparing a list of 'traitors', that is its wartime opponents. They were also deported from Turkey, and their citizenship revoked. Some members of this group, such as Çerkes Ethem, Sami and Eşref, planned and attempted to assassinate Mustafa Kemal, overthrow the government, and then return to Turkey. Their distrust of Mustafa Kemal was more personal than ideological; they were upset that Mustafa Kemal had excluded them from the nationalist cause in order to seize control of the national movement and had not allowed their respected leader, Enver Pasha, to return to Anatolia. On the other hand, the opposition in the post-1923 period provided an opportunity for the republican regime to solidify its power over the people. The protests against those who attempted assassinations became a nationalist ritual, whereby citizens of the young republic came together in the squares around statues of Atatürk to 'curse the traitors'.

One could ask two questions at this juncture: first, why had the Circassians resisted the Kemalists from the Turkish War of Independence period to the creation of Turkish nation state? And secondly, why did they not face similar pressure and violence as Kurds suffered in the early republican period? After the exodus of Circassians to the Ottoman land they were seen as trusted new settlers by the state. Despite the fact that it is not that simple to claim that the Ottoman state had a well-working settlement plan for them, they were, whether intentionally or not, settled in very problematic areas of the empire from the Balkans to Western and Central Anatolia, Diyarbekir, Bitlis, Golan Heights, Vadi-i Rum (today's Amman). Although they faced many difficulties during the exodus and afterwards, such as epidemic and famine, they did not see the Ottoman state as responsible for their tragedy. The state also did not see them as a source of problem.

Some of the Circassian elites already had a close relationship with the Ottoman state before the refugees entered the Ottoman state. They thus integrated themselves in the state and became a state apparatus. Within fifty to sixty years after their exile from the North Caucasus to the Ottoman Empire, the Circassian elites were accommodated within the state. They became the hanım sultan (the mother of Padişah), Paşa, head of army and relatives of the Ottoman Hanedan by marriage – particularly the mother of the last three Ottoman sultans and some of their wives were Circassian. All this led to a privileged position for the Circassian elites in Istanbul more than any other group had at the time. All these created a mutual relationship wherein both sides, the state and the Circassian elites, benefited. The elites held a privileged status due to their rights within the Ottoman household. As mentioned in the Introduction, it was due to this close link that they became one of the first groups that had obtained the right to open a Circassian school in the empire in the post-constitutional revolution era in 1911. Some Circassian elites supported the Ottoman government and the sultan/caliph first against the *Ittihat ve Terakki* and then the *Kuva-yi Milliye* and the Kemalists.

As to the second question – why the Circassians did not face the same level of pressure as the Kurds in the early republican period – although some of the elite Circassians did not support the Kemalist movement and backed the sultan and the Istanbul governments, a group of Circassian military men, bureaucrats and politicians were in the *Kuva-yi Milliye* and Anatolian movement from the beginning. Some of the names were Rauf (Orbay), Bekir Sami (Günsav), Bekir Sami (Kunduh), Yusuf İzzet Paşa, Cemil Cahit (Toydemir) and Emir Marşan Paşa. One could argue that those high-level statesmen and low-level Circassian people in the bureaucracy prevented the state from using force against the Circassians. As it was seen in the previous chapter, when the Ankara government deported the Circassians in the Edremit Region in 1922, Rauf Orbay was a prime minister then and warned the local governor and security officers to be sensitive towards the people. Although the Circassians were deported in very poor conditions, there was no killing and massacre reported at the time.

It can be said that the Circassians lost their unique position in the state in the post-Ottoman period. However, it did not make them the same as the other non-Turkish groups in Turkey. They were not seen as a sub-human group who had to be modernized by the regime as had been the case in the Dersim issue. The Circassians were not densely populated in one region as Kurds in the south-east of Turkey. Furthermore, it is worth mentioning that the existence of some Circassians in the top echelons of the Republican People Party (CHP) management (the ruling party of the single part era) stopped the state from oppressing the Circassian population further. Although they were not in the position of decision makers, it could be said that they were in a position to connect the Circassians with the state. For instance, the general secretary of 1942, Ahmet Fikri Tüzer, and some of the MPs of the time, were of Circassian origin.[1] Therefore, the state did not see ordinary Circassians to be as dangerous as the Kurds in the early republican period.

Although they resisted against the Ankara government in the civil war period due to their connection with the Ottoman sultanate and caliphate, with the conclusion of the civil war the armed Circassian resistance ended. Despite the fact that they had armed people in the army, relatives in the Ottoman household and agents in the Special Organization, it was not an easy task to pursue their resistance to the Kemalists since they were as a group latecomers to Anatolia. They had spent only about sixty to seventy years since their arrival in Anatolia as compared to the hundreds of years of the Kurds' and Turks' existence there. Hence the resistance of the Kurds and the Turks were much more troublesome for the state than Circassians. Only a group of former Circassian Special Organization insurgents and militias, such as

Çerkes Sami and Ethem, continued their opposition and fight against the Ankara government.

Before the single-party regime was established, Turkey missed the huge opportunity to create a state for everyone. While there was a pluralistic structure to the first assembly (1920),[2] its MPs were from a variety of backgrounds, from ulema to notables, bureaucrats and high-ranking military personnel. Although the government encountered difficulties making decisions due to the frequent and lengthy discussions between the different groups in the assembly, the pluralistic structure had to be maintained, since the government required the support of the masses. During the Turkish–Greek War, Mustafa Kemal gradually assumed a dominant, authoritarian position, as an extension of the rights extended to him as commander-in-chief, head of the Assembly and the government (which gave him the right to choose who was going to be an MP).[3] With the defeat of the Greeks (1922), the Kemalists, and especially Mustafa Kemal, did not wish to sustain a pluralistic structure, since opposition was seen as an obstacle preventing them from modernizing the country.

The Kemalist modernist project was not built on pluralism, but rather applied top–down policies to create a nation state. Therefore, the opposition groups were gradually purged from political life and the basis of an authoritarian political system was set down, creating the cult of a powerful leader in the early republican period that has endured in Turkish political life ever since. Although there were developments in the early republican era in social and cultural areas, this type of rule strengthened anti-democratic political culture in Turkish political life.[4] The apparatus of the state was employed as a tool to shape the citizens of the republic. Through bureaucracy, the military and education, the state not only aimed at transforming itself but also at transforming its citizens by interrupting daily life and making decisions for them in terms of the clothes they wore, what books they read, how they should look and what they should think. These things could only be decided by the state.

During the nation-building process (as Anthony Smith emphasizes, 'the homeland becomes a repository of historic memories and associations'),[5] the existence of Circassians displeased the Kemalists. They were like a reminder of the multicultural, multilingual and multi-ethnic past of the Ottoman state and society. They were seen as an obstacle to creating a homogenous nation. To solve the problem they had to be assimilated into Turkish identity. This approach led to the exclusion of some people from the centre by the elites, who held the state apparatus in their hands. Although society had always been diverse, the new state was based on the Kemalist ideology, which, as we have seen in this book, prohibited its citizens from expressing different identities – for instance, through the use of their mother tongues – in public. Due to the oppressive policies in the early republican period, many people were not considered 'true citizens' of the republic. The state was not based on the values of the people; rather, it imposed its own values on the people by force.

Similar to the other citizens of Turkey, the Circassians were restricted by the regime in terms of using their mother tongue and expressing their identities in public. Indeed, it must be underlined that these topics were not openly discussed until the 2000s, either in the Circassian community or in academic circles. The elder Circassians who lived through this catastrophic period preferred to forget what they had experienced, choosing not to mention it to the younger generations. When they spoke about these topics with their friends, any children present were ordered out of the room by the elders.[6]

Another reason for the forgetting of the past was the reconciliation that took place between the Circassians and the state. The Circassians did not suffer from the single party regime as much as other groups within the country. With multiparty elections in 1950, for example, and the coming to power of the Democrat Party, a reconciliation process began between the state and Circassians. The negative image the state had towards the Circassians in the 1920s and 1930s gradually disappeared. Cold War politics also helped to change this image. Turkey and the Soviet Union were on opposite sides, and the latter was now both the 'enemy' of the Turkish state and the Circassians.

The Turkish state and many Circassians also had mutual interests against Soviet Russia. Turkey developed a good relationship with the North Caucasian emigrants who entered Turkey after the collapse of the North Caucasian Republic, from the early 1920s up until the 1970s as part of its foreign policy against Soviet Russia. Due to this relationship between the North Caucasian emigrants and the Turkish state, the latter extended a privileged status to the North Caucasian political emigrants.[7] Although the single-party regime oppressed the Circassians of Turkey, it did not affect the foreign policy agenda, which supported the North Caucasian emigrants. This was a win-win situation for both the Turkish state and the North Caucasian emigrants. While Turkey used the emigrants for its foreign policy, it was used by them as a safe haven in their struggle against Soviet Russia. The emigrants were supported by Turkey in terms of their publications and political mobilization, and in establishing political networks with other Circassian associations in Europe.[8]

In terms of using the emigrants effectively, the Ministry of Foreign Affairs and the military, police and intelligence services worked in coordination.[9] From the 1920s until the end of the 1930s, Turkey was much more independent in terms of creating policy and using emigrants. In 1925, Istanbul was seen as a centre for emigrants by Russia, and thus represented an opportunity to strengthen its own network via intelligence agents.[10] From late 1930 to the mid-1940s onwards, Turkey worked with Great Britain, France, Poland and later Germany against Russia.[11] Although the Circassians had difficulties with the Turkish nation state in the first two decades of the regime, aside from a few minority groups of Circassians, even the anti-Kemalist Circassians had never aimed at establishing an independent state. They fought against Mustafa Kemal and his single-party regime and tried to overthrow it, with the aim of replacing it with a more pluralistic one. They never had fundamental problems with the other peoples living in Anatolia. One can argue that despite some problems in the early republican period, the Circassians did not have an especially negative impact both on the state and society. Therefore, one might also claim that with the arrival of these latest emigrants, the Circassians were given a little bit more freedom, being allowed officially by the state to open the first non-Turkish community association in modern republican history with the Azerbaijanis of Turkey, namely the 'Dost Eli Yardımlaşma Derneği' in 1946.[12] Furthermore, from the intelligence service to the military, the Circassians were not restricted in Turkey and played a role in these state departments post-1950.

Another important topic covered in this book in relation to Circassians in the republican era was the Çerkes Ethem incident. Although a limited reconciliation occurred between the Circassians and the Turkish state in the post 1950s era, the issue of Çerkes Ethem was an ambiguous topic for Circassians. On the one hand, while Çerkes Ethem did not represent all the Circassians in Turkey, and not all Circassians supported him, he nevertheless became a symbol for the Circassians. He was introduced to pupils in schools as a traitor, something that persists in the official curriculum until today. Although there are plenty of interpretations of his life, school texts still rely on Atatürk's *Nutuk*, in which Atatürk accuses Ethem of being an agent who worked for himself and the interests of the other states.

On the other hand, Ethem elsewhere came to have a very positive meaning for some Circassians, especially those who felt themselves close to republican Turkey and were proud of Ethem for having suppressed three very significant incidents, which had saved Ankara from defeat at the hands of anti-nationalists. Indeed, this became part of a newly imagined Circassian identity, which took pride in one of its own having responsible for founding modern Turkey and in the significant numbers of high-ranking soldiers and bureaucrats who participated in the nationalist struggle to fight against the occupation. Ethem's suppression of the incidents strengthened this narrative and became a founding element of Turkey. They used Ethem to prove their 'loyalty' to the Turkish state and its values, but only focused on his early activities from 1919 to December 1920, ignoring his later exclusion from the nationalist circle. The activities post-December 1920 were not considered, since they were seen as too complex and damaging to Ethem's image as a saviour of Turkey, rather than as an assassin or insurgency leader aiming to overthrow Mustafa Kemal.

However, what is interesting here is that the Circassians prefer not to recall that the majority of Circassians were loyal to the sultan/caliph, as were the majority of Anatolia's peoples. This group rose against the nationalists since they did not want to be engaged in war any longer; indeed, they were very war-weary by this time. Furthermore, a group of Circassians, the majority of whom were former Ottoman soldiers and agents, aimed at creating an insurgency in Turkey in opposition to the Kemalists. One of the reasons for the problems noted is that Ethem's life was not evaluated from beginning to end. Some groups and people used part of his life to support their own arguments, either claiming that he was a 'hero', or the reverse, that he was a 'traitor'. This approach also dominates Turkish academia, and there is not yet a well-documented and balanced book or thesis relating to him written in Turkish.[13]

Although some authors believe that very few people still spoke their languages by the 1920s,[14] this doesn't seem to be true. Most of the population used to live in the rural parts of the country until the 1980s. While the Turkish state tried to prevent the use of non-Turkish languages in public, it was not possible for the state to control every village and town in Anatolia. Even in the schools, teachers usually forced their students to speak Turkish in the classroom and in their houses, but they could not prevent their students from speaking their native languages in private places. However, with the increasing urbanization of the population, these languages are being spoken less and less.

Undoubtedly, the Circassians suffered from state oppression in the early republican period, but their suffering was in fact much less when compared to that of the Kurds and other minority groups. However, they did suffer from oppression by the state in ideological terms, as a response to their closeness to the Ottoman state, especially the harem and the military and intelligence services, and because of the Çerkes Ethem incident. For high-ranking Kemalists, politicians and statesman in the early republican period, Circassian identity was associated with either 'backwardness', the Ottoman state or the 'traitor' Çerkes Ethem. They were seen by the republican elites as a reminder of the bad old days of the Ottoman Empire and the civil war between the Ankara and Istanbul governments. On the other hand, because the Circassian population lived in rural areas and villages, their oppression by the state did not result in full assimilation or adoption of the new Turkish identity being promoted in the republican era. Indeed, the Turkish state was not sufficiently well organized to interrupt the daily life of the rural population, and so the Circassians continued to live very close to their own ethnic kin, practising inter-Circassian marriage widely.

It can be argued that the urbanization of the Circassian population after the 1950s had a huge impact on the assimilation of Circassian identity – even more so than the policies of the Kemalists in the early republican period. Prior to this, the Circassians lived in villages where they were isolated from the centre and their identity was protected from the assimilationist policies of the Kemalism. However, with the higher rates of urbanization, the influence of the Kemalist nation state ideology increased on the Circassians because of their increasing interaction with the state in urban life. Thus, when the Kemalist regime was most oppressive, between the 1920s, 1930s and 1940s, the Circassian identity was less affected by its policies, since the Turkish state could no longer control the rural areas as effectively as the urban ones. However, although the Turkish state had begun to be less oppressive from the 1950s onwards, preventing the Circassian identity from assimilation was much more difficult than it had been in the previous period, since the Circassians moved to the cities and were educated en masse under the doctrines of a kind of repressive nation state ideology.

Notes

Chapter 1

1. http://www.cerkesarastirmalari.org/org/cerkesler.
2. See Walter Richmond, *The Circassian Genocide* (New Brunswick: Rutgers University Press, 2013). Justin McCarthy, *Death and Exile: The Ethnic Cleansing of Ottoman Muslims 1821–1922* (Princeton: Darwin Press, 1995). Kemal H. Karpat, 'The Status of the Muslim under European Rule: The Eviction and Settlement of the Çerkes', in *Studies on Ottoman Social and Political History: Selected Articles and Essays by Kemal Karpat*, ed. Kemal Karpat (Leiden: Brill, 2002), 647–75.
3. Circassians were settled from the Balkans to Western, Central and Eastern Anatolia, Diyarbekir, Bitlis, Golan Heights, Vadi-i Rum (today's Amman) by the Ottoman state.
4. Richmond, *The Circassian Genocide*, Genocide, Political Violence, Human Rights Series.
5. Ibid., 8.
6. Ibid., 13.
7. Ibid., 54.
8. Ibid., 18. The overall situation was also described by Russian officers in the following manner: '*Mankind has rarely experienced such disasters and such extremes, but only horror could have an effect on the hostile mountaineers and drive them from the impenetrable mountain thickets.*' p. 54, endnote 1.
9. Benjamin C. Fortna, *The Circassian: A Life of Eşref Bey, Late Ottoman Insurgent and Special Agent* (London: Hurst & Company, 2016), 13.
10. There were number of Abkhazians in the *Çerkes İttihat ve Teavün Cemiyeti* and *Şark-ı Karip Çerkesleri Temini Hukuk Cemiyeti*. It could be seen that to make a clear statement on this terminology was very difficult.
11. Nuri Güçtekin, 'Çerkes Teavün Mektebi (1910-1914)', *Yakın Dönem Türkiye Araştırmaları* 12, no. 23 (2013): 1–21.
12. The term 'Turkish War of Independence' is used by academics and historians in the Turkish context for the wars between Turkish troops and the Allies, Greeks

and Armenians during the 1919–22 period. I will use the words 'Turkish–Greek War of 1919–22' to refer to the western front of the Turkish War of Independence.
13 The CUP was established as a secret society in 1889 and later became a political party (1906). It governed the empire after the military coup of 1913 until 1918.
14 CUP members and its ideology remained influential until the 1950s, though they were gradually replaced by the Kemalists and Kemalism, particularly after the assassination attempt (the so-called 'İzmir Conspiracy') against Mustafa Kemal in 1926. The first three presidents of the country – Mustafa Kemal Atatürk, İsmet İnönü and Celal Bayar–were all one-time members of the CUP.
15 Fikret Başkaya, *Paradigmanın İflası: Resmi İdeolojinin Eleştirisine Giriş: Batılılaşma, Kalkınma, çağdaşlaşma* (İstanbul: Özgür Üniversite, 2012).
16 'Atatürk'ün cenaze namazı, gazeteciye 15 ay hapis cezasına mal oldu' 21 April 2004. http://webarsiv.hurriyet.com.tr/2004/04/21/446534.asp, accessed 21 August 2015.
17 Erik Jan Zürcher, *The Unionist Factor: The Role of the Committee of Union and Progress in the Turkish National Movement, 1905-1926* (Leiden: Brill, 1984). Ryan Gingeras, 'Notorious Subjects, Invisible Citizens: North Caucasian Resistance to the Turkish National Movement in Northwestern Anatolia, 1919–23', *International Journal of Middle East Studies* 40, no. 1 (February 2008): 89–108. Ryan Gingeras, *Sorrowful Shores: Violence, Ethnicity, and the End of the Ottoman Empire, 1912-1923*, Oxford Studies in Modern European History (Oxford; New York: Oxford University Press, 2009). Ryan Gingeras, 'Last Rites for a "Pure Outlaw": Clandestine Service, Historiography and the Origins of the Turkish "Deep State"', *Past and Present*, no. 206 (February 2010): 121–44. Ryan Gingeras, 'The Sons of Two Fatherlands: Turkey, the Soviet Union and the North Caucasian Diaspora, 1918-1923' *European Journal of Turkish Studies [Online]* (2011): 3, 4. Zeynel Abidin Besleney, *The Circassian Diaspora in Turkey: A Political History*, Routledge Studies in Middle Eastern Politics (London: Routledge, 2014). Fortna, *The Circassian*.
18 'Loyalists' are those who were on the side of the sultan/caliph and the Istanbul government. 'Nationalists' or 'Kemalists' are those who supported the movement based in Anatolia and who fought against the Greek occupation. However, Kemalism in that period as a term did not have any secularist and/or authoritarian meanings; these meanings emerged after 1927.
19 Nicholas Sambanis, 'Partition as a Solution to Ethnic War: An Empirical Critique of the Theoretical Literature', *World Politics* 52, no. 4 (July 2000), downloaded from http://muse.jhu.edu/journals/wp/summary/v052/52.4sambanis.html on 9 August 2013, 444.

20 Ibid.
21 Ibid.
22 Ibid.
23 Ibid.
24 J. F. N. Bradley, *Civil War in Russia 1917-1920* (London: BT Batsford, 1975), Peter Holquist, *Making War, Forging Revolution; Russia's Continuum of Crisis 1914-1921* (Cambridge: Harvard University Press, 2002), V. P. Butt, A. B. Murphy and N. A. Myshov, *The Russian Civil War; Documents from the Soviet Archieves* (London: Macmillan Press, 1996) Also see the other important books on the topic; Evan Mawdsley, *The Russian Civil War* (Edinburg: Birlinn Limited, 2008). Geoffrey Swain, *Russia's Civil War* (Gloucestershire: Tempus, 2000).
25 Group of Circassians attempted to set up an autonomous state under the Greek rule in 1922. See Chapter 5.
26 This is known as the 'Fourteen Points' declared by the then president of United States, Woodrow Wilson, in 1918. Article 12 mentions self-determination for non-Turkish people of the Ottoman Empire. See http://avalon.law.yale.edu/20th_century/wilson14.asp.
27 *Kuva-yi Milliye* means 'national forces', the irregular troops of the Ankara government. I also use nationalist, Anatolian movement and resistance movement to refer to that. They generally comprised of irregular troops, paramilitary groups and bandits. They were used by the nationalists (after April 1920, the Great Assembly of Ankara) against loyalists and the Greek occupation. The conflict between loyalists and the *Kuva-yi Milliye* has been regarded as 'infighting' rather than a civil war in Turkish republican historiography. On the other hand, anti-*Kuva-yi Milliye* (anti-nationalists) refer to those people who were loyal to the sultan/caliph in Istanbul. However, in the beginning, Ankara government, especially Mustafa Kemal, attempted to convince people by saying that they were not against the sultan and the caliphate.
28 Rauf Orbay (1881–1964) was of Abkhazian descent. He was a former minister of navy and a leading figure in the Circassian cell in Istanbul. The cell organized the participation of Circassians in the national struggle.
29 1867–1933, comes from a notable Osetian family. He was educated in Galatasaray and was a diplomat and first ministry of foreign affairs of the Anatolian movement/Turkey.
30 He was born in Bandırma/Balıkkesir (1879–1934), of Circassian descent. During the Turkish–Greek War, from 1918 to 1920 he was stationed in Bandırma as a colonel. Muhittin Ünal, *Miralay Bekir Sami Günsav'ın Kurtuluş Savaşı Anıları*

(İstanbul: Cem Yayınları, 1993). Muhittin Ünal, 56. *Fırka Harb Ceridelerinden Miralay Bekir Sami Günsav'ın Kurtuluş Savaşı Anıları 1919-1920* (Ankara: Türk Tarih Kurumu, 2016).

31 (Met, Janutuko) Yusuf İzzet Paşa (1876–1922): A Circassian major general of the nationalist forces. He was in charge of the 14th army corps.

32 (1880–1952), Abkhazian MP of Saruhan for the National Assembly. He was one of those was participated in the national movement from the beginning.

33 (1883–1956) Circassian general, he served in the Libyan, Balkan, First World War and War of Independence.

34 Charles Tilly, 'War Making and State Making as Organized Crime', in *The State: Critical Concepts*, ed. John A. Hall (New York: Routledge, 1994), 519.

35 Anthony D. Smith, *National Identity* (Las Vegas: University of Nevada Press, 1991), viii.

36 Mehmet Beşikçi, *The Ottoman Mobilisation of Manpower in the First World War; Between Voluntarism and Resistance* (Leiden: Brill, 2012). Yücel Yanıkdağ, *'Ill-Fated' Son of the 'Nation': The Ottoman Prisoners of War in Russia and Egypt, 1914-1922* (Unpublished PhD thesis, The Ohio State University, 2002). Yücel Yanıkdağ, 'Ottoman Prisoners of War in Russia, 1914-1922', *Journal of Contemporary History* 34, no. 1 (January 1999): 69–85.

37 Gingeras, *Sorrowful Shores*.

38 'The original (Italian) meaning of bandito is a man "placed outside the law" for whatever reasons, though it is not surprising that outlaws easily became robbers.' E. J. 1917–2012 Hobsbawm, *Bandits*, new edn (London: Abacus, 2001), 12.

39 He was a former agent in the Ottoman Special Organization, one of the leading paramilitary leaders in South Marmara in the days following the First World War, of Circassian descent, born in Emreköy/Balıkesir (1886–1950).

40 Sabri Yetkin, *Ege'de Eşkıyalar*, Tarih Vakfı Yurt Yayınları (Beşiktaş, İstanbul: Türkiye Ekonomik ve Toplumsal Tarih Vakfı, 1996). He was born in İzmir, 1872.

41 Ibid., 92.

42 Anzavur Ahmed (1885–1921) was a Circassian and a member of the Ottoman Special Organization (*Teşkilat-ı Mahsusa*) during the First World War; his name was proposed by (Met, Janutuko) Yusuf İzzet Paşa and Çerkes Üzeyir Bey to the Special Organization. See Semih Nafiz Tansu, *Cumhuriyet Newspaper,* 31 July 1956. 2 Later on, he was made a Paşa by Damat Ferid government in March 1920.

43 Kuşçubaşı Eşref Sencer, 1873–1964. Circassian descent. He was an agent in the Ottoman Special Organization (*Teşkilatı Mahsusa*). In the early days of the Turkish War of Independence he worked for the nationalists and then moved to the opposite side. Fortna, *The Circassian*.

44 He was also known as Çerkes Sami or Kuşçubaşı Sami. He was brother of Kuşçubaşı Eşref, and member of the Ottoman Special Organization. He was killed in a skirmish in Aydın by the gendarme in 1927.
45 Yetkin, *Ege'de Eşkıyalar*, 178.
46 South Marmara is to the south of the Marmara Sea and includes the provinces of Kale-i Sultani, Hüdavendigar and Karesi. Today the term refers to Bursa, Balıkesir and Çanakkale.
47 Gazi Mustafa Kemal (Atatürk), *Nutuk* (Ankara: Türk Tarih Kurumu Basımevi, 1981). Suna Kili, *Kemalism* (Istanbul: School of Business Administration and Economics, Robert College, 1969). Munis Tekinalp, *Kemalizm* (İstanbul: Cumhuriyet Gazete ve Matbaası, 1936). Doğu Ergil, *Milli Mücadelenin Sosyal Tarihi* (Ankara: Turhan Kitabevi, 1981). Anıl Çeçen, *100 Soruda Kemalizm* (İstanbul: Kilit Yayıncılık, 2009).
48 Zürcher, *The Unionist Factor*, 106-17.
49 Nationalists or later on 'Kemalists' are those who supported the movement against the Greek occupation and who were based in Anatolia. However, Kemalism in that period as a term did not have any secularist and authoritarian meanings; these features were taken after 1927.
50 Rahmi Apak, *İstiklal Savaşında Garp Cephesi Nasıl Kuruldu* (İstanbul: Güven Basımevi, 1942), 88-9. Miralay Mehmet Arif Bey, *Anadolu İnkılabı (Mücahedat-ı Milliye Hatıratı 1335-1339)*, ed. Bülent Demirbaş (İstanbul: Arba, 1987).
51 Apak, *İstiklal Savaşında Garp Cephesi Nasıl Kuruldu*, 88-9.
52 Ibid., 88-9.
53 Foti Benlisoy, *Kahramanlar Kurbanlar Direnişçiler Trakya ve Anadolu'daki Yunan Ordusunda Propaganda, Grev ve İsyan (1919 - 1922)* (İstanbul: İstos Yayınevi, 2014), 10, 12, 13.
54 Ibid., 10.
55 Ibid.
56 Particularly, Shapsug and Ubikh tribes fought the Russians until the end of the war. Richmond, *The Circassian Genocide*, 71. It is worthy of mention that two prominent characters in this book were Çerkes Ethem and Kuşçubaşı Eşref, who belonged to the Shapsug and Ubikh tribes respectively. *The Circassian Genocide*, 71.
57 Walter Richmond, *The Northwest Caucasus; Past, Present, Future* (London: Routledge, 2008), 21. Also, for the impact of the class structure in the diaspora, see Eiji Miyazawa, *Memory Politics; Circassians of Uzunyayla, Turkey* (Unpublished PhD thesis, SOAS University of London, ND.)
58 Gingeras, 'The Sons of Two Fatherlands'.

59 Ehud R. Toledano, 'Ottoman Concepts of Slavery in the Period of Reform (1830s-1880s)', in *Breaking the Chains: Slavery, Bondage and Emancipation in Modern Africa and Asia*, ed. Martin A. Klein (Madison: University of Wisconsin Press, 1993), 44.

60 Ryan Scott Gingeras, 'Imperial Killing Fields: Revolution, Ethnicity and Islam in Western Anatolia, 1913–1938' (PhD Thesis, University of Toronto, 2006), 42.

61 Ibid., 48.

62 Michael A. Reynolds, *Shattering Empires: The Clash and Collapse of the Ottoman and Russian Empires, 1908-1918 /* (Cambridge, UK; New York: Cambridge University Press, 2011), 121, Please see a detailed work on the *Teşkilat-ı Mahsusa*, Polat Safi, 'The Ottoman Special Organization – Teşkilat-ı Mahsusa: An Inquiry into Its Operational and Administrative Characteristics' (Unpublished PhD Thesis, Bilkent University, 2012).

63 Fortna, *The Circassian*, 5.

64 Reynolds, *Shattering Empires*, 121.

65 Fortna, *The Circassian*, 16.

66 Gingeras, 'Imperial Killing Fields', 182–3.

67 There were a number of Circassians in the Special Organization during the First World War; however, after the war, a significant number of them took the Ottoman government's side against the nationalists. Gönenli Çerkes Bekir Sıtkı Bey, Anzavur Ahmed, Düzceli Çerkes Maan Ali Bey, Gendarme lieutenant Çerkes Mustafa Bey, Çerkes Ethem, Reşid and Tevfik Beys, Istanbullu Çerkes lieutenant Çerkes Sadeddin Bey, Gönenli Çerkes Ahmed Bey, Gönenli Çakır Efe, Major Tophaneli Çerkes Hüseyin Bey, Kadıköylü Çerkes Agah Bey, Gönenli Ahmed Bey, see Semih Nafiz Tansu, *Cumhuriyet*, 31 July 1956, 2.

68 Sefer Berzeg, *Türkiye Kurtuluş Savaşı'nda Çerkes Göçmenleri (II)* (İstanbul: Nart Yayıncılık, 1990); Muhittin Ünal, *Kurtuluş Savaşında Çerkeslerin Rolü* (İstanbul: Cem Yayınevi, 1996).

69 Çerkes Ethem, *Anılarım* (İstanbul: Berfin Yayınları, 2005), Emrah Cilasun, *Baki İlk Selam* (İstanbul: Agora Kitaplığı, 2009). Ahmet Efe, *Çerkes Ethem* (İstanbul: Bengi Kitap Yayın, 2009), Cemal Şener, *Çerkes Ethem Olayı* (İstanbul: Altın Kitaplar, 2007), Zeki Sarıhan, *Çerkes Ethem İhaneti* (İstanbul: Kaynak Yayınları, 1998). Uluğ İğdemir, *Biga ayaklanması ve Anzavur olayları: günlük anılar* (Ankara: Türk Tarih Kurumu Basımevi, 1973). Gingeras, 'Notorious Subjects, Invisible Citizens'.

70 Ahmet Insel (ed.), *Modern Türkiye'de Siyasi Düşünce Cilt 2 / Kemalizm (Ciltli)*, (İstanbul: İletişim Yayınları, 2011). Event Köker, *Modernleşme, Kemalism ve Demokrasi* (İstanbul: İletişim Yayınları, 2012). Taha Parla, *Ziya Gökalp,*

Kemalizm ve Türkiye'de Korporatizm (İstanbul: İletişim Yayınları, 2006). Taha Parla, *Türkiye'de Siyasal Kültürün Resmi Kaynakları; Kemalist Tek-Parti İdeolojisi ve CHP'nin Altı Ok'u* (İstanbul: İletişim Yayınları, 1995). Füsun Üstel, *İmparatorluktan ulus-devlete Türk milliyetçiliği: Türk Ocakları (1912-1931)* (İstanbul: İletişim, 1997). Ahmet Yıldız, *Ne Mutlu Türküm Diyebilene; Türk Ulusal Kimliğinin Etno-Seküler Sınırları (1919-1938)* (İstanbul: İletişim Yayınları, 2001). Cemil Koçak, *Geçmişiniz İtina ile Temizlenir* (İstanbul: İletişim, 2011). Erik Jan Zürcher, *The Young Turk Legacy and the Nation Building: From the Ottoman Empire to Atatürk's Turkey* (London: I.B. Tauris, 2010).

Chapter 2

1. James McMillan, 'War in Political Violence', in *Political Violence in Twentieth - Century Europe*, ed. Donald Bloxham and Robert Gerwarth (New York: Cambridge University Press, 2011), 58.
2. Enzo Traverso, *A feu et à sang: De la guerre civile européenne 1914-1945* (Paris: Stock, 2007), 129, quoted in Mcmillan, 'War in Political Violence', 58.
3. Enzo Traverso, *A feu et à sang*, seventy-one quoted in Mcmillan, 'War in Political Violence', 64.
4. McMillan, 'War in Political Violence', 65.
5. Ibid.
6. Ibid.
7. Bradley, *Civil War in Russia 1917-1920*. In the Ottoman context it cannot be said that at the beginning the nationalists were initially against the sultan; they were in fact against the supporters of the sultan. The sultan in many ways was seen as above this conflict.
8. Büşra Ersanlı, *İktidar ve Tarih* (İstanbul: İletişim Yayınları, 2003), 108.
9. For the Soviet side of this historiography, see M. Gorky, V. Molotov, K. Voroshilov, S. Kirov, A. Zhdanov and J. Stalin, *The History of the Civil War in the U.S.S.R.* Volume 1 (London: Lawrance & Wishart, 1936). For the Kemalist side, see Kemal (Atatürk), *Nutuk. Tarih IV. Kemalist Eğitimin Tarih Dersleri 1931 – 1941* (İstanbul: Kaynak Yayınları, 2004).
10. Charles King, *Midnight at the Pera Palace: The Birth of Modern Istanbul*, First edn (New York: W. W. Norton and Company, 2014), 224, 225.
11. I am using 'National Movement', National Resistance' and '*Kuva-yi Milliye*' interchangeably to refer to the movement against the Greek occupation and

headed by Mustafa Kemal, Rauf (Orbay), Ali Fuat Paşa (Cebesoy), Kazım Paşa (Karabekir) and Refet (Bele) in Anatolia, but the meaning of 'national' or '*milli*' refers to Ottoman Muslims rather than Turkish ethnicity or Turkish nationalism. The 'national' also covers those who lived on the borders declared with the Mudros Armistice in October 1918 and later on in the National Pact of the Ottoman Parliament in February 1920. 'National' covers the Turks, Kurds, Circassians, Albanians, Lazs, Arabs and Bosnians as the '*Anasır-ı İslam*' – the elements of Islam. The sultan and caliphate were also part of the basic elements of identity for these Muslim elements of the state; shared cultural and religious feelings were more important for the Muslims of the empire, than any idea of *Türklük* (Turkishness). At the beginning of the period, the leading persons of the movement were Ottoman officials. Although there were discussions on Turkishness in the early period of the assembly, the leading people of the movement, particularly Mustafa Kemal, always referred to the *Anasır-ı İslam* in their speeches instead of emphasizing Turkishness. See the session of the assembly in 1 May 1920. http://www.tbmm.gov.tr/tutanaklar/TUTANAK/TBMM/d01/c001/tbmm01001008.pdf.

12 The incidents generally were referred to as '*İç İsyanlar*' 'Domestic Rebellions'. 'Rebellion' as a term is already used to define a domestic problem. It can be said that mainstream Turkish historians used 'domestic rebellions' to avoid to using 'İç Savaş', that is the term for 'Civil War'.

13 Although the First World War caused widespread devastation for the Ottoman Empire, it is not possible to see scholarly works on social life during this period. There are a few studies on this topic, see Yiğit Akın, 'The Ottoman Home Front during World War I: Everyday Politics, Society, and Culture' (Unpublished PhD thesis, Ohio State University, 2011). I would like to thank to Yiğit Akın for sharing his PhD thesis with me.

14 Some CUP members still held important positions in some districts as notables and as officials in the military and bureaucracy. The nationalists, the majority of whom were CUP members, avoided outwardly showing their ties to the CUP. At the Erzurum and Sivas congresses (July–September 1919), propaganda for the CUP was banned. The reason for this was to garner enough support from the people for resistance against the Greeks. See Sina Akşin, *İstanbul Hükümetleri ve Milli Mücadele; Mutlakiyete Dönüş (1918-1919)* (İstanbul: Cem Yayınevi, 1992), 482.

15 Özcan Mert, 'Anzavur'un İlk Ayaklanmasına Ait Belgeler', *Belleten*, 56, no. 217 (1992): 850–1.

16 Mert, 'Anzavur'un İlk Ayaklanmasına', 850–2. Also see Hacim Muhittin Çarıklı, *Balıkkesir ve Alaşehir Kongreleri ve Hacim Muhittin Çarıklı'nın Kuva-yi Milliye Hatıraları (1919-1920)* (Ankara: Türk İnkılap Tarihi Enstitüsü Yayınları, 1967), 77.
17 Zürcher, *The Young Turk Legacy and the National Awakening*.
18 The course was started in 1935 and was taught by Yusuf Kemal Tengirşenk, Mahmut Esat Bozkurt, Recep Peker and Hikmet Bayur in İstanbul and Ankara Universities. Recep Peker, at the same time, was the general secretary of the CHP. See Hıfzı Veldet Velidedeoğlu, *Bir Lise Öğrencisinin Milli Mücadele Anıları* (İstanbul: Varlık Yayınevi, 1971), 67.
19 Outlines of the Turkish History '*Türk Tarihinin Ana Hatları,(Kollektif eser Türk Tarihi Tetkik Heyeti). Mf. Vekâleti yayınları. Devlet matbaası. İstanbul 1930*, the book was prepared by a group which, barring two of them, were MPs from the Republican Party. Ersanlı, *İktidar ve Tarih*, 119–20.
20 Ersanlı, *İktidar ve Tarih*, 26.
21 Genel Kurmay Harp Tarihi Dairesi, *Türk istiklal harbi: iç ayaklanmalar: 1919-1921* (Ankara: Genelkurmay Harp Tarihi Başkanlığı, 1964). Genel Kurmay Harp Tarihi Dairesi, *Genel Kurmay Harp Tarihi Vesikaları Dergisi* (Ankara: Genelkurmay Harp Tarihi Başkanlığı, 1964–77). Genel Kurmay Harp Tarihi Dairesi, *Türk İstiklal Harbi: İstiklal harbinde ayaklanmalar (1919-1921)* (Ankara: Genelkurmay Harp Tarihi Başkanlığı, 1974).
22 Even though in the last decade an increasing number of discussions and criticisms on TV programmes have occurred, as well as writings in popular history books about the Turkish War of Independence and the First World War, there is not much academic study on the topics at hand, except for a few notable exceptions. See: Zürcher, *The Unionist Factor*. Gingeras, *Sorrowful Shores*. Gingeras, 'Notorious Subjects, Invisible Citizens'. Rogan, *The Fall of the Ottomans*. Reynolds, *Shattering Empires*. Aksakal, *The Ottoman Road to War in 1914*.
23 Ersanlı, *İktidar ve Tarih*.
24 Ord. Prof. Hıfzı Veldet (1904–92) was an officer in Ankara in the assembly from 1920 to 1928 until he was sent to Switzerland with a scholarship from the state to study law. He edited and published a modern Turkish version of the Atatürk's *Nutuk*. However, this edition is problematic in terms of accuracy. Hakan Erdem reviewed this edition in his book, *Tarih-Lenk*. Erdem shows that Hıfzı Veldet cut one-fifth of the *Nutuk* in his edition because of what he saw as its 'unimportance' in terms of 'Kemalist Thought'. Erdem says that the Hıfzı Veldet's edition includes

significant anachronistic content as well as changes from the original *Nutuk*. See Gazi M. Kemal Atatürk, *Söylev*, ed. Hıfzı Veldet Velidedeoğlu (İstanbul: Çağdaş Yayınları, 1982). See also Hakan Erdem, *Tarih-Lenk; Kusursuz Yazarlar, Kağıttan Metinler* (İstanbul: Doğan Kitap, 2010), 50–9.

25 *1920 yılı Mart ayı içinde bir gün arkadaşlarımızdan Memduh (Payzın) koşa koşa ve ağlıyarak geldi, 'İstanbul'u İngilizler işgal etmişler, askerlerimizi uykuda bastırarak şehit etmişler' dedi ... Herkes İstanbul'u ve İstanbul'daki yakınlarını düşünüyor, herkes bir şey söylüyor, birbirini teselliye çalışıyordu. İngilizlerden intikam almak, Yunanlılarla savaşmak için nemli gözlerle and içmiştik. İlk telaş ve şaşkınlık geçtikten sonra: 'Mustafa Kemal Paşa her halde bir tedbir almıştır' sonucuna vardık ve durulduk. Ona bir peygambere inanır gibi inanıyorduk.'* Velidedeoğlu, *Bir Lise Öğrencisinin*, 37.

26 When Mustafa Kemal resigned from his duty, he was scared of being arrested as a rebel general by Kazım Karabekir, see Taha Akyol, *Ama Hangi Atatürk* (İstanbul: Doğan Kitap, 2008), 49–53.

27 Adnan Sofuoğlu, *Milli Mücadele Döneminde Kocaeli* (Ankara: AKDTYK Atatürk Araştırma Merkezi, 2006), 32–4.

28 Emel Akal, *Mustafa Kemal, İttihat Terakki ve Bolşevizm: Milli Mücadelenin Başlangıcında* (İstanbul: İletişim Yayınları, 2012), 14.

29 A critic for this approach, Erik J. Zürcher demostrates in his book that National Struggle was a CUP project, Zürcher, *The Unionist Factor*.

30 That is, Mustafa Kemal and those around him.

31 Akal, *Mustafa Kemal, İttihat Terakki ve Bolşevizm Milli Mücadelenin Başlangıcında*, 33.

32 Zürcher, *The Unionist Factor*, 86.

33 Ibid., 101, Rauf Orbay (1881–1964) was of Abkhazian descent. He was a former minister of navy, and a leading figure in the Circassian cell in Istanbul. The cell organized the participation of Circassians in the national struggle. See Ünal, *Miralay Bekir Sami Günsav'ın Kurtuluş Savaşı Anıları*, 41. Emrah Cilasun, *Baki İlk Selam: Çerkes Ethem* (İstanbul: Belge Yayınları, 2004), 36–7.

34 Zürcher, *The Unionist Factor*, 101.

35 Ibid.

36 Kazım Özalp, *Milli Mücadele 1919-1922* (Ankara: Türk Tarih Kurumu, 1971), 13.

37 Kazım Özalp (1882-1968), an Albanian descent. He was the commander of several corps during the Turkish–Greek War, and he was promoted as general after Sakarya battle in 1921.

38 Ibid., 29.

39 He was a former agent in the Ottoman Special Organization, one of the leading paramilitary leaders in South Marmara in the days following the First World War, of Circassian descent, born in Emreköy/Balıkkesir (1886–1950).

40 Balıkesir Congress was one of the important local congress groups which was organized by local nationalists from 26 to 31 July 1919. One of the important decisions of the Congress was 'to fight against the Greeks until they leave Anatolia'. It is noteworthy that in the letters written by participants of the Congress to send to the Western powers, there is no mention of different ethnic groups; there is, however, an emphasis on the 'Turk and Islamic characteristics of Anatolia'. The reasons for using this terminology might be to avoid creating a new problem for the Ottoman state because according to the twelfth principle of Wilson, autonomous provinces which consisted of different ethnic groups were to be established under Turkish rule. See Özalp, *Milli Mücadele*, 46.

41 Özalp, *Milli Mücadele*, 68, 93.

42 Ibid., 68. '*Fransız subaylardan M. Deuran ve İtalyan tabasında Mr. Parciel, o sırada milli kuvvetlerin faaliyetleriyle çok alakadar oldular ve bizlere yakınlık göstererek yardım ettiler.Bundan başka bazı ecnebi subaylar ve memurlar Kuva-yi Milliyenin kuruluş şekli, mevcudu ve faaliyeti hakkında bilgiler almak üzere Balıkesir'e geldiler.Bunlardan bazılarını cephenin belirli noktalarına göndermekte ve milli kuvvetlerimizin harekatını göstermekte bir zarar görmüyordum. Aksine fayda görüyordum.*'

43 Ibid., 93... *Zaten İngilizler, İstiklal muharebesi süresince birçok vaziyetlerde bu gibi sebepler ortaya çıktığı halde, bizimle çarpışmadan daima kaçınmışlardı*, Özalp, *Milli Mücadele*, 93.

44 During that period, except for Ali Fuat Paşa's conflict with British troops on 18 June 1920 in İzmit, there were no serious exchanges of fire between British and *Kuva-yi Milliye* troops. See TTK. Bekir Sami dosya 25, 1409–11.

45 See Ali Kemal`s telegram to the governor of the Karesi. Özalp, *Milli Mücadele*, 33.

46 Özalp, *Milli Mücadele*, 33.

47 Apak, *İstiklal Savaşında Garp Cephesi Nasıl Kuruldu*, 52. Ali Kemal, '*Biz size, sizi ayaklandırmaktan menedecek emirler veririz, çünkü tazyik altındayız. Siz bize dahi isyan ediniz. Milli müdafaa, bir milletin en kudsi hakkıdır.*'

48 Özalp, *Milli Mücadele*, 56–7. Assistance and cooperation from the War Office Istanbul to military units Anatolia were observed by British Officials. See Bilal Şimşir, *İngiliz Belgelerinde Atatürk*. Volume I (Ankara: Türk Tarih Kurumu, 1973–84), 322.

49 Ahmet Demirel, *Birinci Meclis'te Muhalefet: İkinci Grup* (Cağaloğlu, İstanbul: İletişim, 2009), 53–4.
50 Ibid., 53–4.
51 Ergil, *Milli Mücadelenin Sosyal Tarihi*, 70.
52 Ibid., 93.
53 Ibid.
54 Ibid., 275.
55 Fevzi Çakmak (1876–1950) and İsmet İnönü (1884–1973) were two prominent figures of the war. They went to Ankara in April 1920.
56 British forces begin to arrest and exile to Malta those who were in important positions in the empire during the First World War period. On 28 May1919 sixty-seven detainees were exiled. See Ergil, *Milli Mücadelenin*, 91.
57 According to Mert, he was governor of Hüdavendigar (Bursa), Kal`a-i Sultaniye (Çanakkale), Karesi (Balıkkesir) from the end of 1918 to 23 April 1919, and the governor of İzmit from 23 April 1919 to August 1919. See Mert, 'Anzavur'un İlk Ayaklanmasına', 847–972.
58 Kemal Özer, *Kurtuluş Savaşında Gönen* (Balıkesir: Türkdili Matbaası, 1964), 53. Rahmi Apak claims that Anzavur was sent to Balıkesir by the İstanbul government to protect the region from bandits. Apak, *İstiklal Savaşında Garp Cephesi Nasıl Kuruldu*, 95.
59 Özalp, *Milli Mücadele*, 66.
60 Çarıklı, *Balıkesir ve Alaşehir*, 97–100.
61 Mert, 'Anzavur'un İlk Ayaklanmasına', 852.
62 Ibid.
63 Ibid.
64 In Turkey, the existing historiography defines the Anzavur's movement as a rebellion or uprising. However, Anzavur Ahmed did not rebel against the legitimate government of the time. He was an Ottoman official who was against the national movement in Anatolia which, it can be argued, was itself already rebelling against the Ottoman Porte.
65 Çarıklı, *Balıkkesir ve Alaşehir*, 34. Mert, 'Anzavur'un İlk Ayaklanmasına', 862. Zühtü Güven, *Anzavur isyanı; İstiklâl Savaşı tarihinden acı bir safha* (Istanbul: Aydınlık Matbaası, 1948), 45 quoted Mert, 'Anzavur'un İlk Ayaklanmasına', 862.
66 TTK. Bekir Sami dosya 13, 275–7.
67 Gingeras, 'Notorious Subjects, Invisible Citizens', 98.
68 PRO/FO 371/5047 – E 3713/3/44. 23 April 1920.
69 Ibid. '*Anzavur Ahmet Paşa*', İkdam, 26 April 1920, '*Dahili Sütun; Ahmed Anzavur Paşa*', İkdam, 27 April 1920.

70 Mert, 'Anzavur'un İlk Ayaklanmasına', 862. Such as, gang leaders Şah İsmail and Canbazlı Hakkı.
71 Ibid., 865.
72 Ibid.
73 Çarıklı, *Balıkkesir ve Alaşehir*, 97–8.
74 TTK. Bekir Sami dosya 13, 262–4.
75 TTK. Bekir Sami dosya 14, 401. Mert, 'Anzavur'un İlk Ayaklanmasına', 871.
76 ATASE.ATAZB. 11-47, 29/30 October 1335 (1919).
77 Mert, 'Anzavur'un İlk Ayaklanmasına', 868.
78 Ibid., 869.
79 TTK. Bekir Sami dosya 15, 439–41.
80 Özalp, *Milli Mücadele*, 166.
81 Mert, 'Anzavur'un İlk Ayaklanmasına', 875.
82 Ibid., 877.
83 Özer, *Kurtuluş Savaşında Gönen*, 72.
84 TTK. Bekir Sami dosya 15, 477.
85 Mert, 'Anzavur'un İlk Ayaklanmasına', 878.
86 Ibid., 880.
87 Özalp, *Milli Mücadele*, 70–1.
88 Mert, 'Anzavur'un İlk Ayaklanmasına', 881. Hurşit Paşa in particular eulogized the *Kuva-yi Milliye* and added that he would try to provide arms for *Kuva-yi Milliye* in Istanbul. Özalp, *Milli Mücadele*, 79.
89 Özalp says they had already decided that 'the council could do nothing, the only solution was to finish the chaos with the sword'. Özalp, *Milli Mücadele*, 70–1. Mert, 'Anzavur'un İlk Ayaklanmasına', 885.
90 For example, although Anzavur Ahmed was supported by the Sadrazam Damat Ferid Paşa, his government decided to warn Anzavur Ahmed because of the chaos created by him. See 'Biga'ya Heyet', İkdam, 31 March 1920.
91 Özalp, *Milli Mücadele*, 88.
92 Mert, 'Anzavur'un İlk Ayaklanmasına', 886.
93 İğdemir, *Biga Ayaklanması*.
94 Özalp, *Milli Mücadele*, 98–9. Uluğ İğdemir mentions that Circassians from the village of Savaştepe raided Biga on 16 February. There were also Pomaks and *Muhacir*s (Muslims from the Balkans) and many armed villagers in Biga. İğdemir, *Biga Ayaklanması*, 5.
95 İğdemir, *Biga Ayaklanması*, 9.
96 Özalp, *Milli Mücadele*, 98–9.

97 He was killed by Anzavur's forces at the end of February 1920; see TİTE K20G34B34001 29, 3, 1336(1920). Özcan Mert and Uluğ İğdemir also mention the Akbaş arsenal incident in their works, and that Hamdi Bey was killed by the 'rebels' (anti-nationalists). Hamdi tried to protect the arms against the 'bandits'. However, Bekir Sami's telegrams tell us a different story. Yusuf Izzet Paşa sent a telegram to Bekir Sami saying that 'although we established a union in Biga where we had between three hundred or four hundred soldiers, due to Hamdi Bey's arrest of bandit leader Kara Hasan, a reaction occurred among the people to save Kara Hasan from Hamdi Bey. Anzavur Ahmed also benefited from this incident.' TTK. Bekir Sami dosya 18, 743–6.
98 İğdemir, *Biga Ayaklanması*, 87, notes 27.
99 Ibid., 87, notes 27.
100 Özalp, *Milli Mücadele*, 98–9.
101 Gönen was an important place as some events took place there. The commander of the 174th unit, Rahmi Bey, wrote that 'there was no one who did not fire against the soldiers (*Kuva-yi Milliye*,) in Gönen'. TTK. Bekir Sami dosya 20, 939. He also says that the soldiers rejected the orders to fire against the people, and that fifty-four of them deserted. See TTK. Bekir Sami dosya 21, 1025–6.
102 By having Bandırma, he had an opportunity to have direct communication with the Istanbul government via telegram lines. See Özalp, *Milli Mücadele*, 109–10.
103 PRO/FO 371/5167 – 776 – 791 – 793 – 794.
104 İğdemir, *Biga Ayaklanması*, 35. It seems that there are overstatements in some of Uluğ İğdemir's expressions about the activities of the Circassians in Biga. It can be also seen in the book that İğdemir is extremely supportive of the *Kuva-yi Milliye* and against Ahmed Anzavur without making the distinctions between his armed people and ordinary Circassians. 'The Circassian looting cannot be described. Their actions would fill volumes of books. They were stealing their friends' animals while they had gone to the war. Their leader is already a man who steals horses. What can you expect from this kind of group?' İğdemir, *Biga Ayaklanması*, 62.
105 TTK. Bekir Sami dosya 14, 326–9.
106 TTK. Bekir Sami dosya 15, 463–4.
107 TTK. Bekir Sami dosya 22, 1142.
108 Ibid., 1161.
109 Ibid.
110 Ibid.

111 Cilasun, *Baki İlk Selam*, 44.
112 Kazım Özalp also suggested using Albanian bandits against Anzavur Ahmed. The bandits were in the region from long before. Kazım Özalp and Mustafa Kemal aimed to secure the bandits' support by promising them arms and money so as to convince them to become part of *Kuva-yi Milliye* against Anzavur Ahmed. See TTK. Bekir Sami dosya 22, 1175–6.
113 Özalp, *Milli Mücadele*, 113.
114 Ibid., 115. Çerkes Ethem also argued, similar to Kazım Özalp, that 'our first forward patrol entered the district and fired towards the serpebt people until the ship left from the harbour'.

'İlk ve ani kasabaya giren keşif kollarımız vapura iltica etmek üzere gördüğü eşhası mel'uneye ateş etmişler ve vapur hareket edinceye kadar ateşlerine devam ederek vapurun hareketini tesri etmişlerdir.' TTK. Bekir Sami dosya 22, 1138.
115 Özalp, *Milli Mücadele*, 115.
116 Ibid., 125.
117 İğdemir, *Biga Ayaklanması*, 9.
118 TTK. Bekir Sami dosya 21, 1054.
119 A group of Circassians, Ahmed Anzavur, Kel Huseyin and Mirza Beys, sent Hasan Tahsin on 13 May 1920 to ask Bekir Sami about the rumours regarding a plan for the annihilation of the Circassians by Turks in the region. Çarıklı, *Balıkkesir ve Alaşehir*, 102.
120 Çarıklı, *Balıkkesir ve Alaşehir*, 100. Whether or not there existed a 'Turkish–Circassian issue' was indeed a matter of discussion. On 6 January 1920 Mustafa Kemal asked Bekir Sami via telegram whether during the Anzavur incident there was contact between the Circassian bandit leaders, Çerkez Şevket, Şah İsmail, Çerkes Ethem, Yusuf İzzet Paşa and Ahmet Fevzi Paşa. According to Mustafa Kemal this contact among the Circassians and the support from the military officers could have led to a conflict between Turks and Circassians. See TTK. Bekir Sami dosya 16, 598–600.
121 The Damat Ferid Paşa government decided to make him a Paşa in 7 April 1920. They were then planning to give to his soldiers official Ottoman military uniforms. PRO/FO 371/5047 – E 3673/3/44. April 23 1920. Ferid Paşa also tried to convince the British delegates to aid them in terms of military equipment since, he argued, that if Anzavur Ahmed had more arms and munitions, he could be more successful against the nationalists. See the same document. PRO/FO 371/5047 – E 3673/3/44. 23 April 1920.
122 Kazım Özalp believed that Anzavur's success was worse than Greek advance in Anatolia for them. Özalp, *Milli Mücadele*, 112.

123 'Ahmed Anzavur Paşa', *İkdam Gazetesi*, 26 April 1920. It is worthy that both sides saw the other as rebels. Mustafa Kemal also referred to Anzavur as the one who tried to create division among the national forces TİTE. K20G37B37001.

124 Bekir Sami claimed that the *Kuva-yi Milliye* could undermine the Anzavur uprising if they could divide the Circassians in two separate groups in the region. See TTK. Bekir Sami dosya 14, 329 and TTK. Bekir Sami dosya 15, 449–52.

Chapter 3

1 It is also interesting to mention that both the Turkish media and state called them as 'Eylemci' (activist), not hijacker or terrorist.

2 He is a Circassian from Kırkpınar village of Sapanca/İzmit. Sadık Güleç, *Ölüm üçgeni: Bir şehir, Bir Kabadayı, Bir Mafya Babası*, 1. baskı, Profil; Strateji-Analiz (Cağaloğlu, İstanbul: Profil Yayıncılık, 2013).

3 BAŞKAN - Birtakım infazlar, babalar şunlar bunlar hep bu mıntıkada; İzmit, Sakarya, Sapanca, İstanbul üçgeninde oluyor, niye burada oluyor.
MEHMET HADİ ÖZCAN - Havasındandır, bilmiyorum.
BAŞKAN - Havası güzeldir; biz de beğendik havasını da ...
MEHMET HADİ ÖZCAN - Hakikaten burada oluyor ama, ben bakıyorum öyle, hep buradan çıkıyor.
BAŞKAN - Hep havasından değil gibi geliyor bana?

1 March 1997 Hadi Özcan's statement to the Susurluk Investigation Committee, http://www.kocaelimeydan.com/gundem/bir-mafya-babasinin-itiraflari-h11394.html, accessed 21 August 2015.

4 Anti-*Kuva-yi Milliye* movement reached the Yabanaban town of Ankara which was only 30 km far from Ankara. Halide Edib Adıvar, *Türkün Ateşle-Imtihanı: (Istiklâl Savaşı Hâtıraları)* (Istanbul: Çan yayını, 1962), 137, 138, 144.

5 Pro-nationalist, a resistance group which was led by two prominent CUP figures, Kara Kemal and Vasif Bey.

6 Ali Fuat Cebesoy, *Millî Mücadele Hâtıraları*, 2. baskı., Temel Yayınları Sertifika No (İstanbul: Temel, 2010), 440.

7 Ali Fuat Paşa (Cebesoy) 1882–1968. General, diplomat and politician. He was the commander of the western front in the early days of the Turkish War of Independence, and then he was appointed as the ambassador for Turkey in Moscow.

8   Cebesoy, *Millî Mücadele Hâtıraları*, 427.
9   There were girls from the Adapazarı–Düzce region in the Ottoman harem; for an example see the report of a lady from Maan (the family of Kayalar village); see BOA.DH.MKT 2270/81 document 1. 4 May 1320 (1904).
10 Cebesoy, *Millî Mücadele Hâtıraları*, 427–8.
11 Hüsrev Gerede, *Hüsrev Gerede'nin Anıları: Kurtuluş Savaşı, Atatürk ve Devrimler (19 Mayıs 1919-10 Kasım 1938)* (İstanbul: Literatür, 2003), 202–3.
12 Kemal Atatürk, *Nutuk* (Istanbul: Devlet Matbaası, 1934). Volume 3, document 174, 206.
13 Atatürk. Volume 3, document 162, 196–7. Mustafa Kemal believes that these Circassians were backed by the British. Sofuoğlu, *Milli Mücadele Döneminde Kocaeli*, 64–6.
14 Atatürk, *Nutuk*. Document 162, 196. One of these Circassians was Safer Bey, who would change sides and take a position in the local government of Adapazarı.
15 Ibid., Volume 3, document 162, 198–9.
16 BOA.DH.ŞFR. 104/136, 1 Teşrinisani 1335 (1 November 1919). Çerkes Said Bey was the leader of bandits in Adapazarı at the time.
17 BOA.DH.KMS. 53-3/36 document 1, 14 September 1335 (1919).
18 BOA.DH.KMS. 53-3/36 document 2, 16 September 1335 (1919).
19 Ibid.
20 BOA.DH.EUM.AYŞ. 33/ 76, 2 March 1920. BOA.DH.KMS. 53-4/ 47 document 3, 17 April 1336 (1920). Rüknü Özkök, *Milli Mücadele Başlarken Düzce – Bolu İsyanları* (İstanbul: Milliyet Yayın Ltd. Şti. Yayınları Tarih Kitapları Dizisi, 1971), 244.
21 Fortna, *The Circassian*.
22 PRO/FO 371/5047 E3731/3/44, 23 April–24 April 1920, a telegram from Admiral Webb in İstanbul, document no 133. According to the same document, Eşref Bey was released from Malta in February 1920.
23 Mustafa Kemal and İsmet (İnönü) were suspicious about his behaviour as he enjoyed a very close relationship with Enver Paşa. Fortna, *The Circassian*.
24 Sofuoğlu, *Milli Mücadele Döneminde Kocaeli*, 60, 61.
25 PRO/FO 371, 5167, E5039/262/44. 23 April 1920–20 May 1920 a report from Admiral Webb in 23 April 1920, page 106.
26 Özkök, *Milli Mücadele Başlarken Düzce – Bolu İsyanları*, 244.
27 ATASE.İSH. 274/ 23, 13 April 1336 (1920), ATASE.İSH. 527/43, 25 April 1336 (1920). M. Zekai Konrapa, *Bolu Tarihi* (Bolu: Bolu Vilayet Matbaası, 1964), 724. Sina Akşin claims that about four thousand people came together in Ömer Efendi, see Sina Akşin, *İç Savaş ve Sevr'de Ölüm* (İstanbul: Türkiye İş Bankası Yayınları, 2010), 65–6.

28 Captain Avni Efendi and officer Rahiskar Efendi were killed. BOA.DH.EUM. AYŞ. 51, document 2, 24 April 1336 (1920). Özkök, *Milli Mücadele Başlarken Düzce - Bolu İsyanları*, 247, 248.
29 He was a member of the Ottoman Special Organization; during the First World War he served as a major. He was on the Iraq front and served under the *Osmancık* volunteer regiment. See Semih Nafiz Tansu, *Cumhuriyet Newspaper*, 31 July 1956, 2.
30 Akşin, *İç Savaş ve Sevr'de Ölüm*, 65–6.
31 BOA.DH.EUM.AYŞ. 40/51, document 2, 24 April 1336 (1920).
32 Konrapa, *Bolu Tarihi*, 724.
33 Thirty guns and ten thousand shotshells were seized from one military unit. BOA.DH.EUM.AYŞ. 40/51, document 3, 24 April 1336 (1920).
34 The Secret Session Records of the Grand National Assembly, Secret Session 2, 24 April 1920, 8. http://www.tbmm.gov.tr/tutanaklar/TUTANAK/GZC/d01/CILT0 1/gcz01001002.pdf, accessed 14 November 2014.
35 BOA.DH.EUM.AYŞ. 40/51, document 3, 24 April 1336 (1920).
36 BOA.DH.EUM.AYŞ. 39/37, document 3, 24 April 1336 (1920), BOA.DH.EUM. AYŞ. 39-41, document 3.
37 BOA.DH.EUM.AYŞ. 39/41, document 3.
38 BOA.DH.EUM.AYŞ. 39/37, document 3, 24 April 1336 (1920) Berzeg Sefer Bey was a member of a local and well-known family in the region.
39 Eşref also informed Ankara that he had to free the prisoners since armed groups in the region, who according to him was supported by the British, did not leave him any option. Fortna, *The Circassian*. One could speculate that Ankara used this incident and mistakes of Eşref in order to pacify him due to his connection to Enver Paşa, but it is still not clear how and why Eşref left the nationalist side and became an anti-nationalist.
40 Cebesoy, *Millî Mücadele Hâtıraları*, 424–6.
41 Ibid., 426–7, Akşin, *İç Savaş ve Sevr'de Ölüm*, 67–8.
42 Kanbolatzade Said, Abaza Kazım and Halim were also killed along with Mahmut Bey. BOA.DH.EUM.AYŞ. 39/37, 24 April 1920. Sofuoğlu, *Milli Mücadele Döneminde Kocaeli*, 96.
43 BOA.DH.EUM.AYŞ. 39/37, 24 April 1920, document 2.
44 BOA.DH.EUM.AYŞ. 39/41, document 3.
45 Fahri Yetim, 'Milli Mücadele Döneminde İsyanların Gölgesinde Düzce ve Çevresinde Asayiş Sorunları', *Hacettepe Üniv. Cumhuriyet Tarihi Araştırmaları Dergisi*, no. 13 (2011): 66.

46 Except he tries to give some narrow Kemalist explanations in terms of the reasons for the incident, such as 'religious backwardness', or the ignorance of the people, and the activities of 'turbaned Muslim preachers'.
47 BOA.DH.EUM.AYŞ. 39/41, 25 April 1336 (1920).
48 Gerede, *Hüsrev Gerede'nin Anıları*, 194, 195.
49 Ibid., 197, 198.
50 BOA.DH.EUM.AYŞ. 40/79, 15 May 1336 (1920), document 2.
51 Ibid. It is also noteworthy to mention that *Kuva-yi Milliye* was called '*Kuva-yi Bağiyye*' by the Istanbul government, which means the forces of those who rebel against the government.
52 BOA.DH.EUM.AYŞ. 40/20, 6 May 1336 (1920).
53 TİTE. K314G25B25-1001, 23 May 1336 (1920) a letter report from Refet Bey to Ali Fuat Paşa.
54 Cebesoy, *Millî Mücadele Hâtıraları*, 464–5.
55 Ibid., 469. However, in one of the secret session in the assembly on 17 May the MPs were informed that Ali Fuat Paşa had the control on 16 May. See the secret session of the assembly *Grand National Assembly, Secret session 17*, 17 May 1336 (1920). https://www.tbmm.gov.tr/tutanaklar/TUTANAK/GZC/d01/CILT01/gcz01001017.pdf, accessed 14 November 2014, 31.
56 He was also known as İbrahim 'the English' (*İngiliz İbrahim*) due to his relationships with the British. He was a CUP opponent as majority of the post-First-World-War period bureaucrats, who were appointed by the Istanbul government.
57 TİTE. K314G2B2001, 22, 23 May 1336 (1920), a report from the minister of war of the Ankara government, İsmet Bey (İnönü), to Ali Fuat Paşa.
58 ATASE.İSH. 274/4. 23 April 1336 and 25 April 1336 (23–25 April 1920).
59 PRO/FO 371/5048, E4635/3/44, 11th May 1920–12th May 1920, page 29.
60 PRO/FO 371/5047, E4272/3/44, 12 April 1920–6 May 1920, document number 130. A report from the British High Commission in Istanbul.
61 PRO/FO 371/5048, E4635/3/44, 11th May 1920–12th May 1920, page 30.
62 PRO/FO 371/5047, E3673/Z/44, 8th April 1920–23rd April 1920, page 22.
63 PRO/FO 371, 5167, E4510/262/44, 10th May 1920 a report from the director of Military Intelligence, on 1 April 1920, page 66.
64 Sofuoğlu, *Milli Mücadele Döneminde Kocaeli*, 86, 87.
65 PRO/FO 371, 5167, E4510/262/44, 10th May 1920 a report from the director of Military Intelligence, on 1 April 1920, page 48. According to the same document page 49, the Ottoman government sought a way to raise anti-nationalist sentiment in the Kurdish-dominated regions of Anatolia.
66 PRO/FO 371/5048, E5241/3/44, 25 May 1920–26 May 1920, page 117.

67 *Grand National Assembly, Secret session* 21, 29 May 1336 (1920), http://www.tbmm.gov.tr/tutanaklar/TUTANAK/GZC/d01/CILT01/gcz01001021.pdf, accessed 14 November 2014, 41.
68 Ibid., 41.
69 PRO/FO 371/5048, E5552/3/44, 29 May 1920–31 May 1920, a telegram from General Milne, page 197.
70 PRO/FO 371/5048, E5241/3/44, 25 May 1920, page 117.
71 *Grand National Assembly, Secret session* 26, 3 July 1336 (1920), https://www.tbmm.gov.tr/tutanaklar/TUTANAK/GZC/d01/CILT01/gcz01001026.pdf, accessed 14 November 2014, 74.
72 *Grand National Assembly, Secret session* 2, 24 April 1336 (1920), http://www.tbmm.gov.tr/tutanaklar/TUTANAK/GZC/d01/CILT01/gcz01001002.pdf, accessed 14 November 2014, 8–9.
73 Ethem, *Anılarım*, 8.
74 Ibid., 8.
75 Genel Kurmay Harp Tarihi Dairesi, *Türk İstiklâl Harbi: İç ayaklanmalar (1919-1921)* (Genelkurmay Basımevi: Ankara, 1974), 216–17 quoted in Doğu Ergil, *Milli Mücadelenin Sosyal Tarihi*, Bilimsel Eserler Dizisi (Ankara: Turhan Kitabevi, 1981), 295.
76 Cilasun, *Baki Ile Selam*, 43.
77 Ethem, *Anılarım*, 28.
78 Ibid., 30.
79 Ibid.
80 Kuşçubaşı Eşref tried to recruit İbrahim Efendi of Akyazı/Hacı Ahmed Bey village for his nationalist forces. İbrahim Efendi rejected this demand; however, when Ethem came to the region he was sentenced to death due to this. BOA. DH.KMS. 59-1/56, document 2, 24 July 1336 (1920), Ethem, *Anılarım*, 32–3.
81 Ibid., 33.
82 Ibid.
83 Ali Fuat Cebesoy, *Bilinmeyen Hatıralar* (İstanbul: Temel, 2005), 373.
84 Ibid., 374, 375.
85 Ibid., 375, 376.
86 Ibid., 377.
87 Sèvres Peace Treaty (10 August 1920) was imposed by the Allies on the Ottoman Empire. According to this treaty, the Ottoman Empire would be partitioned and colonized by the Allies. It was signed by the Ottoman Empire but it had never been implemented since it was not confirmed by the Ottoman

Assembly (*Meclis-i Mebusan*), and the Ankara government forces defeated the Greeks and declared Turkey's independence.

88   TİTE. K314G25B25-1001, 23 May 1336 (1920). A telegram from Refet Bey to Ali Fuat Paşa. Gerede, *Hüsrev Gerede'nin Anıları*, 198–201.
89   Gerede, *Hüsrev Gerede'nin Anıları*, 198–201. Konrapa, *Bolu Tarihi*.
90   Ethem, *Anılarım*, 35.
91   Konrapa, *Bolu Tarihi*.
92   Adıvar, *Türkün Ateşle-Imtihanı*, 140–1.
93   Ibid., 140–1. Halide Edip claims that Mustafa Kemal agreed with Ethem to the hanging of Sefer Bey. However, Halide Edib and İsmet (İnönü) Bey were against this because Ankara had promised Sefer that they would save him from execution. They convinced Mustafa Kemal to not allow Ethem to hang Sefer.
94   Gerede, *Hüsrev Gerede'nin Anıları*, 200–1. According to Cebesoy, forty-five people were hanged in Adapazarı, Hendek, Düzce and Bolu. See Cebesoy, *Bilinmeyen Hatıralar*, 379. Konrapa, *Bolu Tarihi*, 726.
95   Organized by the İstanbul government (Damad Ferid Pasha) as the army of the caliphate against the nationalists.
96   Ibid., 726.
97   Ibid.
98   Ibid.
99   Ibid., 727.
100 He was a grandson of Beslan Bey who was in exile in Greece with his father Aslan Bey; they stayed in Greece until the 1940s. Interview, 18 April 2015.
101 Kaşen is the name of a friendship between boys and girls among the Circassians. There are two types of kaşen: one is not serious and more akin to being friends; the other one is serious and leads to marriage.
102 Recep Albayrak, *Ethem Bey'in Sürgün Yılları ve Simav Olayları (1919-1948)* (Ankara: Berikan Yayınevi, 2004), 137.
103 BOA.BEO 4639/347908, 29 June 1336 (1920).
104 BOA.BEO 4646/348398, document 2. Some of these anti-nationalist people joined Circassian congress and had to leave Turkey later on; these included number 33 on the list, Maan Mustafa Bey of Adapazarı ('Hain Mustafa').
105 BOA.DH.KMS. 59-1/50, document 6, 29 July 1336 (1920).
106 BOA.DH.KMS. 59-1/50, document 10, 20 July 1336 (1920).
107 Gerede, *Hüsrev Gerede'nin Anıları*, 202.
108 ATASE.İSH. 587/158, document no 158aa, 20 December 1336, 20 December 1920.
109 ATASE.İSH. 587/158, 20 December 1336, 20 December 1920.

110 it is written as Neferin in the records mistakenly.
111 *Grand National Assembly, Open session* 48, 14.81336 (1920), https://www.tbmm.gov.tr/tutanaklar/TUTANAK/TBMM/d01/c003/tbmm01003048.pdf, accessed 14 November 2014, 215-16.
112 Yetim, 'Milli Mücadele Döneminde İsyanların Gölgesinde Düzce ve Çevresinde Asayiş Sorunları', 25.
113 Özkök, *Milli Mücadele Başlarken Düzce – Bolu İsyanları*, 269.
114 Yetim, 'Milli Mücadele Döneminde İsyanların Gölgesinde Düzce ve Çevresinde Asayiş Sorunları', 25.
115 Özkök, *Milli Mücadele Başlarken Düzce – Bolu İsyanları*, 270-6. Yetim, 'Milli Mücadele Döneminde İsyanların Gölgesinde Düzce ve Çevresinde Asayiş Sorunları', 26.
116 Kazım Aras, *İstiklal Savaşında Kocaeli Bölgesindeki Harekat* (İstanbul, 1936), 21 quoted in Özkök, *Milli Mücadele Başlarken Düzce – Bolu İsyanları*, 314-16.
117 Military reports emphasize this movement see ATASE.İSH.1139/105, document no from 105 to 105af, July and August 1921.
118 ATASE.İSH. 950/98, 1337 (1921).
119 ATASE.İSH.1311/53, document no 53, 53a, 20 October 1337 (1921). Some suspicion was directed towards the Circassians who fought for the nationalists in some units ATASE.İSH.1240/52, document no 52, 12 August 1337 (1920).
120 ATASE.İSH. 967/ 54, 2 Teşrinievvel (October), 1336 (1920), from local governor of Bafra to Canik mutasarrıfı. ATASE.İSH. 967/54, Document no 54ae, 10 November 1336 (1920).
121 ATASE.İSH.967/54, document no 54aa, 1 Teşrinisani (November) 1337 (1920).
122 ATASE.İSH. 967/ 54, document 54ae, 10 November 1336 (1920).
123 Akşin, *İç Savaş ve Sevr'de Ölüm*, 67.
124 Ibid.
125 Ibid., 88-9.
126 Abdülkadir Bey, *Çapanoğulları Hadisesi ve Abdulkadir Bey'in Hatıraları*, ed. Ali Şakir Ergin (Ankara: Ahmet Şevki Ergin Kültür ve Hizmet Vakfı Yayınları, 2006), 162.
127 Ibid., 165.
128 Ibid., 25.
129 Ibid., 41.
130 Ibid., 43, footnote 7. According to another story they left the city because they would be exiled to Ankara due to their ties to the Zile incident in May 1920. Ibid., 46-7.

131 Ibid., 52–3.
132 *Grand National Assembly, Secret session* 26, 3 July 1336 (1920), https://www.tbmm.gov.tr/tutanaklar/TUTANAK/GZC/d01/CILT01/gcz01001026.pdf, accessed 14 November 2014, 63.
133 Akşin, *İç Savaş ve Sevr'de Ölüm*, 88–9.
134 Indeed, the Greek forces attacked the western front a week later on 22 June. In the secret session of 3 July 1920 İsmet stated that the Greeks begun military action in İzmir in 22 June 1920 *Grand National Assembly, Secret session* 26, 3 July 1336 (1920), http://www.tbmm.gov.tr/tutanaklar/TUTANAK/GZC/d01/CILT01/gcz01001026.pdf, accessed 14 November 2014, 52. Sina Akşin claims that the attack was on 21 June 1920 see Akşin, *İç Savaş ve Sevr'de Ölüm*, 88–9.
135 Ethem, *Anılarım*, 47.
136 Ibid. 48.
137 Akşin, *İç Savaş ve Sevr'de Ölüm*, 90.
138 Ergin, *Çapanoğulları Hadisesi ve Abdulkadir Bey'in Hatıraları*, 160–70.
139 Akşin, *İç Savaş ve Sevr'de Ölüm*, 90.
140 Ergin, *Çapanoğulları Hadisesi ve Abdulkadir Bey'in Hatıraları*, 106, footnote 33. Zübeyir Uzun, 'Milli Mücadele'de Çerkez Ethem ve Kuva-Yı Seyyare'nin Faaliyetleri (1919–1920)' (Master Thesis, Selçuk University, 2008), 69.
141 Ergin, *Çapanoğulları Hadisesi ve Abdulkadir Bey'in Hatıraları*, 107.
142 Ibid., 61.
143 Ibid., 76.
144 'Yozgat İsyanı' Ömer Faik Boran, 58. Quoted in Ergin, *Çapanoğulları Hadisesi ve Abdulkadir Bey'in Hatıralar*, 211. Ali Şakir Ergin gave some part of this work in his book.
145 Bey, *Çapanoğulları Hadisesi ve Abdulkadir Bey'in Hatıraları*, 205.
146 Ibid., 120–3.
147 Ibid., 81–94.
148 Ibid.
149 Ibid., 125.
150 Ethem, *Anılarım*, 62–3.
151 Ibid., 63.
152 Ibid., 66.
153 Akşin, *İç Savaş ve Sevr'de Ölüm*, 90.
154 Ibid.

Chapter 4

1. http://uyg.tsk.tr/ataturk/ata_album/albuyuk/index.htm, image 25.
2. http://www.haberturk.com/gundem/haber/823156-genelkurmay-cerkez-etheme-sansur-mu-uyguladi, accessed 19 April 2018.
3. Later on these MPs established second group in the assembly. See Demirel, *Birinci Meclis'te Muhalefet*. Ahmet Demirel, *Birinci Meclis'te Mustafa Kemal'in Muhalifleri* (İstanbul: Ufuk yayınları, 2013).
4. Akal, *Mustafa Kemal, İttihat Terakki ve Bolşevizm Milli Mücadelenin Başlangıcında*, 122.
5. Ibid., 14.
6. Ethem was a member of the Special Organization, and his family had links with the executive members of the CUP. His father Ali Bey was the founder of the İzmir branch of the CUP.
7. Akal, *Mustafa Kemal, İttihat Terakki ve Bolşevizm Milli Mücadelenin Başlangıcında*, 44.
8. Masayuki Yamauchi, *The Green Crescent under the Red Star: Enver Pasha in Soviet Russia 1919-1922*, Studia Culturae Islamicae (Tokyo: Institute for the Study of Languages and Cultures of Asia and Africa, 1991).
9. Ali Fuat Cebesoy, *Moskova Hatıraları: (21/11/1920-2/6/1922)* (Istanbul: 'Vatan' Neşriyatı, 1955), 61.
10. *Grand National Assembly, Secret session* 84, 16 October 1336 (1920), https://www.tbmm.gov.tr/tutanaklar/TUTANAK/GZC/d01/CILT01/gcz01001084.pdf, accessed 14 November 2014, 159.
11. Akal, *Mustafa Kemal, İttihat Terakki ve Bolşevizm Milli Mücadelenin Başlangıcında*, 92.
12. Ibid.
13. Yamauchi, *The Green Crescent under the Red Star*, 19.
14. Ibid., 37.
15. Ibid., 34.
16. Akal, *Mustafa Kemal, İttihat Terakki ve Bolşevizm Milli Mücadelenin Başlangıcında*, 106–15.
17. Kâzım Karabekir, *İstiklâl Harbimizde Enver Paşa ve Ittihat Terakki Erkânı* (İstanbul: Menteş Matbaası, 1967), 132–7.
18. Cebesoy, *Moskova Hatıraları*, 159.
19. Ibid., 163.
20. Ibid., 163–4.

21   Ibid., 171–2.
22   Murat Bardakçı, *Enver* (İstanbul: İş Bankası Kültür Yayınları, 2015), 279–80.
23   I use 'Enverists' as the supporters of Enver Paşa.
24   Akal, *Mustafa Kemal, İttihat Terakki ve Bolşevizm Milli Mücadelenin Başlangıcında*, 255–6.
25   Cebesoy, *Moskova Hatıraları*, 314.
26   Zürcher, *The Unionist Factor*, 123.
27   Efe, *Çerkez Ethem*, 23. Enver was also seen as a leading person in the army by some of his close men, such as Kuşçubaşı Eşref, and the Enver–Mustafa Kemal struggle started from the war in Libya and continued until Enver was killed. See Fortna, *The Circassian*, 19.
28   In late 1930s Tarık Mümtaz Göztepe, who was declared as personae non grata by the Turkish government in 1924 due to his anti-nationalist activities during the Turkish–Greek War, did an interview with Çerkes Ethem in Amman, Jordan. In the interview Ethem expressed that he was working to bring back Enver Paşa to Anatolia in 1920 to replace Mustafa Kemal. He aimed to bring Mustafa Kemal to the court to sentence him for his involvement and mismanagement of the Yozgat incident. However, because of his older brother Reşid's interference, Ethem could not succeed to try Mustafa Kemal and bring about Enver's return to Anatolia. Tarık Mümtaz Göztepe, *Osmanoğulları'nın Son Padişahı Sultan Vahideddin Mütareke Gayyasında* (İstanbul: Sebil Yayınevi, 1969).
29   Cebesoy, *Moskova Hatıraları*, 223.
30   Ibid., 234–5.
31   Ibid., 227.
32   Zürcher, *The Unionist Factor*, 129.
33   Cebesoy, *Moskova Hatıraları*, 244–5.
34   Karabekir, *İstiklâl Harbimizde Enver Paşa ve Ittihat Terakki Erkânı*, 132–7.
35   Zürcher, *The Unionist Factor*.
36   TİTE. K58G69B69001, 26 Teşrinievvel 1338 (26, Ekim, 1922). The date was the letters registered at that date by the Intelligence Service of Ankara. These two letters could be among the very last letters of Enver Paşa since he was killed on 4 August 1922.
37   TİTE. K58G69B69001, 26 Teşrinievvel 1338 (26, Ekim, 1922).
38   Mitat Çelikpala, 'Search for a Common North Caucasian Identity: The Mountaineers' Attempts For Survival and Unity Response to the Russian Rule' (PhD thesis, Bilkent University, 2002), 63.
39   Ibid., 64.

40　Ibid., 64–6.
41　Ibid., 72–3.
42　Ibid., 74.
43　Reynolds, *Shattering Empires*, 221.
44　Ibid., 195.
45　*Harb Tarihi Vesikaları Dergisi*, year 5, issue 19, 15 March 1956. Document no 388, 2.
46　Ibid.
47　*Harb Tarihi Vesikaları Dergisi*, year 5, issue 19, 15 March 1956. Document no 388, 3.
48　Cebesoy, *Moskova Hatıraları*. 8.
49　*Harb Tarihi Vesikaları Dergisi*, year 5, issue 19, 15 March 1956. Document no 389.
50　*Harb Tarihi Vesikaları Dergisi*, year 5, issue 19, 15 March 1956. Document no 303, 2.
51　*Harb Tarihi Vesikaları Dergisi*, year 5, issue 19, 15 March 1956. Document no 302, 2–3.
52　Salâhi Ramadan Sonyel, *Turkish Diplomacy, 1918-1923: Mustafa Kemal and the Turkish National Movement*, Sage Studies in 20th Century History (London: Sage Publications, 1975), 47.
53　ATASE.İSH. 912/51, document no ai, aia, 27 December 1920. ATASE.İSH. 912/51, document ac, ad. Some of the names in this document are not fully legible. The names were Cemaleddin Usalof, Mehmed Asıve … zade, Mehmed … zade, Mikail Askerzade, Yusuf Kemalzade, İbrahim Kemalzade, Davud Malikzade, Ali Malikzade, Atalay Çerkeszade, Mehmed Mustafazade, Şemseddin Hatif, Mahmud Hatif, Sultan … and … Kazım (the ellipses in these names indicate that the names aren't fully legible). The names were recorded on 23 December 1920 by the officials from Ankara government. ATASE.İSH. 912/51, document ac.
54　ATASE.İSH. 912/51, document ai, aia 27 December 1920. ATASE.İSH. 912/51, document aa 7 January 1337 (1920).
55　ATASE.İSH. 912/51, 5–6 February 1337 (1920).
56　ATASE.İSH. 912/51, document ag 19–20 January 1921.
57　Mete Tunçay, *Türkiye'de Sol Akımlar: 1908-1925*, Ankara Üniversitesi. Siyasal Bilgiler Fakültesi Yayınları (Ankara: Ankara Üniversitesi – Siyasal Bilgiler Fakültesi Yayınları, 1967), 85.
58　Emel Akal, *İştirakiyuncular, Komünistler ve Paşa Hazretleri Moskova-Ankara-Londra Üçgeninde* (İstanbul: İletişim Yayınları, 2014), 62.

59 Uzun, 'Milli Mücadele'de Çerkez Ethem ve Kuva-Yı Seyyare'nin Faaliyetleri (1919–1920)', 81.
60 Cebesoy, *Millî Mücadele Hâtıraları,* 514, 528.
61 Ibid., 515.
62 Tunçay, *Turkiye'de Sol Akımlar,* 85.
63 Ibid., 127, endnote 91.
64 Ethem's irregular forces were called as *Kuva-yi Seyyare* (Mobile Forces). The actual number of the armed people were about five thousand – only five hundred of them were foot soldiers, the rest of the forces were cavaliers.
65 Cebesoy, *Moskova Hatıraları,* 78–9.
66 Ibid., 82.
67 Stefanos Yerasimos, *Türk-Sovyet İlişkileri; Ekim Devriminden 'Milli Mücadele'ye* (İstanbul: Gözlem Yayınevi, 1979), 630, 634, 635.
68 Ibid., 630–4.
69 Reynolds, *Shattering Empires,* 255.
70 *Grand National Assembly, Secret session 26,* 3 July 1336 (1920), https://www.tbmm.gov.tr/tutanaklar/TUTANAK/GZC/d01/CILT01/gcz01001026.pdf, accessed 14 November 2014, 72.
71 Cebesoy, *Moskova Hatıraları,* 36.
72 Uzun, 'Milli Mücadele'de Çerkez Ethem ve Kuva-Yı Seyyare'nin Faaliyetleri (1919–1920)', 102.
73 Yerasimos, *Türk-Sovyet İlişkileri; Ekim Devriminden 'Milli Mücadele'ye,* 528–9.
74 Tunçay, *Turkiye'de Sol Akımlar,* 85.
75 Zürcher, *The Unionist Factor.*
76 Uzun, 'Milli Mücadele'de Çerkez Ethem ve Kuva-Yı Seyyare'nin Faaliyetleri (1919–1920)', 96.
77 Cemal Şener, *Çerkes Ethem Olayı* (Istanbul: Ant Yayınları, 1990), 107.
78 Later on, after Çerkes Ethem was excluded from the national movement, Ethem, Tevfik, Reşit and some of Ethem's friends – Manyaslı Şevket (Takığ), Lieutenant İbrahim, gendarme lieutenant Sami, Halil, police officer Artin, Çerkes Ahmet, Reşat and Colonel Abdullah – were sentenced to death by an Ankara government's court on 9 May 1921 due to their activities in the Green Army Society; see Uzun, 'Milli Mücadele'de Çerkez Ethem ve Kuva-Yı Seyyare'nin Faaliyetleri (1919–1920)', 103.
79 Zürcher, *The Unionist Factor.*
80 Ibid., 127.
81 M. Şükrü Hanioğlu, *Atatürk: An Intellectual Biography* (Princeton: Princeton University Press, 2011), 1.

82 King, *Midnight at the Pera Palace*, 54–5.
83 Demirel, *Birinci Meclis'te Muhalefet*, 25–8.
84 Mustafa Kemal mentioned Ethem's name for the first time in the assembly when he said, 'He is a talented (*kıymetli*) friend of us. We were grateful of him because of his actions against Anzavur.' The Secret Session Records of the Grand National Assembly, Secret Session' 8, 1 May 1336 (1920), 6, http://www.tbmm.gov.tr/tutanaklar/TUTANAK/GZC/d01/CILT01/gcz01001008.pdf, accessed 14 August 2016.
85 Demirci Efe was a local armed leader. He also resisted the Greek occupation.
86 'The Open Session Records of the Grand National Assembly, Open Session' 54, 21 August 1336 (1920), 366–7, https://www.tbmm.gov.tr/tutanaklar/TUTANAK/TBMM/d01/c003/tbmm01003054.pdf, accessed 29 June 2016.
87 Uzun, 'Milli Mücadele'de Çerkez Ethem ve Kuva-Yı Seyyare'nin Faaliyetleri (1919–1920)', 108.
88 Ibid.
89 Cebesoy, *Millî Mücadele Hâtıraları*, 507.
90 Uzun, 'Milli Mücadele'de Çerkez Ethem ve Kuva-Yı Seyyare'nin Faaliyetleri (1919–1920)', 108.
91 Cebesoy, *Millî Mücadele Hâtıraları*, 508.
92 Ibid., 507.
93 'The Open Session Records of the Grand National Assembly, Open Session' 54, 21 August 1336 (1920), 366–7, https://www.tbmm.gov.tr/tutanaklar/TUTANAK/TBMM/d01/c003/tbmm01003054.pdf, accessed 29 June 2016.
94 Cebesoy, *Millî Mücadele Hâtıraları*, 508.
95 Ibid.
96 Uzun, 'Milli Mücadele'de Çerkez Ethem ve Kuva-Yı Seyyare'nin Faaliyetleri (1919–1920)', 112.
97 Cebesoy, *Millî Mücadele Hâtıraları*, 559–62.
98 Mustafa Kemal's speech in the Grand National Assembly, see 'The Secret Session Records of the Grand National Assembly, Secret Session' 125, 29 December 1336 (1920), 276, https://www.tbmm.gov.tr/tutanaklar/TUTANAK/GZC/d01/CILT01/gcz01001125.pdf, accessed 23 August 2015.
99 Kazım Özalp, *Milli Mücadele 1. Cilt 1919-1922* (Ankara: Türk Tarih Kurumu, 1998), 166.
100 'The Secret Session Records of the Grand National Assembly, Secret Session' 125, 29 December 1336 (1920), 276, https://www.tbmm.gov.tr/tutanaklar/TUTANAK/GZC/d01/CILT01/gcz01001125.pdf, accessed 23 August 2015.
101 Atatürk, *Nutuk*, 51.

102 (Met, Janutuko) Yusuf İzzet Paşa (1876–1922) was a Circassian major general of the nationalist forces. He was in charge of the 14th army corps.
103 TTK. Bekir Sami dosya 16, 598–600.
104 'The Secret Session Records of the Grand National Assembly, Secret Session' 125, 29 December 1336 (1920), 276, https://www.tbmm.gov.tr/tutanaklar/TUTANAK/GZC/d01/CILT01/gcz01001125.pdf, accessed 23 August 2015.
105 In *Nutuk*, Mustafa Kemal criticized Ali Fuat Paşa for his guerrilla uniform. Some of the military men were affected by Bolshevik ideas at the time; they did not prefer to wear their military rank on their uniforms. As a head of the western front Ali Fuat also did not wear his military ranks which Mustafa Kemal said was something that surprised him when they met in Ankara. However, Mustafa Kemal did not hesitate to send Ali Fuat to Moscow to negotiate with Bolsheviks. Atatürk, *Nutuk*. 52. However, Ali Fuat Paşa rejects this claim, and he also emphasizes that Mustafa Kemal distorted the facts. See Cebesoy, *Bilinmeyen Hatıralar*, 447, 450.
106 Cebesoy, *Millî Mücadele Hâtıraları*, 582.
107 Cebesoy, *Bilinmeyen Hatıralar*, 445–6.
108 Ibid., 446.
109 İsmet moved to Ankara to join the movement in April 1920 after the assembly was opened. He was also criticized for not joining the Anatolian movement from the beginning and for or his move to Ankara.
110 Özalp, *Milli Mücadele 1. Cilt 1919-1922*, 166–7.
111 Ibid., 167.
112 Ethem, *Anılarım*, 110.
113 Ibid.
114 Şener, *Çerkes Ethem Olayı*, 163–4.
115 Ethem, *Anılarım*, 117.
116 Ibid.
117 27 November 1920. *Harp Tarihi Belgeleri Dergisi*, year 24, issue 73, September 1975, Document no 1574, 8–9.
118 Özalp, *Milli Mücadele 1. Cilt 1919-1922*, 167.
119 *Harp Tarihi Belgeleri Dergisi*, year 24, issue 73, September 1975, Document no 1574, 8–9.
120 The meeting was hold in 5 December 1920. See the details Oğuz Aytepe, 'Milli Mücadele'de Bilecik Görüşmesi', *Ankara Üniversitesi Türk İnkılâp Tarihi Enstitüsü Atatürk Yolu Dergisi*, no. 33–4 (May–November 2004): 23–31.
121 Özalp, *Milli Mücadele 1. Cilt 1919-1922*, 168.

122 Ibid.
123 Ethem, *Anılarım*, 122.
124 Ibid., 124–6.
125 Ibid., 122–3.
126 Ibid., 124.
127 Ibid., 126.
128 'The Secret Session Records of the Grand National Assembly, Secret Session' 111, 09 December 1336 (1920), 258, https://www.tbmm.gov.tr/tutanaklar/TUTANAK/GZC/d01/CILT01/gcz01001111.pdf, accessed 23 August 2015.
129 Özalp, *Milli Mücadele 1. Cilt 1919-1922*, 168.
130 Ibid., 169.
131 Atatürk, *Nutuk*, volume 2, 27.
132 Şener, *Çerkes Ethem Olayı*, 47.
133 24 December 1920 (24 December 36). *Harp Tarihi Belgeleri Dergisi*, year 24, issue 73, September 1975, Document no 1582, 38.
134 'The Secret Session Records of the Grand National Assembly, Secret Session' 125, 29 December 1336 (1920), 281, https://www.tbmm.gov.tr/tutanaklar/TUTANAK/GZC/d01/CILT01/gcz01001125.pdf, accessed 23 August 2015. Members of a local group in Akhisar were arrested by the local gendarme forces; however, later on, the gendarme station was raided by Ethem and those locals were executed by shooting BOA.DH.KMS. 53-4/32, 12 February 1336 (1920). It has to be mentioned that in the official document Ethem's name was recorded as 'Çerkes Ethem'. Some historians claim that 'Çerkes/Circassian' was put before his name after he split up with Mustafa Kemal to accuse all Circassians in republican Turkey as they were 'traitors' like Çerkes Ethem. It meant that he was already known as Çerkes Ethem.
135 27 December 1920 (27 December 1336). *Harp Tarihi Belgeleri Dergisi*, year 24, issue 73, September 1975, Document no 1585, 50.
136 7 December 1920 (7 December 1336). *Harp Tarihi Belgeleri Dergisi*, year 24, issue 73, September 1975, Document no 1576, 16.
137 7 December 1920 (7 December 1336). *Harp Tarihi Belgeleri Dergisi*, year 24, issue 73, September 1975, Document no 1576, 17.
138 Celal, Kılıç Ali, Eyüp Sabri, Vehip and Ethem's brother Reşit was in the council. Atatürk, *Nutuk*, 75.
139 Atatürk, *Nutuk*, 76–7.
140 27 December 1920 (27 December 1336). *Harp Tarihi Belgeleri Dergisi*, year 24, issue 73, September 1975, Document no 1584, 47.

141 Atatürk, *Nutuk*, 78, 79.
142 Ibid., 77–9.
143 *Harp Tarihi Belgeleri Dergisi*, year 24, issue 73, September 1975, Document no 1584, 47.
144 30 December 1920 (30 December 1336). *Harp Tarihi Belgeleri Dergisi*, year 24, issue 73, September 1975, Document no 1587, 56.
145 'The Secret Session Records of the Grand National Assembly, Secret Session' 126, 30 December 1336 (1920), 294–6, https://www.tbmm.gov.tr/tutanaklar/TUTANAK/GZC/d01/CILT01/gcz01001126.pdf, accessed 23 August 2015.
146 30 December 1920 (30 December 1336). *Harp Tarihi Belgeleri Dergisi*, year 24, issue 73, September 1975, Document no 1587, 56.
147 31 December 1920 (31 December 1336). *Harp Tarihi Belgeleri Dergisi*, year 24, issue 73, September 1975, Document no 1589, 62.
148 'The Secret Session Records of the Grand National Assembly, Secret Session' 123, 27 December 1336 (1920), 270, the date of the telegram 27 December 1336 (1920), https://www.tbmm.gov.tr/tutanaklar/TUTANAK/GZC/d01/CILT01/gcz01001123.pdf, accessed 23 August 2015.
149 'The Secret Session Records of the Grand National Assembly, Secret Session' 111, 09 December 1336 (1920), 261, the date of the telegram 5 January 1337 (1921), https://www.tbmm.gov.tr/tutanaklar/TUTANAK/GZC/d01/CILT01/gcz01001111.pdf, accessed 23 August 2015.
150 'The Secret Session Records of the Grand National Assembly, Secret Session' 126, 30 December 1336 (1920), 292, https://www.tbmm.gov.tr/tutanaklar/TUTANAK/GZC/d01/CILT01/gcz01001126.pdf, accessed 23 August 2015.
151 Ibid., 293.
152 Ibid., 305.
153 Uzun, 'Milli Mücadele'de Çerkez Ethem ve Kuva-Yı Seyyare'nin Faaliyetleri (1919–1920)', 171.
154 Ibid., 172.
155 27 December 1920 (27 December 1336). *Harp Tarihi Belgeleri Dergisi*, year 24, issue 73, September 1975, Document no 1584, 47.
156 Ibid.
157 'The Secret Session Records of the Grand National Assembly, Secret Session' 126, 30 December 1336 (1920), 292, https://www.tbmm.gov.tr/tutanaklar/TUTANAK/GZC/d01/CILT01/gcz01001126.pdf, accessed 23 August 2015.

158 Form lieutenant Sami and the governor Demirci İbrahim Ethem's meeting which was held on 13 January 1921. See İbrahim Ethem Akıncı, *Demirci Akıncıları*, Yayınlar (Ankara: Türk Tarih Kurumu Basımevi, 1978), 25.
159 Atatürk, *Nutuk*, 80. *Anadolu İnkılabı (Mücahedat-I Milliye Hatıratı 1335-1339)*, 58.
160 23 January 1921 (23 February 1337). *Harp Tarihi Belgeleri Dergisi*, year 24, issue 73, September 1975, Document no 1593, 76.
161 Ibid.
162 Özalp, *Milli Mücadele 1. Cilt 1919-1922*, 170.
163 Ethem, *Anılarım*, 141.
164 Ibid., 143.
165 Ibid., 148–50.
166 Ibid., 155.
167 Ibid., 148–50.
168 'The Open Session Records of the Grand National Assembly, Open Session' 131, 8 January 1337 (1921), 225, https://www.tbmm.gov.tr/tutanaklar/TUTANAK/TBMM/d01/c007/tbmm01007131.pdf and 'The Secret Session Records of the Grand National Assembly, Secret Session' 125, 29 December 1336 (1920), 286, https://www.tbmm.gov.tr/tutanaklar/TUTANAK/GZC/d01/CILT01/gcz01001125.pdf, accessed 23 August 2015.
169 'The Open Session Records of the Grand National Assembly, Open Session' 131, 8 January 1337 (1921), 227, https://www.tbmm.gov.tr/tutanaklar/TUTANAK/TBMM/d01/c007/tbmm01007131.pdf, accessed 23 August 2015.
170 Ibid., 227. It is worth imagining how difficult it must have been for someone to work or collaborate with all of these dissimilar groups.
171 ATASE.İSH. 945/152, 7 Kanunisani (January) 1337 (1921).
172 ATASE.İSH. 770/35,35aa. 19 January 1337 (1921).
173 'The Open Session Records of the Grand National Assembly, Open Session' 131, 8 January 1337 (1921), 227, https://www.tbmm.gov.tr/tutanaklar/TUTANAK/TBMM/d01/c007/tbmm01007131.pdf, accessed 23 August 2015, 228.
174 'The Secret Session Records of the Grand National Assembly, Secret Session' 137, 24 January 1337 (1921), 353, https://www.tbmm.gov.tr/tutanaklar/TUTANAK/GZC/d01/CILT01/gcz01001137.pdf, accessed 23 August 2015.

Chapter 5

1 Sadrazam Mahmut Şevket Paşa was killed on 11 June 1913. After his murder, the CUP used this killing to silence the opposition in the empire. A significant

number of military men and bureaucrats were retired or exiled to the peripheries of the empire by the CUP. See Ali Birinci, *Hürriyet ve İtilaf Fırkası : II. Meşrutiyet Devrinde İttihat ve Terakki'ye Karşı Çıkanlar* (İstanbul: Dergâh Yayınları, 2012), 229.

2 Berzeg, *Türkiye Kurtuluş Savaşı'nda Çerkes Göçmenleri (II)*. He had to leave the empire in the days following the assassination of Mahmut Şevket Paşa due to his participation in the assassination. (Interview with Baki Çule, in 18 April 2015, Düzce. Baki Çule is the grandson of İbrahim Hakkı's brother Arslan Bey.)

3 PRO/FO 608/113, 21 August 1919, document no 332.

4 Porte means 'gate' in French. It (the monumental entrance gate of the Ottoman Government Departments in Istanbul) symbolizes the Ottoman government.

5 Berzeg, *Türkiye Kurtuluş Savaşı'nda Çerkes Göçmenleri (II)*. İbrahim Hakkı Bey's wife Pakize Hanım was the granddaughter of Pertev Paşa (d. 1785–1837) and daughter of Marşan Fersah Paşa. The family had a good reputation in Egypt. (Interview with Baki Çule, in 18 April 2015, Düzce.)

6 BOA.DH.KMS. 60-1/34, document 1, 28 Kanunievvel 36 (28 December 1920).

7 Ibid.

8 BOA.DH.KMS. 60-1/34, document 2, 28 Kanunievvel 36 (28 December 1920).

9 BOA.DH.KMS. 60-2/16, document 1, 6 Kanunisani 37 (6 January 1921).

10 BOA.DH.KMS. 60-2/16, document 6, 29 March 1337 (29 March 1921), and BOA.DH.KMS. 60-2/16 document 5, 14 March 1337 (14 March 1921).

11 PRO/FO 371/5167 E5255/262/44, 21 April 1920, document 129.

12 PRO/FO 608/113, 8 August 1919, document no 334.

13 BOA.DH.KMS. 60-1/34, document 4, 2 Kanunisani 1337 (2 January 1921).

14 BOA.DH.KMS. 60-1/19 document 1, 22 Teşrinisani 1336 (22 November 1920).

15 Ibid.

16 Ibid.

17 BOA.DH.KMS. 60-1/19 document 2, 22 Teşrinisani 1336 (22 November 1920).

18 http://www.kocaeli.gov.tr/ortak_icerik/1/tarih/kocaeli%20tarihi/index.html, page 4.

19 BOA.DH.KMS. 60-2/39, document 1, 29 June 1337 (21 June 1921).

20 Çule İbrahim Hakkı, Efkar-ı Umumiyeye Bir İzah ve Muarızlara Cevab, Şark-ı Karib Çerkesleri Temin-i Hukuk Cemiyeti Beyanname ne Nizamname-i Esasiyesi, Çerkeslik Hareket ve Teşebbüs-i Ahirinin Esbab ve Sevaiki Tarihçesi, 1922. As can be seen, İbrahim Hakkı used three different titles for the booklet. I will use the first one to refer to the booklet.

21 Ibid., 3.

22 Ibid.
23 Ibid., 4.
24 Ibid., 5.
25 Ibid., 6.
26 Ibid. Most of these towns were taken by Çerkes Ethem's forces from the loyalists for Ankara.
27 Can Erdem, 'İbrahim Hakkı Bey'in İzmit Mutasarrıflığı', *Yakın Dönem Türkiye Araştırmaları Dergisi*, sayı 5. Cilt3 (2004 s): 105–24; pp. 109–10.
28 Ibid., 111.
29 Ibid., 114.
30 Ibid., 115–16.
31 Çule İbrahim Hakkı, Efkar-ı Umumiyeye Bir İzah ve Muarızlara Cevab, Şark-ı Karib Çerkesleri Temin-i Hukuk Cemiyeti Beyanname ne Nizamname-i Esasiyesi, 13.
32 Ibid., 13.
33 Erdem, 'İbrahim Hakkı Bey'in İzmit Mutasarrıflığı', 105–24, 109–10.
34 Çule İbrahim Hakkı, Efkar-ı Umumiyeye Bir İzah ve Muarızlara Cevab, Şark-ı Karib Çerkesleri Temin-i Hukuk Cemiyeti Beyanname ne Nizamname-i Esasiyesi, 14.
35 'Ottomanness' (*Osmanlıcılık*) was a political project which proposed that the different ethnic and religious groups of the Ottoman Empire could under a single identity (Ottoman) with peace under the Ottoman Empire.
36 Çule İbrahim Hakkı, Efkar-ı Umumiyeye Bir İzah ve Muarızlara Cevab, Şark-ı Karib Çerkesleri Temin-i Hukuk Cemiyeti Beyanname ne Nizamname-i Esasiyesi, 13.
37 Ibid., 17.
38 Ibid.
39 Ibid., 17, 18.
40 Ibid., 14.
41 Gingeras, 'Notorious Subjects, Invisible Citizens'.
42 Çule İbrahim Hakkı, Efkar-ı Umumiyeye Bir İzah ve Muarızlara Cevab, Şark-ı Karib Çerkesleri Temin-i Hukuk Cemiyeti Beyanname ne Nizamname-i Esasiyesi, 17.
43 Ibid.
44 The exile of the Circassians was the result of the Russian occupation of the North Caucasus, which was the homeland of the Circassians. During the exile, from 1850s to the 1870s, one-third of the exiled, around a million Circassians, were

either killed by the Russian forces or died on the way due to the lack of sufficient preparation .

45 Çule İbrahim Hakkı, Efkar-ı Umumiyeye Bir İzah ve Muarızlara Cevab, Şark-ı Karib Çerkesleri Temin-i Hukuk Cemiyeti Beyanname ne Nizamname-i Esasiyesi, 17.
46 TİTE. K63G104B104001, 22 August 1337 (1921).
47 Çerkes Ragıb was an anti-nationalist and the brother-in-law of Mizancı Murat (1854–1917); he murdered a person in Kadıköy/Istanbul on 23 April 1337 (1921), and was imprisoned by the British. Later on he was released from the prison and worked in a very determined way for the British in Istanbul and in Eastern Thrace; one can speculate that he had a deal with British as per which in exchange for his release he worked for the British in Anatolia. In April 1924 he was put into the '*Yüzellilik*' list. BOA. DH.KMS. 61-1/35 document 5, 9 May 1337 (1921).
48 ATASE. İSH 1481/ 140, 28 August 1337 (1921).
49 TİTE. K63G104B104001, 22 August 1337 (1921).
50 ATASE.İSH. 1163/164, document no 164, 164a, 164aa, 164aaa, 14 August 1337 (1920). Interview with Müşir Fuad Paşa by Tevhid-i Efkar newspaper.
51 Ibid., document no 164, 164a, 164aa, 164aaa, 14 August 1337 (1920). Interview with Müşir Fuad Paşa by *Tevhid-i Efkar* newspaper.
52 Özer, *Kurtuluş Savaşında Gönen*, 129.
53 Ibid.
54 Ibid., 131.
55 Ibid., 129.
56 Traditionally every single Circassian family has a lineage name (*Sülale ismi* in Turkish).
57 Gingeras, *Sorrowful Shores*, 124–7. I would thank to Dr Gingeras for allowing me to use his translation of the declaration.
58 Çule İbrahim Hakkı, Efkar-ı Umumiyeye Bir İzah ve Muarızlara Cevab, Şark-ı Karib Çerkesleri Temin-i Hukuk Cemiyeti Beyanname ne Nizamname-i Esasiyesi, 17.
59 Ibid., 22.
60 BOA.DH.KMS. 60-3/26, document 2, 3 Kanunievvel 1337 (3 December 1921).
61 According to one military intelligence report, Ethem and Anzavurzade Kadir worked to set up a Circassian government in the region. They also invited Çerkes Bekir, Reşid, Eşref, Ragıb and lieutenant Bahadır from İstanbul. ATASE.İSH. 1485/2, 3 Teşrinievvel (October) 1337 (1921). However, it is not clear what they

meant by using the term 'Circassian government' – it is not clear whether it referrred to the Circassian Congress or not.

62 BOA.DH.KMS. 60-3/26, document 2, 3 Kanunievvel 1337 (3 December 1921).
63 Çule İbrahim Hakkı, Efkar-ı Umumiyeye Bir İzah ve Muarızlara Cevab, Şark-ı Karib Çerkesleri Temin-i Hukuk Cemiyeti Beyanname ne Nizamname-i Esasiyesi, 26. Vakit newspaper 29 rebiülevvel 1340–30 Teşrinisani 1337.
64 While Talustan Bey was the head of the association, İbrahim Hakkı was its vice precedent. 'An explanation to the public', Çule İbrahim Hakkı, 32.
65 Çule İbrahim Hakkı, Efkar-ı Umumiyeye Bir İzah ve Muarızlara Cevab, Şark-ı Karib Çerkesleri Temin-i Hukuk Cemiyeti Beyanname ne Nizamname-i Esasiyesi, 9 Rebiülahır 1340, 32.
66 Ibid., 30.
67 Akıncı, *Demirci Akıncıları*, 360. Efe, *Çerkez Ethem*, 460.
68 Akıncı, *Demirci Akıncıları*, 216–17.
69 Some Circassians were also involved in banditry activities under the Greek-controlled Thrace. Maanzade Ali Bey, Bağzade Refik Bey, Parmaksız Torunzade Nezih Bey, Bağ Osman Bey, Karabigalı Kara Mustafa (one of Ferid Paşa's servants) and Koçzade Şerif Bey were the leaders of the bandits. TİTE. K53G71B71-3001, 04 October 1338 (1922).
70 TİTE. K57G55B55a001, 09 July 1338 (1922).
71 TİTE. K50G180B180001, 18 June 1338 (1922).
72 Just a year after Ethem was excluded from the national movement, the situations of other opposing Circassians and Abkhazians and of Eşref Bey were discussed in Ankara. The Ministry of War asked the Cabinet if they would be free to come to Anatolia in the case of their pardon. On 22 January 1922, the Cabinet declared that they would not be allowed to come to Anatolia. Ankara insisted that they should be far away from Anatolia. BCA. 30 18 1 1.4.45.16, 22, 1 January 1338 (1922).
73 Çerkes Hasan, Kazım, İbrahim, Hasan Fehmi and Ragıb were some of them TİTE. K59G137B137-1001, 1 July 1338 (1922).
74 Cilasun, *Baki ilk Selam*, no page number.
75 ATASE.İSH. 1666/88, document no aa, 23 June 1339. According to an intelligence report, there were three hundred anti-nationalists in Midilli who left İzmit for Midilli after the Ankara government's forces took the city in July 1921. They consisted of Muslims, Circassians and Rums. TİTE. K48G17B17-1001, 23 May 1338 (1922).
76 The Greeks in particular helped them to create chaos in Western Anatolia BOA. HR.İM. 81/57, 23 August 1339 (1923).

77 ATASE.İSH. 1667/87 and 87aa, 24 July 39.
78 Ibid.
79 ATASE.İSH. 1666/88, document no aa, 23 June 1339.
80 Ibid.
81 Ibid.
82 Ibid.
83 PRO/FO/ E11493/8401/44, document no 140, 141, 11 September 1923.
84 BOA.HR.İM. 77/44, document 2, 29 June 1923.
85 ATASE.İSH. 1666/53, document no aa, 03 May 1339 (1923).
86 Ibid.
87 Ibid.
88 Ibid.
89 *Mülazim-i evvel Mehmet Ali Çetesi, Kel Aziz Çetesi, Kanlı Mustafa Çetesi* see Mehmet Fetgerey Şoenu, *Tüm Eserleri* (Kafdav: Ankara, 1997), 224–5.
90 In some of the records he was known as Çerkes Ethem's brother, which was not true, but he was very close to Çerkes Ethem. He was from Mürüvetler village of Manyas, also known as Takığ Şevket or Mürüvetlerli Şevket.
91 Mançaoğlu Edhem oğlu Ali was one of them. He was from Kızılcaören village of Kütahya. Later on, he was sentenced by the Independent Court (*İstiklal Mahkemesi*) for a month due to his activities in Şevket's gang. IM_T5_K004_D066_G001_0000 - IM_T5_K004_D066_G001_0008. January–September 1337 (1921).
92 ATASE.İSH. 1666/26, document no al, 04 February 1339 (1923) According to this document, Çerkes Ethem was in Germany at that time.
93 ATASE.İSH. 1666/26, document no al and ak, 27 December 1338/ ATASE.İSH. 1667/7, 21 January 39 (1923). According to the same report Ethem was in Limni and ready to come to the region after Şevket's attack. However, another intelligence report claims that Ethem was in Germany with his brother. ATASE.İSH. 1666/26, document no al, 04 February 1339 (1923).
94 ATASE.İSH. 1667/7, 21 January 1339 (1923).
95 Ibid.
96 ATASE.İSH. 1666/26, document no al and ak, 27 December 1338 (1922).
97 Ibid.
98 ATASE.İSH. 1666/26, document no am, ama.
99 BCA. 2017-03-29 (1) 0012, 1 September 1339 (1923).
100 ATASE.İSH. 1666/26, document no al and ak, 27 December 1338 (1922).
101 ATASE.İSH. 1666/26, document no ah, 29 December 1338 (1922).

102 ATASE.İSH. 1666/26, document no ad, 18 January 1339 (1923) and ATASE.İSH. 1666/26, document no ab, ac. It is also important to mention that the Ankara government saw Georgians, like the Circassians, as a threat. It was feared that Georgians would join the Circassians' armed groups. ATASE.İSH. 1666/26, document no aa.
103 ATASE.İSH. 1666/26, document no ac.
104 ATASE.İSH. 1534/139, document no aa, 28 November 1338 (1922)–07 December 1338 (1922).
105 BCA. 2017-03-29 (1) 0004, 11 January 1339 (1923).
106 BCA. 2017-03-29 (1) 0006, (no date) In Konya they were delivered as one house per village. BCA. 2017-03-29 (1) 0011, 14 February 1339 (1923). In Niğde eight families were sent to one district, four families to another district, three families to another district, and one family was sent to the Bor district. BCA. 2017-03-29 (1) 0013, 27 March 1339 (1923).
107 BCA. 2017-03-29 (1), 0007, 0008, 14 January 1339 (1923).
108 Oral History project by Kuban Kural, 'Unutulan Geçmişin Peşinde: "Gönen – Manyas Çerkes Sürgünü"', interview with Gürol Demir, http://www.gusips.net/analysis/sozlutarih/4338-gurol-demir-babam-yillar-sonra-kayseri-de-surgun-deyken-dayimin-oturdugu-evi-buldu.html, accessed 01 March 2015.
109 Ibid.
110 Şoenu, *Tüm Eserleri*, 224–5.
111 Fetgerey claims that Şevket's aunt's husband was not punished since he was not Circassian. Şoenu, *Tüm Eserleri*, 224–5.
112 Kural, 'Unutulan Geçmişin, interview with Gürol Demir http://www.gusips.net/analysis/sozlutarih/4338-gurol-demir-babam-yillar-sonra-kayseri-de-surgun-deyken-dayimin-oturdugu-evi-buldu.html, accessed 01 March 2015.
113 Şoenu, *Tüm Eserleri*, 225–7.
114 Ibid.
115 Fetgerey Şoenu, *Tüm Eserleri* (Ankara: Kafdav, 1997), 226–7.
116 Gingeras, *Sorrowful Shores*, 146.
117 Several people from this village were executed by shooting by the *Kuva-yi Milliye* Kemal Özer, *Kurtuluş Savaşında Gönen*, 74.
118 Özer, *Kurtuluş Savaşında Gönen*, 72. A lieutenant, Mehmet Ziya Şahan, informed Kemal Özer about these villages. Most of these villages were deported by Ankara to Eastern and Central Anatolia in May and June 1923.
119 Ibid., 72. Kemal Özer learned this information from the first secretary of the local court in Gönen, Sadık Aydınıoğlu.

120 Şoenu, *Tüm Eserleri*, 193-4.
121 BCA. 30 18 1 1.7.18.16, 7 May 1923.
122 Ibid.
123 Merve Tram, Kollektif Cezalandırmanın Tarihi ve Bugününden Bir Kesit, http://www.gusips.net/blogger/2244-kolektif-cezalandirmanin-tarihi-ve-bugununden-bir-kesit.html, accessed 01 March 2015.
124 Şoenu, *Tüm Eserleri*, 231-2.
125 Ibid., 222-3.
126 From this village forty-five people died due to the conditions they faced during their exile. Kural, 'Unutulan Geçmişin, interview with Hakkı Acı, http://www.gusips.net/analysis/sozlutarih/4336-hakki-aci-yaslilar-hic-bahsetmiyorlardi-bu-konulardan-eskiden-yasakli-konulardi-bir-yerde.html.
127 Şoenu, *Tüm Eserleri*, 232-4. Muratlar, Keçeler, Üçpınar, Keçidere and Sızı were the villages where people participated in the Ahmed Anzavur-led unrest. Özer, *Kurtuluş Savaşında Gönen*, 72.
128 Ibid., 240.
129 Şoenu, *Tüm Eserleri*, 235.
130 For example, Nauke Reşit from Bölceağaç village. He fought with the nationalists. He was suffering from tuberculosis. Reşit was sent to his village to rest. However, he was also exiled. He died in Afyon during the exile due to his sickness. Şoenu, *Tüm Eserleri*, 240.
131 First letter to Mustafa Kemal ATASE. İSH. 430/12, 20 June 1339 (1923), the second letter to Kazım Paşa, 11 August 1923 see Ünal, 56. *Fırka Harb Ceridelerinden Miralay Bekir Sami Günsav'ın Kurtuluş Savaşı Anıları 1919-1920*.
132 Şoenu, *Tüm Eserleri*, 241.
133 Özer, *Kurtuluş Savaşında Gönen*, 100-1.
134 Kural, 'Unutulan Geçmişin, interview with Hasan Tekin, http://www.gusips.net/analysis/sozlutarih/4334-hasan-tekin-hayvan-vagonlarina-insanlari-balik-istifi-yerlestirmisler.html.
135 Karaağaçalan, Tuzakçı, Hacımenteş, Çaloba, Ayvalıdere, Obaköy, Kumköy, Ayvalık, Bayramiç, Balcı villages of Gönen. Darıca, Işıklar, Hacıyakup, Süleymanlı, Durak, Çakırca, Elkesen, Çavuşköyü, Kızık, Kulak, Eskimanyas, Tatarköyü, Haydar, Eşen, Ergili, Salur, Hamamlı, Muradiye, Geyikler, Karacalarçiftliği villages of Manyas. Şoenu, *Tüm Eserleri*.
136 Şoenu, *Tüm Eserleri*, 235-8.

Chapter 6

1. Arsen Avagyan, *Türk Dış Siyasetinde Kuzey Kafkasya Siyasi Muhacereti (1920-1971)* (İstanbul: Belge Yayınları, 2013), 9.
2. Ibid., 16–17.
3. It is also worthy of mention that some Circassian figures, such as Kuşçubaşı Eşref, were turned into heroes by Turkish popular culture. Kuşçubaşı Eşref was mistakenly mentioned many times in the famous Turkish popular TV series *Kurtlar Vadisi* (*The Valley of the Wolves*) as the founder of the Ottoman Intelligence Service (*Teşkilat-ı Mahsusa*).
4. Avagyan, *Türk Dış Siyasetinde Kuzey Kafkasya*, 18.
5. Ibid., 10.
6. Gingeras, 'The Sons of Two Fatherlands', 12.
7. Ahmet T. Kuru, *Secularism and State Policies towards Religion: The United States, France, and Turkey*, Cambridge Studies in Social Theory, Religion, and Politics (Cambridge; New York: Cambridge University Press, 2009), 14.
8. King, *Midnight at the Pera Palace*, 191.
9. İzzet Aydemir, http://kaffed.org/bilgi-belge/tarih/item/226-yuzellilikler-listesi-ve-cerkesler.html. accessed on 03 August 2016.
10. Hakan Ozoglu, *From Caliphate to Secular State: Power Struggle in the Early Turkish Republic: Power Struggle in the Early Turkish Republic* (Westport: Praeger, 2011), http://site.ebrary.com/lib/alltitles/docDetail.action?docID=10508639, 22.
11. Kamil Erdeha, *Yüzellilikler Yahut Milli Mücadelenin Muhasebesi* (İstanbul: Tekin Yayınevi, 1998), 18.
12. Turkish politician and diplomat, 1878–1971.
13. *Turkish Grand National Assembly, Secret session 39*, 16 April 1924, https://www.tbmm.gov.tr/tutanaklar/TUTANAK/GZC/d02/CILT04/gcz02004039.pdf. accessed 07 September 2016, 435.
14. Ibid.
15. Ibid., 439.
16. Ibid.
17. Erdeha, *Yüzellilikler Yahut Milli Mücadelenin Muhasebesi*, 67.
18. *Turkish Grand National Assembly, Secret session 39*, 16 April 1924, https://www.tbmm.gov.tr/tutanaklar/TUTANAK/GZC/d02/CILT04/gcz02004039.pdf, accessed 07 September 2016, 436.
19. Ibid.
20. Ibid., 437.

21 Ibid., 435.
22 Ibid., 443.
23 Ibid.
24 Ibid., 445, 446.
25 Ibid., 437.
26 Ibid., 449, 450.
27 Ibid., 441.
28 It can be also said that some members of the Çapanoğlu family were forced to stay in Ankara after their uprising in 1920. Therefore, it might have been assumed by the government that the family has already been pacified in Ankara.
29 Ozoglu, *From Caliphate to Secular State*, 32–3.
30 BCA. 30 18 1 1.4.45.16, 22, 1 January 1338 (1922).
31 Birinci, *Hürriyet ve İtilâf Fırkası*, 39.
32 Ibid., 213.
33 Ibid., 229.
34 Erdeha, *Yüzellilikler Yahut Milli Mücadelenin Muhasebesi*, 75. Amit Bein, *Ottoman Ulema, Turkish Republic: Agents of Change and Guardians of Tradition* (Stanford University Press, 2011), 102, 103.
35 Erdeha, *Yüzellilikler Yahut Milli Mücadelenin Muhasebesi*, 61.
36 Ozoglu claims that this group was selectively chosen since not every Cabinet member who worked for the *Kuva-yi İnzibatiyye* was put into the list. This included people such as Cemil Paşa (Topuzlu), minister of public works, and Ahmet Reşit (Rey), the minister of interior. Ozoglu, *From Caliphate to Secular State*, 47.
37 *Resmi Ceride*, 7 January 1925, 3, 4.
38 Şaduman Halıcı, 'Yüzellilikler', *Yüksek Lisans Tezi* (Anadolu Üniversitesi Sosyal Bİlimler Enstitüsü, 1998), 29.
39 BTCA. 030_01_88_551_9 – 1, 2, 3. A letter from Kuşçubaşı Eşref Bey to Finance Minister Hasan Polatkan (Eşref mistakenly used the title '*Başvekilim*', meaning 'my prime minister'; however, Hasan Polatkan was not the prime minister, he was the finance minister) in 10 June 1953.
40 Halıcı, 'Yüzellilikler', 69.
41 http://www.resmigazete.gov.tr/arsiv/68.pdf. Halıcı, 'Yüzellilikler', 31.
42 http://www.resmigazete.gov.tr/arsiv/398.pdf. Halıcı, 'Yüzellilikler', 31.
43 Halıcı, 'Yüzellilikler', 32.
44 Ibid.
45 BCA. 030_10_00_00_15_84_11_1, 2, 10 March 1938.

46 BCA. 030_10_00_00_44_283_6_1-7, 13 May 1938.
47 Evren Dede, http://www.azinlikca.net/yazarlar/evren-dede/bat-trakyada-150likler-i-.html, accessed 18 August 2016.
48 PRO/FO 371/9120 E 611/34/44. PRO/FO 371/9120 E 2953/34/44.
49 PRO/FO 317/7919 E 14515/27/44, 158–62.
50 Caner Yelbaşı, *Bir Muhalifin Portresi*, http://ajanskafkas.com/gorus/bir-muhalifin-portresi-hafiz-ali-resad/, accessed 02 August 2016. According to Cemal Kutay, Çerkes Ethem dictated his memoirs to Hafız Reşad, and Hafız Reşad sent the memoirs to Kutay. Cemal Kutay, *Çerkez Ethem Dosyası* (İstanbul: Boğaziçi Yayınevi, 1977), 39.
51 Erdeha, *Yüzellilikler Yahut Milli Mücadelenin Muhasebesi*, 124.
52 Ibid., 97.
53 Halıcı, 'Yüzellilikler', 170–1.
54 Ibid.
55 BCA. 30 10 0 0.106.695.29, 11 June 1925. BCTA, 30 10 0 0.106.695.30-1, 7–8 July 1925.
56 BCA. 30 10 0 0.106.695.30-2, 28 June 1925.
57 Tülay Duran, '150 Liklerin Gizli Mektupları (III)', *Belgelerle Türk Tarihi Dergisi; Dün/Bugün/Yarın* (Kasım November 1999), 66. 28 November 1928.
58 Halıcı, 'Yüzellilikler', 171–4.
59 Ibid., 176.
60 Ibid., 174.
61 Ibid., 175.
62 Ibid.
63 BCA. 030_10_00_00_110_740_11, 07 March 1927.
64 Çerkes Ethem, 'Çerkes Ethem meydan okuyor', in Derin Tarih, February 2015, 57–8.
65 Duran, '150 Liklerin Gizli Mektupları (III)', 71, 25 December 1930 and page 73, 22 January 1932.
66 Ibid., 73. 24 February 1932.
67 Ibid., 73.
68 Ibid., 24 March 1932.
69 Ibid., 2 January 1932, 22 January 1922. Ibid., 75. endnote 4. A young male member of Ottoman Dynasty.
70 Duran, '150 Liklerin Gizli Mektupları (V)', January 2000. 52. Sometimes Ethem used nick names instead of to write his own name on the letters.
71 Ibid., 53. 9 June 1932.

72 Zürcher, *The Unionist Factor*, 144.
73 BCA. 030-0-010-000-000-107-702-2.2, 22 August 1926.
74 Ibid.
75 He was also known as Çerkes Sami, Kuşçubaşı Sami.
76 Erdeha, *Yüzellilikler Yahut Milli Mücadelenin Muhasebesi*, 108.
77 Düzceli Hakkı (1882–1928). He was born in Düzce/Bıçkı village, married and had eight children. He fought in the Balkan War and in the Caucasian front of the First World War and then he came back to Istanbul and became an official. In the post-First-World-War period he was also in the Adapazarı and İzmit regions. He left the region probably with (Çule) İbrahim Hakkı in June 1921 for Midilli. *Cumhuriyet*, 27 August 1927, 1, 6 November 1927, 3, and 19 January 1928, 3.
78 Düzceli Mecid was the nephew of Hakkı. He was from the Bıçkı village of Düzce, see *Cumhuriyet*, 27 August 1927, 1, and 19 January 1928, 3. According to his statement in court, he was taken as a hostage by the Greeks in Bursa during the Turkish–Greek War, and then he was sent to Midilli and Athens.
79 Sökeli Mecid, according to his statement in court, fought in Hüseyin the shepherd's group during the Turkish–Greek War. He was taken hostage by the Greeks and stayed in Midilli. See *Cumhuriyet*, 6 November 1927, 3.
80 *Cumhuriyet*, 6 November 1927, 3. 7 November 1927, 2.
81 *Milliyet*, 1 September 1927, 2.
82 *Cumhuriyet*, 31 Ağustos 1927, 1, 2. 'Çerkes Sami was slithering like a snake. He did not have fatherland (vatansız)' *Milliyet*, 29 August 1927, 1, 4.
83 The Prime Ministry Republican Archive (BTCA) records, particularly the court records, have not been opened yet on this incident. Newspapers are the only source for the trial. *Cumhuriyet* and *Milliyet* newspapers published most of the court records when the trial happened.
84 Due to his father's opposition to Abdülhamid II, his father was exiled to Mecca; Mekki was born there in 1901. According to his statement, he fought for the *Kuva-yi Milliye* under Edib Bey in Salihli during the Turkish–Greek War. Later on, Mustafa Kemal ordered his arrest. It is not known when he was released exactly, but after his release he lived in Istanbul/Üsküdar. See *Cumhuriyet*, 7 November 1927, 1, 2.
85 *Cumhuriyet*, 6 September 1927, 1. 7 September 1927, 1.
86 *Cumhuriyet*, 4 October 1927, 2.
87 *Cumhuriyet*, 6 November 1927, 1.
88 Ibid., 1, 3. *Milliyet*, 6 November 1927, 3.
89 *Cumhuriyet*, 6 November 1927, 3.

90 Ibid. 7 November 1927, 2.
91 *Cumhuriyet*, 6 November 1927, 3.
92 *Cumhuriyet*, 8 September 1927, 1, 2. 11 September 1927, 4.
93 *Cumhuriyet*, 6 November 1927, 3. *Milliyet,* 6 November 1927, 1.
94 *Cumhuriyet*, 7 November 1927, 2.
95 https://www.tbmm.gov.tr/tutanaklar/TUTANAK/TBMM/d03/c002/tbmm0300 2030.pdf, 12 January 1928.
96 *Cumhuriyet,* 7 November 1927, 2.
97 Same as with Sami's case, the Prime Ministry Republican Archive (BTCA) records, particularly the court records, have not been opened yet on this incident. Therefore, I used the *Cumhuriyet* newspaper.
98 Yahya was from the Yukarıotluk village of Çarşamba/Samsun, born in 1316 (1898) and from the Sapsugh 'Şapsığ' branch of Circassians, a farmer and workman.
99 Ali Saip Ursavaş (1885–1939), colonel, MP from CHP, and head of Independent Court.
100 Üzeyir was owner of a farm in Maraş.
101 '*Eşref kılıç ile başlamış olduğu tarihi yine kılıçla kapatacaktır*'. *Cumhuriyet*, 8 February 1936, 8.
102 *Cumhuriyet*, 8 February 1936, 8.
103 Ibid., 9.
104 It is also mentioned that 'not only was the host obliged to defend the guest even at the cost of his own life, he [it] was forbidden to inquire about the guest's background'. Richmond, *The Circassian Genocide*, 5. Note 14 cited from Khan-Girey, Zapiski o Cherkesii. Nal'chik: El'brus, 1978, 298–305.
105 *Cumhuriyet*, 8 February 1936, 10.
106 Ibid., 11.
107 Ibid., 10.
108 It is worth mentioning that although the beginning of the dispute is not known exactly; before or after the alleged assassination attempt there was an argument over the land between Üzeyir and Ali Saip (Ursavaş) from the 1930s. According to the statements of Üzeyir Bey's son and grandson, their land in Kesikli and Mecidiye villages of Adana (now Osmaniye after 1996) was seized by Ali Saip, just as he did to some other Circassians of the region. Ali Saip used his position as MP and head of the Independent Tribunal to seize Circassian land in the region. Üzeyir Bey's son took the case to court; however, although the trial started in the early 1950s, it has not finished yet. The European Human Rights

Court (EHRC) was also involved in the trial process, and it was decreed by the court that €19.20 compensation should be paid to the heirs of Üzeyir Bey in 2009. Haşim Söylemez 'Çerkezlerin Toprak Kavgası', *Aksiyon*, 03 June 2000. www.aksiyon.com.tr/dosyalar/newsDetail_openPrintPage.action?newsId=506 223, accessed 31 January 2016. For the decision of EHRC http://blog.kararara .com/aihsnin-8-maddesinin-ve-1-nolu-protokolun-1-maddesinin-ihlal-edil digi-iddiasi/, accessed 31 January 2016.

109 *Cumhuriyet*, 8 February 1936, 10.
110 Ibid., 9.
111 *Cumhuriyet*, 19 October 1935, 1.
112 *Cumhuriyet*, 27 October 1935, 1, 7. 20 October 1935, 1, 8. 28 October 1935, 1, 6. *Son Posta*, 28 October 1935, 1, 7.
113 *Cumhuriyet*, 19 October 1935.
114 *Son Posta*, 27 October 1935, 6.
115 *Cumhuriyet*, 22 October 1935, 1.
116 *Son Posta*, 30 October 1935, 6.
117 *Cumhuriyet*, 20 October 1935, 1.
118 *Son Posta*, 27 October 1935, 1.
119 *Son Posta*, 25 October 1935, 1.
120 *Cumhuriyet*, 30 October 1935, 1. *Son Posta*, 27 October 1935, 6.
121 *Cumhuriyet*, 6 November, 1935, 1, 7.
122 *Cumhuriyet*, 10 January 1936, 1, 9.
123 *Cumhuriyet*, 8 February 1926, 7.
124 *Cumhuriyet*, 7 February 1936, 9.
125 *Son Posta*, 17 January 1936, 7.
126 *Cumhuriyet*, 18 February 1936, 7.
127 Halıcı, 'Yüzellilikler', 100.
128 *Cumhuriyet*, 18 February 1936, 1.
129 Ahmet İnsel, *Giriş*, Modern Türkiye'de Siyasî Düşünce (Cağaloğlu, İstanbul: İletişim, 2011), 18, 19.
130 Ibid., 22.
131 Mesut Yeğen, 'The Kurdish Question in Turkish State Discourse', *Journal of Contemporary History*, October 1999, 557.
132 Ibid., 559.
133 Ibid.
134 Mesut Yeğen, 'Turkish Nationalism and Kurdish Question', *Ethnic and Racial Studies*, November 2006, 126.

135 Yeğen, 'The Kurdish Question in Turkish State Discourse', 567.
136 Mesut Yeğen, 'Citizenship and Ethnicity in Turkey', *Middle Eastern Studies*, November 2006, 56. The law stayed in use until 1965.
137 Ibid., 56.
138 *Resmi Gazete* (Official Newspaper), Number 2733, 21 June 1934, 1, 2.
139 Soner Çağaptay, *Islam, Secularism, and Nationalism in Modern Turkey: Who Is a Turk* (New York: Routledge, 2006), 63.
140 It can be said that the abolishment of the caliphate actuated the activities of the Kurdish nationalists to gain support from the religious Kurds. The Kurdish nationalists convinced the religious Kurds that the Kurds did not have a reason any more to live under the new republic of Turkey.
141 Yeğen, 'Turkish Nationalism and Kurdish Question', 127.
142 Yeğen, 'The Kurdish Question in Turkish State Discourse', 561.
143 Ibid., 563.
144 The obsession of the regime with the use of Turkish language and the ban of the Arabic script were not taken seriously by even the members of the Republican Party. It was declared by the party general secretary that in the congress/meetings of the partys some members took their notes in Arabic letters. They had to be warned by the party management. BCA. 490-1-0-0_728-493-1. Document 12. 11 October 1944.
145 BCA. 10-0-0 / 69-457-14 1. Date 1932. The intelligence report of first inspectorship.
146 BCA. 030_10_00_00_70_461_1_4, 5. Date 24 August 1937.
147 BCA. 030_10_00_00_70_461_1_6. Date 24 August 1937.
148 BCA. 030_10_00_00_68_452_4_7. Date 24 August 1937.
149 BCA. 030_10_00_00_68_452_4_14. Date 24 August 1937.
150 BCA. 030_10_00_00_68_452_4_6. Date 24 August 1937.
151 Ibid. Cemil Koçak gives exact numbers, in the first region 741,325 Kurds, in the second region 299,055 Kurd, in the fourth region 198,508 Kurd used tol ive. Bülent Varlık, Umumi Müfettişler Toplantı Tutanakları 1936 (Cemil Koçak'ın Önsözü ile), Dipnot Yayınları, İstanbul, 2010, 15.
152 BCA. 030_10_00_00_72_471_12_2. Date 15 September 1945. From the Ministry of Interior to the Prime Ministry, report of fourth General Inspectorship.
153 BCA. 030_10_00_00_72_471_12_7. Date 15 September 1945. From the Ministry of Interior to the Prime Ministry, report of fourth General Inspectorship.

154 BCA. 490_01_607_104_2_1 and 2, 24 May 1937–26 March 1937.
155 BCA. 490_01_607_104_2_2, 26 March 1937.
156 BCA. 030_0_18_01_01_013_24_5_001, 18 April 1925.
157 Ibid.
158 BCA. 030_0_18_01_02_13_54_010, 24 July 1930.
159 BCA. 030_0_18_01_02_13_54_010, 24 July 1930.
160 BCA. 030_0_18_01_01_017_88_20_001, 31 January 1926.
161 This law was in force until it was abrogated on 1 July 1964, http://www.resmigazete.gov.tr/arsiv/11742.pdf, accessed 07 September 2016.
162 BCA. 30 18 1 1.30.60.6, 3 October 1928.
163 BCA. 030_0_18_01_02_41_91_012, 3 December 1933.
164 BCA. 030_18_01_02_85_102_2, 3 December 1938.
165 BCA. 490_01_607_104_1_1 and 2, 17 June 1935.
166 BCA. 490_01_607_104_1_1 and 2, 17 June 1935.
167 BCA. 490_01_607_104_1_1, 17 June 1935.
168 Soner Çağaptay, *Islam, Secularism and Nationalism in Modern Turkey: Who Is a Turk?*, Routledge Studies in Middle Eastern History (London: Routledge, 2005), 114, 115.
169 BCA. 030-0-010-000-000-105-688-20, 1 December 1925.
170 Sefer E. Berzeg, *Çerkes-Vubıhlar; Soçi'nin İnsanları (Portreler)* (Ankara: Kuban Matbaacılık Yayıncılık, 2013).
171 Ada Holland Shissler, 'Beauty Is Nothing to Be Ashamed Of: Beauty Contests as Tools of Women's Liberation in Early Republican Turkey', *Comparative Studies of South Asia, Africa and the Middle East* 24, no. 1 (2004): 107–22.
172 *Cumhuriyet*, 2 August 1932, 1.
173 *Cumhuriyet*, 3 August 1932, 1.
174 *Cumhuriyet*, 9 August 1932, 1.
175 *Cumhuriyet*, 11 August 1932, 1, 4.
176 *Akşam,* 2 August 1932, 2. 7 August 1932, 1, 4.
177 Mekki Sait, 'Yedigün', 31 May 1933. 14, 15. Thanks to Rengin Yurdakul of Şamil Foundation for this information.
178 *Cumhuriyet*, 20 May 1933, 3.
179 Keriman Halis was engaged to Dr Orhan Bey on 13 July 1937. *Cumhuriyet*, 14 July 1937, 3. Later on Keriman Halis also asked *Cumhuriyet* that they not use her picture and caricature; she had now become history and was working on her own agendas. *Cumhuriyet*, 26 February 1936, 6.
180 BCA. 030_0_18_01_01_021_67_017, 1 November 1926.

181 BCA. 030_0_18_01_02_29_44_016, 9 June 1932.
182 *Turkish Grand National Assembly, Open session* 83, 29 June 1938, https://www.tbmm.gov.tr/tutanaklar/TUTANAK/TBMM/d05/c026/tbmm05026083.pdf, 481, 482.
183 According to Ozoglu, Sadullah Sami attempted to come back to Turkey; however, until 11 June 1957 he was not allowed to enter the Turkish state. Ozoglu, *From Caliphate to Secular State*.
184 Celal Bayar was himself a member of Committee of Union and Progress (CUP) and Ottoman Special Organization (Teşkilatı Mahsusa). He might personally know some of those who were in the list of 150'ers.
185 *Turkish Grand National Assembly, Open session* 83, 29 June 1938, https://www.tbmm.gov.tr/tutanaklar/TUTANAK/TBMM/d05/c026/tbmm05026083.pdf, 472, 473.
186 Ibid., 482, 483.
187 Ibid., 483.
188 Ibid., 481, 482.
189 Erdeha, *Yüzellilikler Yahut Milli Mücadelenin Muhasebesi*, 174, 181, 211.
190 Ibid., 182.
191 Feridun Kandemir, *Atatürk'e İzmir Suikastinden Ayrı 11 Suikast* (İstanbul: Ekicigil Basımevi, 1955).
192 Halıcı, 'Yüzellilikler', 248–53.
193 Ibid.
194 Sedat Bingöl, *150'likler Meselesi (Bir İhanetin Anatomisi)* (İstanbul: Bengi Yayınları, 2010), 211.
195 Halıcı, 'Yüzellilikler', 185–6.
196 Ibid., 186.
197 Ibid., 186, 187.
198 Ibid.
199 Ibid., 280.
200 Ibid., 189, 190.
201 Ibid.

Chapter 7

1 Cemil Koçak, *CHP Genel Sekreterliği (1930-1945)* (İstanbul: Alfa, 2018), 200, 202, 218.

2 Demirel, *Birinci Meclis'te Muhalefet*.
3 Ibid., 231.
4 Ibid., 608.
5 Smith, *National Identity*, 9.
6 I met with two people who were sons of two *personae non gratae* (Yüzellilik) in Düzce and Gümülcine (Greece) – Çule Baki Özcan and Sedat Reşat. I heard the same story from both of them. They told me that they were not allowed by their fathers to listen to their conversations on these topics.
7 Avagyan, *Türk Dış Siyasetinde Kuzey Kafkasya*, 14, 15.
8 Ibid.
9 Ibid., 16, 17.
10 Ibid., 128.
11 Ibid., 16, 17.
12 Ibid., 18.
13 See Şaduman Halıcı, *Ethem* (İstanbul: E Yayınları, 2016) and for its critic see Caner Yelbaşı, 'Kitap Değerlendirme: Ethem, Şaduman Halıcı', *Divan Disiplinlerarası Çalışmalar Dergisi* 23, no. 44 (January 2018): 128–42.
14 Çağaptay, *Islam, Secularism, and Nationalism in Modern Turkey*, 16.

Bibliography

Archives

ATASE, Askeri Tarih ve Stratejik Etüt Başkanlığı Arşivleri, The Military Archive in Ankara

    İstiklal Harbi Koleksiyonu (İSH)
    Atatürk Koleksiyonu (ATAZB)

BCA, Başbakanlık Cumhuriyet Arşivleri, Prime Ministry's Turkish Republican Archives

BOA, Başbakanlık Osmanlı Arşivleri, Prime Ministry's Ottoman Archive

    Bab-ı Ali Evrak Odası (BEO)
    Dahiliyye Nezareti
        Emniyet – i Umumiye Müdüriyeti (DH.EUM)
            Asayiş Kalemi (DH.EUM.AYŞ)
            Birinci Şube (DH.EUM.1.Şb)
            İkinci Şube (DH.EUM.2.Şb)
            Altıncı Şube (DH.EUM.6.Şb)
            Seyrüsefer Kalemi (DH.EUM.SSM)
        İdare-i Umumiye Evrakı (DH.İ.UM)
        Kalemi Müdüriyet (DH.KMS)
        Mektubi Kalemi (DH.MKT)
        Şifre Kalemi (DH.ŞFR)
    Hariciye Nezareti
        İstanbul Murahhaslığı (HR.İM)
        Siyasi (HR.SYS)
        İradeler

PRO/FO, Public Record Office/Foreign Office, London; Kew Gardens

TİTE, Ankara Üniversitesi Türk İnkılap Tarihi Enstitüsü Arşivi, Ankara University, History of Turkish Revolution Institute Archive

TTK Bekir Sami Dosya, Bekir Sami (Günsav) Bey'in Kişisel Belgeleri, Personal Documents of Bekir Sami Günsav in Turkish Historical Society Archive in Ankara.

Published archive sources

Genelkurmay Başkanlığı Harb Tarihi Vesikaları Dergisi, Turkish Armed Forces General Staff; Journal of Military History Documents

Online sources

01.03.1997 Hadi Özcan's statement to the Susurluk Investigation Committee, http://www.kocaelimeydan.com/gundem/bir-mafya-babasinin-itiraflari-h11394.html
Atatürk'ün cenaze namazı, gazeteciye 15 ay hapis cezasına mal oldu' 21 April 2004. http://webarsiv.hurriyet.com.tr/2004/04/21/446534.asp
Dede Evren, http://www.azinlikca.net/yazarlar/evren-dede/bat-trakyada-150likler-i-.html
http://blog.kararara.com/aihsnin-8-maddesinin-ve-1-nolu-protokolun-1-maddes inin-ihlal-edildigi-iddiasi/
http://uyg.tsk.tr/ataturk/ata_album/albuyuk/index.htm
http://www.cerkesarastirmalari.org
http://www.gusips.net/analysis/sozlutarih/4334-hasan-tekin-hayvan-vagonlarina-insanlari-balik-istifi-yerlestirmisler.html
http://www.gusips.net/analysis/sozlutarih/4336-hakki-aci-yaslilar-hic-bahsetmiyo rlardi-bu-konulardan-eskiden-yasakli-konulardi-bir-yerde.html
Interview with Hasan Tekin
http://www.gusips.net/analysis/sozlutarih/4338-gurol-demir-babam-yillar-sonra-kayseri-de-surgundeyken-dayimin-oturdugu-evi-buldu.html
Interview with Hakkı Acı
http://www.haberturk.com/gundem/haber/823156-genelkurmay-cerkez-etheme-sans ur-mu-uyguladi
http://www.kocaeli.gov.tr/ortak_icerik/1/tarih/kocaeli%20tarihi/index.html
http://www.resmigazete.gov.tr/arsiv
https://www.tbmm.gov.tr/kutuphane/tutanak_sorgu.html
Kural Kuban, Oral History project, 'Unutulan Geçmişin Peşinde: 'Gönen-Manyas Çerkes Sürgünü', http://www.gusips.net/analysis/desc/4325-unutulan-gecmisin-pesinde-gonen-manyas-cerkes-surgunu.html
Interview with Gürol Demir
Söylemez Haşim, 'Çerkezlerin Toprak Kavgası', Aksiyon, 03 June 2000. www.aksiyo n.com.tr/dosyalar/newsDetail_openPrintPage.action?newsId=506223

TBMM, Türkiye Büyük Millet Meclisi Açık ve Kapalı Celse Zabıtları, Turkish Grand National Assembly Open and Closed Sessions Records

Tram, Merve, Kollektif Cezalandırmanın Tarihi ve Bugününden Bir Kesit, http://www.gusips.net/blogger/2244-kolektif-cezalandirmanin-tarihi-ve-bugununden-bir-kesit.html

Yelbaşı Caner, Bir Muhalifin Portresi, http://ajanskafkas.com/gorus/bir-muhalifin-portresi-hafiz-ali-resad/

News papers and magazines

Akşam
Cumhuriyet
İkdam
Milliyet
Son Posta
Yedigün

Books and manuscripts

Abdülkadir Bey. *Çapanoğulları Hadisesi ve Abdulkadir Bey'in Hatıraları*, edited by Ali Şakir Ergin. Ankara: Ahmet Şevki Ergin Kültür ve Hizmet Vakfı Yayınları, 2006.

Adıvar, Halide Edib. *Türkün Ateşle-İmtihanı: (Istiklâl Savaşı Hâtıraları)*. İstanbul: Çan yayını, 1962.

Adıvar, Halide Edib. *Ateşten Gömlek: Sakarya Ordusuna*. 4 üncü basılış. İstanbul: Ahmet Halit Kitabevi, 1943.

Ahmed, Feroz. *The Young Turks: The Committee of Union and Progress in Turkish Politics, 1908-1914*. New York: Columbia University Press, 2010.

Akal, Emel. *İştirakiyuncular, Komünistler ve Paşa Hazretleri Moskova-Ankara-Londra Üçgeninde*. İstanbul: İletişim Yayınları, 2014.

Akal, Emel. *Mustafa Kemal, İttihat Terakki ve Bolşevizm Milli Mücadelenin Başlangıcında*. İstanbul: İletişim Yayınları, 2012.

Akbaş, Rahmi. *Söğütlü Jandarma Onbaşı Ali'nin Milli Mücadele Anıları*. İstanbul: Yeditepe Yayınevi, 2011.

Akın, Yiğit. 'The Ottoman Home Front during WWI: Everyday Politics, Society, and Culture'. PhD, Ohio State University, 2011.

Akıncı, İbrahim Ethem. *Demirci Akıncıları*. Yayınlar. Ankara: Türk Tarih Kurumu Basımevi, 1978.

Aksakal, Mustafa. *The Ottoman Road to War in 1914: The Ottoman Empire and the First World War.* Cambridge Military Histories. New York: Cambridge University Press, 2008.
Akşin, Sina. *İç Savaş ve Sevr'de Ölüm.* İstanbul: Türkiye İş Bankası Yayınları, 2010.
Akşin, Sina. *İstanbul Hükümetleri ve Milli Mücadele; Mutlakiyete Dönüş (1918-1919).* İstanbul: Cem Yayınevi, 1992.
Akyol, Taha. *Atatürk'ün İhtilal Hukuku.* İstanbul: Doğan Kitap, 2012.
Akyol, Taha. *Ama Hangi Atatürk.* İstanbul: Doğan Kitap, 2008.
Albayrak, Recep. *Ethem Bey'in Sürgün Yılları ve Simav Olayları (1919-1948).* Ankara: Berikan Yayınevi, 2004.
Apak, Rahmi. *İstiklal Savaşında Garp Cephesi Nasıl Kuruldu.* İstanbul: Güven Basımevi, 1942.
Arslan, Ali. 'Ülkenin Kurtarılmasında Kuvayı Milliye'nin Görüşü ve Yalnız Siyaseten Müdafaanın İflası (1918-1920)'. In *İstanbul'dan Çıkış; Milli Mücadeleye Giriş*, 7-28. İstanbul: Paraf Yayınları, 2010.
Atatürk, Kemal. *Atatürk: Gizli Oturumlardaki Konuşmalar.* Üçüncü basım. İstanbul: Kaynak Yayınları, 1997.
Atatürk, Kemal. *Atatürk'ün Söylev ve Demeçleri.* Ankara: Atatürk Arastırma Merkezi, 1989.
Atatürk, Kemal. *Gazi Mustafa Kemal Atatürk'ün 1923 Eskişehir-İzmit Konuşmaları.* Ankara: Türk Tarih Kurumu, 1982.
Atatürk, Kemal. *Nutuk.* İstanbul: Devlet Matbaası, 1934.
Atatürk ile Yazışmalar. Doğumunun 100. Yılında Atatürk Yayınları. Ankara: Kültür Bakanlığı, 1981.
Avagyan, Arsen. *Türk Dış Siyasetinde Kuzey Kafkasya Siyasi Muhacereti (1920-1971).* İstanbul: Belge Yayınları, 2013.
Avagyan, Arsen. *Osmanlı İmparatorluğu ve Kemalist Türkiye'nin Devlet-İktidar Sisteminde Çerkesler; XIX. Yüzyılın İlk Yarısından XX. Yüzyılın İlk Çeyreğine.* Çev. Ludmilla Denisenko. İstanbul: Belge Uluslararası Yayıncılık, 2004.
Ayhan, Aydın, and Hasan Ali Göksoy. *Kendi Yurdunda Esir Olmak; İşgal Yıllarında Balıkkesir.* Balıkkesir: Dileksan Kağıtçılık, 2011.
Aytepe, Oğuz. 'Milli Mücadele'de Bilecik Görüşmesi'. *Ankara Üniversitesi Türk İnkılâp Tarihi Enstitüsü Atatürk Yolu Dergisi*, no. 33-34 (November 2004): 23-31.
Baddeley, John Frederick 1854-1940. *The Russian Conquest of the Caucasus.* Richmond, Surrey (Britain): Curzon Press, 1999.
Bardakçı, Murat. *Enver.* İstanbul: İş Bankası Kültür Yayınları, 2015.
Başkaya, Fikret. *Paradigmanın İflası: Resmi İdeolojinin Eleştirisine Giriş: Batılılaşma, Kalkınma, Çağdaşlaşma.* İstanbul: Özgür Üniversite, 2012.
Bell, James S. *Journal of a Residence in Circassia.* Vol. 1. London: Edward Moxon, 1840.

Benlisoy, Foti. *Kahramanlar Kurbanlar Direnişçiler Trakya ve Anadolu'daki Yunan Ordusunda Propaganda, Grev ve İsyan (1919 – 1922)*. İstanbul: İstos Yayınevi, 2014.

Berzeg, Sefer E. *Çerkes-Vubıhlar; Soçi'nin İnsanları (Portreler)*. Ankara: Kuban Matbaacılık Yayıncılık, 2013.

Berzeg, Sefer E. *Türkiye Kurtuluş Savaşı'nda Çerkes Göçmenleri (II)*. İstanbul: Nart Yayıncılık, 1990.

Beşikçi, Mehmet. *The Ottoman Mobilisation of Manpower in the First World War: Between Voluntarism and Resistance*. Leiden; Boston: Brill, 2012.

Besleney, Zeynel Abidin. *The Circassian Diaspora in Turkey: A Political History*. London: Routledge, 2014.

Besleney, Zeynel Abidin. 'A Political History of Circassian Diaspora in Turkey 1864-2011'. SOAS, University of London, 2012.

Bilge, Sadık. *Osmanlı Çağı'nda Kafkasya 1454 – 1829; Tarih, Toplum, Ekonomi*. İstanbul: Kitabevi Yayınları, 2012.

Bingöl, Sedat. *150'likler Meselesi (Bir İhanetin Anatomisi)*. İstanbul: Bengi Yayınları, 2010.

Birinci, Ali. *Hürriyet ve İtilâf Fırkası: II. Meşrutiyet Devrinde İttihat ve Terakki'ye Karşı Çıkanlar*. İstanbul: Dergâh Yayınları, 2012.

Brandley, John Frederick N. *Civil War in Russia 1917-1920*. London: BT Batsford, 1975.

Bruinessen, M. Martin van. *Kurdish Ethno-Nationalism versus Nation-Building States: Collected Articles*. İstanbul: Isis Press, 2000.

Bruinessen, M. M. van. *Mullas, Sufis and Heretics: The Role of Religion in Kurdish Society: Collected Articles*. İstanbul: Isis Press, 2000.

Bruinessen, M. M. van. *Agha, Shaikh and State: The Social and Political Structures of Kurdistan*. London: Zed Books, 1992.

Butbay, Mustafa. *Kafkasya Hatıraları*. Türk Tarih Kurumu Yayınları. Ankara: Türk Tarih Kurumu Basımevı, 1990.

Butt, V. P., A. B. Murphy and N. A. Myshov. *The Russian Civil War; Documents from the Soviet Archieves*. London: Macmillan Press, 1996. https://www.palgrave.com/it/book/9780333593196.

Çağaptay, Soner. *Islam, Secularism and Nationalism in Modern Turkey: Who Is a Turk?* London: Routledge, 2005.

Çarıklı, Hacim Muhittin. *Balıkesir ve Alaşehir Kongreleri ve Hacim Muhittin Çarıklı'nın Kuvayı Millîye Hatıraları: (1919-1920)*. Ankara: Ankara Üniversitesi Basımevi, 1967.

Cebesoy, Ali Fuat. *Millî Mücadele Hâtıraları*. İstanbul: Temel, 2010.

Cebesoy, Ali Fuat. *Bilinmeyen Hatıralar*. İstanbul: Temel, 2005.

Cebesoy, Ali Fuat. *Kuvâ-Yı Milliye'nin İçyüzü: Olaylar, Kişiler, Vesikalar*. İstanbul: Temel, 2002.

Cebesoy, Ali Fuat. *Moskova Hatıraları: (21/11/1920-2/6/1922)*. İstanbul: 'Vatan' Neşriyatı, 1955.
Çeçen, Anıl. *100 Soruda Kemalizm*. İstanbul: Kilit Yayıncılık, 2009.
Çelikpala, Mitat. 'Search For a Common North Caucasian Identity: The Mountaineers' Attempts For Survival and Unity Response to the Russian Rule'. PhD Thesis, Bilkent University, 2002.
Çerkes Ethem. *Anılarım*. İstanbul: Berfin Yayınları, 2005.
Çetinkaya, Doğan. *The Young Turks and the Boycott Movement: Nationalism, Protest and the Working Classes in the Formation of Modern Turkey*. London: I.B. Tauris, 2013.
Çiçek, M. Talha. *War and State Formation in Syria: Cemal Pasha's Governorate during WWI, 1914-1917*. New York: Routledge, 2014.
Cilasun, Emrah. *'Baki ile Selam' Çerkes Ethem*. İstanbul: Belge Yayınları, 2004.
Criss, Nur Bilge. *Istanbul under Allied Occupation 1918-1923*. Leiden: Brill, 1999.
Çule, İbrahim Hakkı. *Efkar-ı Umumiyeye Bir İzah ve Muarızlara Cevab, Şark-ı Karib Çerkesleri Temin-i Hukuk Cemiyeti Beyanname ne Nizamname-i Esasiyesi, Çerkeslik Hareket ve Teşebbüs-i Ahirinin Esbab ve Sevaiki Tarihçesi*, 1922.
Demirel, Ahmet. *Cumhuriyet Tarihinin Bilinmeyen Gerçekleri*. İstanbul: Ufuk Yayınları, 2014.
Demirel, Ahmet. *Birinci Meclis'te Mustafa Kemal'in Muhalifleri*. İstanbul: Ufuk yayınları, 2013.
Demirel, Ahmet. *İlk Meclis'in Vekilleri: Milli Mücadele Döneminde Seçimler*. İstanbul: İletişim, 2010.
Demirel, Ahmet. *Birinci Meclis'te Muhalefet: İkinci Grup*. İstanbul: İletişim, 2009.
Ditson, George L. *Circassia; or a Tour to the Caucasus*. New York: Stringer & Townsend, 1850.
Duran, Tülay. '150 Liklerin Gizli Mektupları (III)'. *Belgelerle Türk Tarihi Dergisi; Dün/Bugün/Yarın*, Kasım 1999.
Efe, Ahmet. *Kuşçubaşı Eşref*. İstanbul: Bengi Kitap Yayın, 2010.
Efe, Ahmet. *Çerkez Ethem*. İstanbul: Bengi Kitap Yayın, 2009.
Erdeha, Kamil. *Yüzellilikler Yahut Milli Mücadelenin Muhasebesi*. İstanbul: Tekin Yayınevi, 1998.
Erdem, Can. 'İbrahim Hakkı Bey'in İzmit Mutasarrıflığı'. *Yakın Dönem Türkiye Araştırmaları Dergisi* 3, no. 5 (2004): 105-24.
Erdem, Y. Hakan. *Tarih-Lenk; Kusursuz Yazarlar, Kağıttan Metinler*. İstanbul: Doğan Kitap, 2010.
Ergil, Doğu. *Milli Mücadelenin Sosyal Tarihi*. Ankara: Turhan Kitabevi, 1981.
Ersanlı, Büşra. *İktidar ve Tarih*. İstanbul: İletişim Yayınları, 2003.
Ertem, Bayan Gönül. *Dancing to Modernity: Cultural Politics of Cherkess Nationhood in the Heartland of Turkey*. PhD Thesis, University of Texas Austin, 2000.

Evan, Mawdsley. *The Russian Civil War*. Edinburg: Birlinn Limited, 2008.

Fortna, Benjamin C. *The Circassian: A Life of Eşref Bey, Late Ottoman Insurgent and Special Agent*. London: Hurst & Company, 2016.

Fortna, Benjamin C., Katsikas, Stefanos, et al. *State-Nationalisms in the Ottoman Empire, Greece and Turkey: Orthodox and Muslims, 1830-1945*. New York: Routledge, 2013.

Gelvin, James L. *Divided Loyalties: Nationalism and Mass Politics in Syria at the Close of Empire*. Berkeley: University of California Press, 1998.

Genel Kurmay Harp Tarihi Dairesi. 'Genel Kurmay Harp Tarihi Vesikaları Dergisi', 1952-69.

Genel Kurmay Harp Tarihi Dairesi. *Türk İstiklal Harbi: İstiklal Harbinde Ayaklanmalar (1919-1921)*. Ankara: Genelkurmay Harp Tarihi Başkanlığı, 1974.

Genel Kurmay Harp Tarihi Dairesi. *Türk İstiklal Harbi: İç Ayaklanmalar: 1919-1921*. Ankara: Genelkurmay Harp Tarihi Başkanlığı, 1964.

Gerede, Hüsrev. *Hüsrev Gerede'nin Anıları: Kurtuluş Savaşı, Atatürk ve Devrimler (19 Mayıs 1919-10 Kasım 1938)*. İstanbul: Literatür, 2003.

Gingeras, Ryan. *Heroin, Organised Crime, and the Making of Modern Turkey*. Oxford University Press, 2014.

Gingeras, Ryan. 'The Sons of Two Fatherlands: Turkey, the Soviet Union and the North Caucasian Diaspora, 1918-1923'. *European Journal of Turkish Studies* (2011): 2-17. https://journals.openedition.org/ejts/4424.

Gingeras, Ryan. 'Last Rites for a "Pure Outlaw": Clandestine Service, Historiography and the Origins of the Turkish 'Deep State'. *Past and Present*, no. 206 (February 2010): 121-44.

Gingeras, Ryan. *Sorrowful Shores: Violence, Ethnicity, and the End of the Ottoman Empire, 1912-1923*. Oxford Studies in Modern European History. Oxford; New York: Oxford University Press, 2009.

Gingeras, Ryan. 'Notorious Subjects, Invisible Citizens: North Caucasian Resistance to the Turkish Nationalist movement in Northwestern Anatolia, 1919-23'. *International Journal of Middle East Studies* 40, no. 1 (February 2008): 89-108.

Gingeras, Ryan. 'Imperial Killing Fields: Revolution, Ethnicity and Islam in Western Anatolia, 1913-1938'. PhD Thesis, University of Toronto, 2006.

Gorky, M., K. Molotov, et al. *The History of the Civil War in the U.S.S.R.* Vol. 1. London: Lawrence & Wishart, 1936.

Göztepe, Tarık Mümtaz. *Osmanoğulları'nın Son Padişahı Sultan Vahideddin Mütareke Gayyasında*. İstanbul: Sebil Yayınevi, 1969.

Göztepe, Tarık Mümtaz. *Osmanoğulları'nın Son Padişahı Vahideddin-Gurbet Cehenneminde*. İstanbul: Sebil Yayınevi, 1991.

Güçtekin, Nuri. 'Çerkes Teavün Mektebi (1910-1914)'. *Yakın Dönem Türkiye Araştırmaları* 12, no. 23 (2013): 1-21.

Güleç, Sadık. *Ölüm Üçgeni: Bir Şehir, Bir Kabadayı, Bir Mafya Babası*. İstanbul: Profil Yayıncılık, 2013.
Halıcı, Şaduman. *Ethem*. İstanbul: E Yayınları, 2016.
Halıcı, Şaduman. 'Atatürk'e Suikast Girişimi: Hacı Sami ve Çetesi'. *Çağdaş Türkiye Tarihi Araştırmaları Dergisi* XIII, no. 27 (Güz 2013): 105–21.
Halıcı, Şaduman. 'Yüzellilikler'. Yüksek Lisans Tezi, Anadolu Üniversitesi Sosyal Bilimler Enstitüsü, 1998.
Hanioğlu, M. Şükrü. *Atatürk: An Intellectual Biography*. Princeton: Princeton University Press, 2011.
Hanioğlu, M. Şükrü. 'The Second Constitutional Period, 1908 - 1918', in *The Cambridge History of Turkey, Turkey in the Modern World*, edited by Reşat Kasaba, 62–111. Vol. 4. Cambridge: Cambridge University Press, 2006.
Hobsbawm, Eric John 1917–2012. *Bandits*. New edn. London: Abacus, 2001.
Holquist, Peter. *Making War, Forging Revolution; Russia's Continuum of Crisis 1914-1921*. Cambridge: Harvard University Press, 2002.
İğdemir, Uluğ. *Biga Ayaklanması ve Anzavur Olayları: Günlük Anılar*. Türk Tarih Kurumu Yayınları. Ankara: Türk Tarih Kurumu Basımevi, 1973.
Ihrig, Stefan. *Atatürk in the Nazi Imagination*. Cambridge: The Belknap Press of Harvard University Press, 2014.
Jongerden, Joost, and Jell Verheij. *Social Relations in Ottoman Diyarbekir, 1870-1915*. Boston: Brill, 2012.
Jwaideh, Wadie. *The Kurdish Nationalist Movement: Its Origins and Development*. Syracuse: Syracuse University Press, 2006.
Kandemir, Feridun. *Atatürk'e İzmir Suikastinden Ayrı 11 Suikast*. İstanbul: Ekicigil Basımevi, 1955.
Karabekir, Kazım. *İstiklal Harbimizde Enver Paşa ve İttihat ve Terakki Erkânı*. İstanbul: Menteş Matbaası, 1967.
Karpat, Kemal. 'The Status of The Muslim under European Rule: The Eviction and Settlement of the Çerkes', in *Studies on Ottoman Social and Political History: Selected Articles and Essays*. Leiden: Brill, 2002.
Kesbi Haşim, Mehmet Efendi. *Ahval-I Anapa ve Çerkes; Anapa ve Çerkesya Hatıraları Yayına Hazırlayan Mustafa Özsaray*. İstanbul: Kafkas Vakfı, 2012.
Kili, Suna. *Kemalism*. İstanbul: Robert College, 1969.
King, Charles. *Midnight at the Pera Palace: The Birth of Modern Istanbul*. New York: W.W. Norton and Company, 2014.
Klein, Janet. *The Margins of Empire: Kurdish Militias in the Ottoman Tribal Zone*. Stanford: Stanford University Press, 2011.
Koçak, Cemil. *CHP Genel Sekreterliği (1930-1945)*. İstanbul: Alfa, 2018.
Koçak, Cemil. *Umumi Müfettişlikler*. İstanbul: İletişim Yayınları, 2016.

Koçak, Cemil. *Geçmişiniz İtina İle Temizlenir*. İstanbul: İletişim Yayınları, 2011.
Koçak, Cemil. *Belgelerle Heyeti Mahsusalar*. İstanbul: İletişim Yayınları, 2005.
Köker, Levent. *Modernleşme, Kemalism ve Demokrasi*. İstanbul: İletişim Yayınları, 2012.
Konrapa, M. Zekai. *Bolu Tarihi*. Bolu: Bolu Vilayet Matbaası, 1964.
Kuru, Ahmet T. *Secularism and State Policies toward Religion: The United States, France, and Turkey*. Cambridge; New York: Cambridge University Press, 2009.
Longworth, John Augustus. *A Year among the Circassians*. Vol. I and II. London: Elibron Classics, 2003.
Mango, Andrew. *Atatürk*. London: John Murray, 1999.
McCarthy, Justin. *Population History of the Middle East and the Balkans*. İstanbul: The Isis Press, 2002.
McCarthy, Justin. *The Ottoman Peoples and the End of Empire*. London: New York: Arnold, 2001.
McCarthy, Justin. *Death and Exile: The Ethnic Cleansing of Ottoman Muslims 1821-1922*. Princeton: Darwin Press, 1995.
McCarthy, Justin. *Muslims and Minorities: The Population of Ottoman Anatolia and the End of the Empire*. New York: New York University Press, 1983.
McMillan, James. 'War in Political Violence', in *Political Violence in Twentieth – Century Europe*, edited by Robert Gerwarth. New York: Cambridge University Press, 2011.
Miralay Mehmet Arif Bey. *Anadolu İnkılabı (Mücahedat-I Milliye Hatıratı 1335-1339)*, edited by Bülent Demirbaş. İstanbul: Arba, 1987.
Miyazawa, Eiji. 'Memory Politics: Circassians of Uzunyayla, Turkey'. PhD Thesis, SOAS, University of London, 2004.
Nihat, Karaer. *Tam Bir Muhalif / Refik Halid Karay -Yüzellilikler Meselesi*. Temel Yayınları, 1998.
Özalp, Kazım. *Milli Mücadele 1. Cilt 1919-1922*. Ankara: Türk Tarih Kurumu, 1998.
Özcan, Mert. 'Anzavur'un İlk Ayaklanmasına Ait Belgeler'. *Belleten* 56, no. 217 (1992): 847–972.
Özer, Kemal. *Kurtuluş Savaşında Gönen*. Balıkkesir: Türkdili Matbaası, 1964.
Özkök, Rüknü. *Milli Mücadele Başlarken Düzce – Bolu İsyanları*. İstanbul: Milliyet Yayın Ltd. Şti., 1971.
Ozoglu, Hakan. *From Caliphate to Secular State: Power Struggle in the Early Turkish Republic: Power Struggle in the Early Turkish Republic*. Westport: Praeger, 2011. http://site.ebrary.com/lib/alltitles/docDetail.action?docID=10508639.
Palanithurai, Ganapathi. *Ethnic Identity and National Loyalty of an Ethnic Group: A Case Study of Tamil Nadu*. New Delhi: Concept Pub. Co., 2005.
Parla, Taha. *Ziya Gökalp, Kemalizm ve Türkiye'de Korporatizm = The Social and Political Thought of Ziya Gökalp*. İstanbul: Deniz Yayınları, 2009.

Parla, Taha. *Corporatist Ideology in Kemalist Turkey: Progress or Order?* Syracuse: Syracuse University Press, 2004.

Parla, Taha. *Türkiye'de Siyasal Kültürün Resmî Kaynakları.* İstanbul: İletişim Yayınları, 1991.

Payaslı, Volkan, and Olcay Özkaya Duman. 'Bir Yüzelliliğin Halep Gezi Notlarından Günceler: Tarık Mümtaz Yazganalp (Göztepe)'. *Turkish Studies* 9, no. 4 (Spring 2014): 967–83.

Reynolds, Michael A. *Shattering Empires: The Clash and Collapse of the Ottoman and Russian Empires, 1908-1918.* Cambridge; New York: Cambridge University Press, 2011.

Richmond, Walter. *The Circasian Genocide:* New Brunswick: Rutgers University Press, 2013.

Richmond, Walter. *The Northwest Caucasus: Past, Present, Future.* New York: Routledge, 2008.

Robert, Olsen. *The Emergence of Kurdish Nationalism and the Sheikh Said Rebellion, 1880 – 1925.* Austion: University of Texas, 1989.

Rogan, Eugene. *The Fall of the Ottomans: The Great War in the Middle East.* New York: Basic Books, 2015.

Sait, Mekki. 'Yedigün'. İstanbul, 31 May 1933.

Sambanis, Nicholas. 'Partition as a Solution to Ethnic War: An Empirical Critique of the Theoretical Literature'. *World Politics* 52, no. 4 (July 2000): 437–83.

Sarıhan, Zeki. *Çerkes Ethem İhaneti.* İstanbul: Kaynak Yayınları, 1998.

Şener, Cemal. *Çerkes Ethem Olayı.* İstanbul: ANT Yayınları, 1990.

Shissler, Ada Holland. 'Beauty Is Nothing to be Ashamed of: Beauty Contests as Tools of Women's Liberation in Early Republican Turkey', *Comperative Studies of South Asia, Africa and Middle East* 24, no. 1 (2004): 107–22.

Şoenu, Mehmet Fetgerey. *Tüm Eserleriyle Mehmet Fetgeri Şoenu.* Ankara: Kafdav Yayınları, 2007.

Sofuoğlu, Adnan. *Milli Mücadele Döneminde Kocaeli.* Ankara: AKDTYK Atatürk Araştırma Merkezi, 2006.

Sonyel, Salâhi Ramadan. *Turkish Diplomacy, 1918-1923: Mustafa Kemal and the Turkish Nationalist Movement.* London: Sage Publications, 1975.

Spancer, Edmund. *Travels in the Western Caucasus Including A Tour Through Imeretia, Mingrelia, Turkey, Moldavia, Galicia, Silesia and Moravia in 1836.* Vol. I and II. London: Elibron Classics, 2003.

Spencer, Edmund. *Travels in Circassia, Kirim Tartary in 1836.* Vol. I and II. London: Henry Colburn, 1838.

Şimşir, Bilâl N. *İngiliz Belgeleriyle Sakarya'dan İzmir'e, 1921-1922.* İstanbul: Milliyet Yayınları, 1972.

Smith, Anthony D. *National Identity*. Las Vegas: University of Nevada Press, 1991.
Stoddard, Philip H. 'The Ottoman Government and the Arabs, 1911 to 1918: A Preliminary Study of the Teşkilat-I Mahsusa'. Princeton University, 1963.
Süleyman Şefik Paşa. *Hatıratım/ Başıma Gelenler ve Gördüklerim / 31 Mart Vakʾası*. Sadeleştiren Hümeyra Zerdeci. İstanbul, 2004.
Swain, Goeffrey. *Russia's Civil War*. Gloucestershire: Tempus, 2000.
Talât Paşa, 1874–1921. *Talât Paşa'nın Anıları*. İstanbul: İletişim Yayınları, 1990.
Tarih IV. Kemalist Eğitimin Tarih Dersleri 1931 – 1941. İstanbul: Kaynak Yayınları, 2004.
Tekinalp, Munis. *Kemalizm*. İstanbul: Cumhuriyet Gazete ve Matbaası, 1936.
Tevfik, Rıza. *Biraz Da Ben Konuşayım*. İstanbul: İletişim Yayınları, 2008.
Tilly, Charles. 'War Making and State Making as Organized Crime', in *The State: Critical Concepts*, 508–30. London: Routledge, 1994.
Toledano, Ehud R. 'Ottoman Concepts of Slavery in the Period of Reform (1830s-1880s)', in *Breaking the Chains: Slavery, Bondage and Emancipation in Modem Africa and Asia*, edited by Martin A Klein, 37–63. Madison: University of Wisconsin Press, 1993.
Tunçay, Mete. *Turkiye' de Sol Akımlar: 1908-1925*. Ankara: Ankara Üniversitesi – Siyasal Bilgiler Fakültesi Yayınları, 1967.
Turfan, M. Naim. *Rise of the Young Turks: Politics, the Military and Ottoman Collapse*. London: I.B. Tauris, 2000.
Turfan, M. Naim. *The Politics of Military Politics: Political Aspects of Civil-Military Relations in the Ottoman Empire, with Special Reference to the 'Young Turk' era*. PhD Thesis, University of London, 1983.
Uçman, Abdullah. *Bir 150'liğin Mektupları Ali İlmi Fani'den Rıza Tevfik'e Mektuplar*. İstanbul: Kitabevi Yayınları, 2012.
Ünal, Muhittin. *56. Fırka Harb Ceridelerinden Miralay Bekir Sami Günsav'ın Kurtuluş Savaşı Anıları 1919-1920*. Ankara: Türk Tarih Kurumu, 2016.
Ünal, Muhittin. *Kurtuluş Savaşında Çerkeslerin Rolü*. İstanbul: Cem Yayınevi, 1996.
Ünal, Muhittin. *Miralay Bekir Sami Günsav'ın Kurtuluş Savaşı Anıları*. İstanbul: Cem Yayınları, 1993.
Üstel, Füsun. *İmparatorluktan Ulus-Devlete Türk Milliyetçiliği: Türk Ocakları (1912-1931)*. İstanbul: İletişim Yayınları, 1997.
Uzun, Zübeyir. 'Milli Mücadele'de Çerkez Ethem ve Kuva-Yı Seyyare'nin Faaliyetleri (1919–1920)'. Master Thesis, Selçuk University, 2008.
Varlık, Bülent. *Umumi Müfettişler Toplantı Tutanakları-1936*. Ankara: Dipnot Yayınları, 2010.
Velidedeoğlu, Hıfzı Veldet. *İlk Meclis ve Milli Mücadele'de Anadolu*. İstanbul: Çağdaş Yayınları, 1990.

Velidedeoğlu, Hıfzı Veldet. *Bir Lise Öğrencisinin Milli Mücadele Anıları*. İstanbul: Varlık Yayınevi, 1971.

Waller, Michael. 'The Paradoxes of Political Loyalty in Russia'. In *Political Loyalty and the Nation-State*, edited by Michael Waller and Andrew Linklater, 205–21. London: Routledge, 2003.

Yamauchi, Masayuki. *The Green Crescent under the Red Star: Enver Pasha in Soviet Russia 1919-1922*. Tokyo: Institute for the Study of Languages and Cultures of Asia and Africa, 1991.

Yanıkdağ, Yücel. 'Il-Fated' Son of the "Nation": The Ottoman Prisoners of War in Russia and Egypt, 1914-1922'. PhD Thesis, Ohio State University, 2002.

Yanıkdağ, Yücel. 'Ottoman Prisoners of War in Russia, 1914-1922'. *Journal of Contemporary History* 34, no. 1 (January 1999): 69–85.

Yeğen, Mesut. 'Citizenship and Ethnicity in Turkey'. *Middle Eastern Studies* 40, issue 6 (November 2006): 51–66.

Yeğen, Mesut. 'Turkish Nationalism and Kurdish Question'. *Ethnic and Racial Studies* 30, no. 1 (November 2006): 119–51.

Yeğen, Mesut. 'The Kurdish Question in Turkish State Discourse'. *Journal of Contemporary History* 34, no. 4 (October 1999): 555–68.

Yelbaşı, Caner. 'Kitap Değerlendirme: Ethem, Şaduman Halıcı'. *Divan Disiplinlerarası Çalışmalar Dergisi* 23, no. 44 (January 2018): 128–42.

Yerasimos, Stefanos. *Türk-Sovyet İlişkileri; Ekim Devriminden 'Milli Mücadele'ye*. İstanbul: Gözlem Yayınevi, 1979.

Yetim, Fahri. 'Milli Mücadele Döneminde İsyanların Gölgesinde Düzce ve Çevresinde Asayiş Sorunları'. In *Hacettepe Üniv. Cumhuriyet Tarihi Araştırmaları Dergisi*, no. 13 (2011): 54–69.

Yıldız, Ahmet. *Ne Mutlu Türküm Diyebilene; Türk Ulusal Kimliğinin Etno-Seküler Sınırları (1919-1938)*. İstanbul: İletişim Yayınları, 2001.

Zürcher, Erik Jan. *The Young Turk Legacy and the Nation Building: From the Ottoman Empire to Atatürk's Turkey*. London: I.B. Tauris, 2010.

Zürcher, Erik Jan. *Turkey: A Modern History*. London: I.B. Tauris, 2004.

Zürcher, Erik Jan. *Political Opposition in the Early Turkish Republic: The Progressive Republican Party, 1924-1925*. Leiden; New York: E.J. Brill, 1991.

Zürcher, Erik Jan. *The Unionist Factor: The Role of the Committee of Union and Progress in the Turkish Nationalist movement, 1905-1926*. Leiden: Brill, 1984.

Index

Abdülhamid II 13–15, 60, 144, 161
Abdullah, King of Jordan 172
Abkhaz 2, 75, 105
Abkhazian 2, 14, 18, 41, 45, 47, 48, 57, 58, 104, 129, 136
Adapazarı 3, 7, 11, 17, 36, 38, 41–7, 49–57, 59, 62, 64, 65, 84, 97, 99, 102–4, 106, 108, 109, 113, 117–20, 128, 129, 131, 138, 140, 176
Adige 2, 105
Aegean Sea 51, 102, 118, 130, 177
alaylı 16, 33
Albanian 9, 10, 23, 27, 30–2
Albayrak, Hakan 3
Aleppo 141, 144, 145, 164, 173
Ali, Maan 16, 47, 58, 113, 140
Ali Fuat Paşa 44, 49, 55, 73, 76, 84–7
Alliance 6, 11, 26, 27
Amman 144, 146, 151, 153, 172, 173, 178
amnesty 58, 130, 131, 171–3
Anadolu İhtilal Cemiyeti 116
Anatolia 2, 3, 6, 8, 9, 11–13, 16–18, 22, 23, 25–31, 38, 39, 43, 45, 49–52, 54, 61, 64, 68–74, 76, 79–83, 85–9, 91, 94, 96, 97, 99, 100, 103, 105, 107–13, 115–19, 121–5, 128–34, 136, 147–9, 160, 161, 164, 172, 176–9, 182, 183
Anatolian movement 27, 64, 68, 72, 76, 83, 85, 86, 88, 105, 132, 178
Anatolian Revolutionary Society 116, 117
Ankara 3, 5–7, 9–11, 16–18, 22, 28, 30, 35, 37, 42–9, 51–65, 67–74, 77–83, 86–93, 95–7, 99–101, 103–8, 114–18, 120–5, 128–36, 144–8, 150, 151, 153, 155, 162–5, 171–3, 176, 177, 179, 180, 183, 184
Ankara government 5, 9, 16–18, 35, 42–4, 47–9, 51, 52, 55–9, 61, 63–5, 69–74, 77–9, 81, 84, 87, 89–92, 95, 97, 99–102, 106–8, 115–22, 124, 128–31, 135, 144, 146, 147, 163–5, 176, 177, 179, 180

anti-nationalist 7, 16–18, 23, 28, 30–2, 36, 37, 39, 42–4, 46–52, 54, 55, 57–60, 64, 65, 68, 83, 88, 92, 94, 97, 99, 100, 104, 108, 115–22, 124, 129–32, 134–7, 144, 148, 164, 176, 183
Anzavur, Ahmed 3, 4, 7, 10, 15–17, 30–9, 49–51, 53, 54, 58, 62, 64, 86, 97, 99, 108, 115, 117, 118, 120, 121, 131, 134, 176
Armenian 3, 26, 27, 44, 64, 68, 75, 82, 91, 102, 111, 124, 134, 135, 144, 147, 152, 157
assassination 15, 26, 90, 100, 106, 117, 120, 128, 130, 136, 147–53, 155, 158, 159, 164, 177
assembly, (Turkish Grand National Assembly/TGNA) 16–18, 35, 52, 54, 58–61, 64, 68, 71, 73, 78, 80–3, 86, 88–97, 105, 129, 131–3, 135, 137, 142, 143, 146, 150, 152, 170, 171, 173, 180
assimilation 123, 127, 160, 161, 184
Association for the Strengthening of Near Eastern Circassian Rights (ASNEC) 99, 105, 107
Atatürk, Mustafa Kemal 3, 6, 9, 11, 17, 22–7, 30, 35, 38, 45, 48, 49, 51, 52, 55, 56, 61, 63, 64, 67–9, 71–83, 85–97, 103, 111, 117, 123, 128–30, 145–50, 152–5, 157–9, 163, 165, 172–4, 176, 177, 180, 182, 183
Athens 116–19, 144
Aydın 32, 109, 113, 114, 133

Balıkesir 27, 28, 31, 33, 109, 113, 141, 173, 174
Balkan Wars 2, 12, 30, 45, 70, 82, 175
banditry 45, 59, 121, 162
bandits 9, 10, 23, 27, 31, 33, 37, 39, 44, 53, 58, 59, 67, 69, 70, 92, 94, 96, 99, 100, 102, 122, 130, 131–4
Bandırma 36, 52, 81, 108, 109, 113, 117, 124, 141, 147, 174
Başkaya, Fikret 3

Bayar, Celal   89, 95, 143, 171, 173
Bedirhani, Celadet   172
Behiç, Hakkı   78, 81, 89
Bekir,Çerkes   16, 46, 108, 141
Bekir Sami (Günsav)   6, 27, 31, 32, 36, 37, 86, 123, 179
Bekir Sami (Kunduh)   6, 71, 75, 76, 179
Bele, Refet   17, 55, 62, 69, 85–8, 91, 93–6, 117, 147, 176
Berlin   70, 71, 73
Berzeg, Sefer   7, 47–9, 55–7
Biga   35, 37, 38, 108, 109, 113, 118, 121, 122, 140
Bilecik   89, 90, 95, 106, 113
Black Sea   44, 51, 59, 63, 69, 79, 87, 107, 109, 118, 146, 161
Bolshevik   5, 22, 69–82, 86, 91, 97, 128, 147, 176
Bolu   46–50, 56–8, 103, 108, 109, 137, 139
Bölükbaşı, Deniz   172
Bölükbaşı, Rıza Tevfik   137, 138, 172
Bozkurt, Mahmut Esad   24
British   2, 8, 21, 22, 25, 28–32, 35, 50–2, 68–71, 74, 76, 79, 82, 86, 87, 97, 100–2, 104, 106–9, 116, 117, 121, 131, 144, 145, 166
British forces   25, 28, 30, 31, 35, 51, 52, 79, 82, 104, 107, 109, 144, 145
Broski, Kürt Emin   172
Bucak, Sedat   41
bureaucracy   1, 2, 6, 14–16, 44, 70, 106, 107, 136, 179, 180
bureaucrats   3, 11, 15, 26, 35, 41, 47, 72, 78, 91, 92, 99, 101, 105, 114, 130, 131, 133, 161, 172, 178, 180, 183
Bursa   32, 50, 78, 85, 109, 113, 138, 139, 141

caliph/caliphate   5, 16, 31–3, 36, 39, 44, 49, 52, 54, 61, 103, 105, 108, 111, 114, 133, 147, 160, 178, 179, 183
Çanakkale   51, 121, 139
Canbulat, İsmail   82
Çapanoğlu   17, 59–63, 65, 88, 135, 176
The Caucasus Revolutionary Committee   15
cavaliers   80
Cemil Cahit (Toydemir)   6, 179
centralization   159, 161

Çerkes Teavün Cemiyeti   108, 120
Cevat Paşa (Çobanlı)   27
chaos   2, 6, 11, 22, 31, 35, 57, 62, 100, 116, 125, 133, 144, 177
Chechnian   41
Chechnya   41
Circassian language   170
Circassians   1–184
citizenship   8, 42, 133–6, 142, 163, 164, 171, 173, 177
civil war   4, 5, 11, 16, 19, 21, 22, 43, 50–2, 64, 65, 70, 91, 96, 97, 130, 176, 179, 184
Cold War   128, 145, 181
Colonel Mahmut   48
Committee of Union and Progress (CUP)   2, 5, 6, 11, 12, 16, 18, 23, 25, 26, 28, 29, 31–3, 36, 37, 45, 60, 64, 68, 69–72, 78, 81, 82, 99–101, 116, 127, 129, 132, 136, 137, 148, 149, 175, 176
conflict   3–5, 8–12, 17, 21–3, 26, 28, 31–5, 38, 39, 43, 44, 51, 53, 69, 73, 75, 86, 90, 93, 106

Dahiliye Nezareti (Ministry of Interior)   33, 34, 57, 101, 104, 137, 160
Damad Ferid Paşa   50–2, 54, 100, 103, 104, 138, 141
Dardanelles   32
Davut (Çerkes)   16, 115
Demirci (Town)   84
Demirci Mehmet Efe   37, 83
Democrat Party   129, 172, 173, 181
Dersim   124, 146, 149, 162, 179
Dost Eli Yardımlaşma Derneği   182
Düzce   3, 7, 11, 17, 38, 41–53, 55–9, 61–5, 82, 83, 97, 99, 102–4, 106, 108, 109, 113, 118, 128, 129, 131, 164, 176

early republican period   3, 8, 19, 25, 127–9, 143, 150, 160, 164, 165, 174, 178–82, 184
Eastern Anatolia   25, 26, 100, 121, 123, 125, 130
Edremit   35, 51, 119, 120, 179
Efe, Çakırcalı Ahmet   10
Efendi, Abdülmecid   147, 149
Efendi, Mustafa Sabri   137, 138, 141, 158
Eğilmez, Cafer Tayyar   27
Enver Paşa   6, 15, 17, 68–78, 82, 147, 177

Erzurum 27, 72
Eskişehir 50, 73, 78, 88–90, 95, 97, 109, 113, 140, 158, 171
Esma Hanım village 164
Eşref, Kuşçubaşı 6, 9, 10, 13, 15, 18, 46, 48, 49, 72–4, 116–18, 122, 129, 136, 139, 147–51, 177
Ethem, Çerkes 3, 4, 6, 9, 10, 13, 15, 16–19, 27, 34, 37, 39, 43, 49, 52–7, 59, 61–5, 67–70, 72–4, 78, 80–97, 99, 109, 114, 116–18, 122, 129, 132, 135, 136, 139, 145–7, 149–56, 158, 163, 164, 171–4, 176, 177, 180, 182–4
ethnicity 7, 9, 38, 39, 105, 119
exile 1, 4, 8, 9, 13, 15, 23, 26, 30, 60, 63, 75, 82, 99, 107, 109, 121–4, 136, 144, 146, 178

Fevzi Paşa (Çakmak) 27, 34, 61, 83, 117
First World War 2, 4, 5, 7, 8, 10–13, 15, 16, 21–6, 28–30, 33, 37, 39, 43–5, 52, 62, 69, 70, 72, 75, 79–82, 100, 101, 114, 132, 134, 136, 137, 175
French 3, 24, 27, 51, 75, 131, 141, 145, 153, 166, 173
Fuad Paşa 108

Galib, Yahya 60, 64
Gediz 83, 85, 95, 96
gendarme 3, 10, 13, 33, 47, 48, 50, 55–7, 59, 119, 120, 148, 149
Gerede, Hüsrev 47, 48, 55, 56, 58, 78
German 24, 69, 122, 173, 182
Golan Heights 178
Gönen 3, 4, 9, 18, 34–6, 38, 39, 56, 86, 99, 100, 107, 109, 113, 115, 117, 118, 120–5, 131, 133, 134, 140–2, 170
Greece 109, 117, 121, 134, 144–6, 148, 156, 158, 163
Greek army 9, 13, 84, 111, 134, 135
Greek occupation 3, 5, 6, 12, 18, 23, 25–7, 29, 31, 32, 38, 39, 43, 53, 82, 84, 87, 92, 101, 106, 107, 109, 115, 131, 135, 139
Green Army 17, 69, 77, 78, 80, 81
Gümülcine 137, 138, 144, 145, 158, 163

Hakuç Çerkes Canbolat 163
Harbiye Nezareti (War Office) 27, 32, 34, 35

harem 14, 19, 44, 58, 184
Hendek 17, 38, 41, 44, 47–9, 58, 103, 109, 113, 139
Heyet-i Temsiliye 25
High Treason Law 132
historiography 4, 8, 9, 11, 22–6, 35, 42, 67, 72, 77, 131, 145, 173
Hurşit Paşa 34

İbrahim Hakkı (Çule) 18, 49, 58, 100–9, 113, 114, 129, 137, 139, 144, 145, 176
identity 2, 4, 5, 7, 8, 19, 82, 103, 105, 123, 127–30, 152, 159–62, 165, 168, 170, 174, 175, 180, 183, 184
Independent Tribunal (İstiklal Mahkemeleri) 171
İngiliz Muhipleri Cemiyeti 143
intelligence service 19, 119, 128, 159, 164, 182, 184
irregular forces 12, 67, 80, 82, 83, 88, 89, 91, 97
Islamic socialism 71
Islamic unity 38, 72–4
İsmail, Şah 34, 86, 108
İsmet (İnönü) 17, 51, 53, 61, 69, 83, 85–97, 117, 176
Istanbul government 17–19, 22, 28, 30, 34, 35, 44, 45, 47–9, 51, 52, 57, 89, 94, 95, 101, 103–6, 130, 132, 178, 184
Italy 2, 21, 27
İzmir 11, 26, 27, 81, 99, 109, 114, 117–19, 134, 139–41, 147–9, 177
İzmit 3, 18, 42, 44, 46, 49, 50, 58, 78, 100–9, 113, 114, 120, 137, 139, 149, 163, 176

Jordan 127, 144, 146, 151–3, 172

Kaptan, Yahya 73
Karacabey 31, 32, 36, 109
Karakol 25, 26, 44
Karesi 122, 134
Kazım Karabekir 27, 64, 72, 74, 148
Kemal, Ali 28, 94, 136, 171
Kemalism 3, 4, 184
Kemalists 5, 8, 10, 18, 19, 22, 24, 26, 99, 107, 111, 113, 115, 119, 128, 129, 136, 144, –146, 152, 158, 159, 171–4, 178–80, 183, 184
Keriman Halis 130, 165–7, 169, 174
Kirmasti 31, 32, 36, 38, 109, 115, 140

Index

Kurdish   62, 127, 144, 146, 147, 152, 160–2
Kurdish issue   161
Kurdish language   161, 162
Kurds   1, 3, 19, 113, 127, 146, 149, 151, 161, 162, 178, 179, 184
Kuşadası   148
Kütahya   73, 84, 87, 89, 90, 93, 95, 96, 109, 113, 139, 148
Kuva-yi İnzibatiye   56, 132
Kuva-yi Milliye   6, 16, 23, 27, 28, 31–8, 42, 45–58, 60, 62–4, 84, 101–3, 105, 106, 124, 150, 178

Lausanne Peace Treaty   116, 145
Lenin, Vladimir   22, 71
Liberal Entente   29, 60, 99, 134, 136–8, 140, 175, 176
loyalists   5, 13, 16, 22, 39

Madanoğlu, Cemal   172
Madanoğlu, Mustafa   141, 172
Mahmut Şevket Paşa   106, 136
Manyas   3, 4, 9, 18, 34, 38, 39, 53, 56, 86, 96, 99, 100, 107, 109, 117–19, 121–5, 131, 133, 134, 142, 165
Mecid, Düzceli   148–50
Mecid, Sökeli   148–50
Mersinli Cemal Paşa   27
Mesai   71
Midilli   102, 103, 105–7, 113, 115, 116, 120, 130, 144, 163
military court   62–4, 83, 88, 135, 142, 143
military and financial support   77, 80, 176
mobilization   7, 11, 23, 38, 43, 45, 90, 127, 182
Mocan, Şevket   172
Moscow   70, 71, 73, 74, 86, 87
Mücadele-i Milliye'ye İştirak Etmeyen Memurin Hakkında Kanun   143
Mudros Armistice   11, 52, 69, 81, 100, 131

Nail, Yenibahçeli   72, 73
national history   22, 24
nationalist   3–7, 11, 12, 14, 16–18, 21–3, 25–8, 30–2, 35–9, 42–55, 57–65, 67–9, 71, 73, 74, 79, 81, 84–6, 92, 95, 97, 100, 102, 103, 105, 106, 108, 114, 115, 117–23, 129, 132, 135–7, 147, 148, 160, 166, 176, 177, 183

nationalization   18
national struggle   6, 11, 16, 26
nation-building   8, 18, 130, 159–61, 180
North Caucasian emigrants   128, 181
North Caucasian Republic   73–7, 181
North Caucasus   1, 13, 15, 69, 73–5, 77, 81, 82, 107, 110, 128, 164, 178
Nur, Rıza   136
Nurettin Paşa   27
Nutuk   11, 23, 24, 85, 93, 94, 183

Okyar, Fethi   82
Orbay, Rauf   6, 27, 179
Osman, Topal   90
Ottoman government   2, 6, 7, 13, 28, 32, 33, 42, 44, 50, 59, 76, 100–2, 104, 106, 110, 112, 114, 118, 171
Ottoman military   1, 12–15, 43
Ottoman State/Empire   1, 2, 5, 7–11, 13–15, 18, 19, 21, 22, 27– 29, 32, 35, 55, 70, 75, 76, 79, 81, 82, 105–7, 114, 118, 127, 129, 137, 148, 175, 178, 180, 184
Özalp, Kazım   27, 33, 37, 89, 90, 96, 123
Özcan, Mehmet Hadi   41, 42

paramilitary   6, 7, 9, 11–13, 15, 21, 23, 26, 27, 29, 37, 43, 52, 53, 56, 72, 73, 81, 82, 89, 91, 101, 123, 175, 176
Peker, Recep   24
personae non gratae   18, 128, 129, 132, 136
Pomaks   32, 86
Porte (Ottoman)   5, 14, 30, 38, 44, 75, 101–4, 106, 107, 110, 111, 114, 175, 176
Pşimafo Kosof   77

Quneytra   164

rebellion   11, 13, 21, 22, 150, 161, 162
refugees   7, 30, 111, 128, 178
Reşad, Hafız   144
resistance   1, 6, 9–12, 22, 23, 25–9, 35, 37, 39, 53, 69–71, 73, 75, 79, 83, 84, 91, 92, 94, 111, 137, 161, 179
Reşit (Çerkes)   6, 17, 18, 52, 72, 73, 78, 85, 89, 90, 95–7, 109, 113, 114, 117, 118, 129, 139, 145, 146, 149, 151–3, 171–4
Revolution   5, 15, 18, 21, 22, 24, 72, 74, 75, 78, 111, 116, 117, 123, 133, 136, 144, 147, 167, 171, 178

Rıfat, Mevlanzade   136, 140, 145
Russia   5, 15, 21, 22, 41, 71, 73–80, 127, 128, 181, 182
Russian   1, 5, 10, 13, 15, 21, 30, 41, 52, 70–5, 77–80, 82, 86, 107, 110, 128

Sabri, Eyüb   78
Saib, Ali   151–3
Sait, Kanbulat   46, 47
Sakız   117, 118
Sami, Hacı (Çerkes/Kuşçubaşı)   10, 18, 72, 74, 129, 139, 145, 147–50, 155, 174, 177, 180
Şarkı Karip Çerkesleri Temin-i Hukuk Cemiyeti   105
Sazak, Emin   171
scarcity   12, 22
secularization   7, 159
Şevket, Takığ   86, 109, 118–22, 142, 177
Sèvres Peace Treaty   55, 132, 138
Simav   83, 84
Şirin, Maan   7, 113, 140
Slavery   13, 14
Şoenu, Mehmet Fetgerey   123
South Marmara   7, 8, 10, 11, 13, 16, 23, 27–30, 32, 35, 38, 39, 49, 50, 52, 62, 84, 109, 115–22, 124, 128, 130, 131, 176, 177
Soviet Union   181
Special Organization *(Teşkilat-ı Mahsusa)*   6, 7, 15, 16, 20, 30, 32, 33, 46, 52, 69, 70, 75, 99, 116, 179
Stalin, J.   22, 71
Suad, Neguç Yusuf   164
Şükrü (Yenibahçeli)   44, 72
Susurluk   33, 41, 96, 115, 116, 139, 141
Syria   76, 81, 110, 144–6, 151–3, 163, 164, 170, 173

Tabiyet-i Osmaniyye Kanunnamesi   135
Tajikistan   74, 147
Talustan Bey   43, 113, 114
tax/taxation   31, 35, 38, 47, 48, 53, 84, 162
Tevfik (Çerkes)   17, 18, 69, 85, 88, 89, 91–3, 95–7, 104, 118, 129, 139, 145, 146, 153, 173
Thessalonica   118, 144, 163

Trabzon   41, 44, 72, 73, 77, 79, 141, 149
Turkification   111, 160
Turkish General Staff   24, 67
Turkish Grand National Assembly (TGNA)   16–18, 35, 52, 54, 58–61, 64, 68, 71, 73, 78, 80–3, 86, 88–97, 105, 129, 131–3, 135, 137, 142, 143, 146, 150, 152, 170, 171, 173, 180
Turkish history   1, 21, 175
Turkish identity   8, 160, 175, 180, 184
Turkish nation state   4, 19, 127, 161, 175, 178, 182
Turkish Republic   7, 8, 15, 42, 145, 149, 162
Turkish War of Independence   2, 3, 7, 8, 11, 19, 23, 24, 128, 130, 147, 160, 178
Türkiye Komünist Fırkası   80

Ubikh   2, 14, 56, 57
Umumi Müfettişlikler   161
uprising   17, 22, 46, 49, 52, 53, 55, 57, 60, 61, 64, 97, 116, 119, 121, 128, 130, 135, 146, 147, 149–51, 164
Uzuntarla   163

Vahidettin, Sultan   54, 102, 103, 119, 132, 137, 149
Vehip Paşa   145, 149
Velidedeoğlu, Hıfzı Veldet   25
Venizelos   13

Western Anatolia   2, 9, 11, 18, 29, 39, 73, 82, 88, 94, 99, 100, 103, 109, 113, 115–19, 121, 123, 129, 131, 176, 177
western front   17, 68, 69, 78, 82, 83, 85–8, 90, 91, 93, 95, 97, 119
Western Thrace   46, 144, 145, 158
White army   22

Yalova   50, 103, 113, 140
Yeni Dünya (Newspaper)   78
Young Turks   144
Yozgat   3, 17, 41, 43, 56, 59–64, 80, 83, 88, 97, 135, 163
Yusuf İzzet Paşa   6, 76, 86, 179
Yusuf Kemal (Tengirşenk)   71, 79
Yüzellilikler   18

www.ingramcontent.com/pod-product-compliance
Lightning Source LLC
Chambersburg PA
CBHW070029010526
44117CB00011B/1754